Cooking with Mena

Cooking with Mena: Favorite Italian Recipes from Calabria & Sicily
Copyright © 2014 Filomena Castriciano

First Edition November 2014
ISBN: 978-0-692-29259-4

All rights reserved. No part of this book may be reproduced or transmitted in any form or by any means, electronic or mechanical, including photocopying, recording, or any information storage or retrieval system, without permission in writing from the publisher.

Published by
Roma Press, Lansing, MI

Cover pictures by Marcia Besonen
Interior recipe pictures by Filomena Castriciano.
Book and Cover Design by Julie Taylor

Printed by Versa Press, East Peoria, IL in the United States of America
25 24 23 22 21   4 5 6 7 8

DEDICATION

For my Mamma and Papá, who gave me life and helped me live it.

And to God, whose presence makes all things possible.

With appreciation for the loving support of my husband, Sostine.

To My Children

AnneMarie, Elisabeth, and Filomena Francesca

You are the Joy of my Life.

And My Grandchildren

Isabella, Matthew, Adriana, and Mario

Nonna Loves You.

ACKNOWLEDGEMENTS

No book is ever possible without family and friends. For me, *Cooking with Mena* has been a true labor of love. I would like to thank my husband, Sostine, for being so loving, patient and kind; my daughters, AnneMarie, Elisabeth, and Filomena Francesca, for being the joys of my life; and my grandchildren, Isabella, Matthew, Mario, and Adriana, for being my life's most precious gift. I am also eternally grateful to Mamma and Papá—Rita Gallo Baldino and Mario Baldino—for showing me that the right mix of hard work and love is the recipe for any dream. I love you all!

So many amazing people helped me to bring this book together. I believe that God gave me the friends and family who were there for me every step of the way. I am so lucky and so very thankful. My deepest thanks go out to my best friends Mary Sasse and to my sister Silvana Dann for helping me translate and edit recipes from Italian to English, especially those from Mamma, our Nonna, and Mamma's sisters Emilia and Ida. Many thanks, also, to my "neighbors and friends" Julianna, Nancy and Mary Scodeller for fine-tuning my words; to my friends Donna Vorce and Wanda Beers for their help in writing recipes; for Mamma's sisters and my aunts Emilia and Ida for their recipes and guidance in the kitchen; and to my brother Gino Baldino for being there for me. I would also like to express my gratitude to all my customers at Roma Bakery and Deli whose appreciation of fine foods and traditions has been a constant inspiration for more than forty years.

My deepest thanks go to my amazing and meticulous editor Boni Federici and her husband Gino Federici. I don't know where I would be without them. Special thanks to Marcia Besonen for her photography on the cover of this book. Finally, I would like to thank other members of my editorial and production team for their hard work and talents including Rhonda Every, my typist and assistant Lexie Johnson, my copy editor Emma Ewusi, my writer and storyteller Ann Kammerer, and my book designer Julie Taylor. Thank you for your immense help in making this book a reality Mille grazie!

Mena Castriciano
Lansing, Michigan

TABLE OF CONTENTS

Introduction	xi
Antipasti, Soups & Dips	1
Egg Dishes	39
Fish	47
Meat	65
Poultry	89
Vegetables	103
Pasta & Rice	113
Salads	141
Sauces	169
Doughs & Breads	187
Desserts & Cookies	199
Photographic History	243
Index	264

INTRODUCTION

SAUCES, PASTAS, SWEETS AND SAVORY DISHES ARE HER LIFE.

"It's who I am," says Mena Castriciano who has been preparing and cooking foods for more than fifty years.

As a business owner, wife, mother and daughter, Mena's identity comes from growing up in southern Italy where she traversed hilly terrain to watch her father work as a millwright and butcher. Her passion for cooking ignited as she helped her mother prepare meals for a family of seven in a small, unheated kitchen, without running water.

This book of recipes, Mena says, is her dream, something she has envisioned since the day her mother showed her how to make her very first lasagna. The recipes in *Cooking with Mena* are like stories from family, friends and customers of Roma Bakery and Deli—the iconic business she runs with her husband, Sostine, in Lansing, Michigan.

"What is food if it's not about family and friends?" she says. "This book is my gift to everyone who has filled my life with love and care—which are also the two essential ingredients to Italian cooking."

Mena at one year old with her Papá, Mario Baldino.

My Mamma, Rita, in Italy.

EARLY LIFE

When Mena recalls her early life in southern Italy, she fills the mind's eye with images of narrow streets, white stone homes, and the slopes of hills cut with winding footpaths. The room fills with imagined aromas of sauces and herbs, and a virtual potpourri of vegetables, fruits, fish and meat on a small wooden family table.

In the late 1940s and early 1950s, Italy was still fragile from two World Wars—particularly the last that left much of Italy in poverty. Through age twelve, Mena lived a simple life framed by daily chores and subsistence. Their family of seven—five children, Mamma and Papá—all lived in a tiny two-room house in Caricchio—a village near Cosenza in the southern region of Calabria. The home had no running water or heat, and they shared a bath with other renters of multiple-family buildings that terraced the hills.

The family home in Caricchio. The Baldinos lived in the front apartment that had tall windows and balconies while two other families lived in apartments in the back. Mena and her siblings often ate the olives that grew up the side of the home. Her father sometimes cured sausages upstairs by hanging the meats from the attic ceiling.

Mena was named for her paternal grandmother, Nonna Filomena Bozzo. As the oldest child, Mena became a natural caregiver. Mena helped to cook, sew, and clean alongside her mother, Rita Gallo Baldino and her maternal grandmother Annunziata Bonofiglio Gallo. Every morning, Mena walked to a nearby church where she filled cisterns with drinking water. She also collected rainwater for occasional baths and cleaning. When she could, she went to school. No matter the day, she was always nearby to take care of her younger brothers and sisters: Luigi (Gino), Silvana, Marianna and Loredana (Lori).

To Mena, her life made sense. She loved her parents, and she loved being the daughter they depended on. Her father, Mario Baldino, worked two jobs: one in a flour mill, the other as a butcher. Mena remembers watching her father leave in the mornings, how he bundled up to take the long trek over the mountains to another little city. There, she says, Mario would help farmers butcher pigs, carefully applying his special knife, fork and seasonings to prepare meat for sausage, pancetta, capicolla and prosciutto.

When the flour mill closed, Mena's Papá picked up more work as a butcher to make ends meet. To Mena, his work was an incredible odyssey; a profession where he left home with simple tools and sometimes came back with delicious cuts of meat. Those meats, she said, were unexpected treats that complimented the pasta, vegetables and fruits she prepared with her mother. To this day, Mena still remembers the warm savory taste of a morsel of sausage on a cold winter night.

Just like she helped her mother, Mena helped her father. She followed the winding trail he made up the mountain, providing the extra set of hands he

Mena's Papá Mario Baldino (right) and his friend Peppino in the flourmill in Cosenza. Mario worked as both a millwright and butcher to support his young family in Italy.

INTRODUCTION

needed to bring meats back to Caricchio. Sometimes she would arrive while he was still hard at work. Pulling up a stool, she watched as he handled his tools with care and respect. It was then, she said, that she grew to appreciate the origins of food and to understand the gifts she could bring to others through cooking.

"Papá was number one," Mena says. "We had very little, but he and Mamma worked hard to give us what we needed."

A snapshot of Cosenza from one of Mena's return trips to Italy. Her childhood home in Caricchio was about a half-mile to the right. Serra is on the hills where her father sometimes worked.

COMING TO AMERICA

While hard workers and accepting of life's challenges, Mena's parents always held fast to their dreams. Those dreams, Mena says, were built on the belief that one day they would reunite with the family members who had left Calabria for a better life in America.

Mario's father, Luigi Baldino, had moved to the United States in 1921. He left behind his wife, Filomena Bozzo Baldino; three children, Assunta, Mario, and Giovannina; and his own parents, and began laying plans to quickly bring them to a new land. But decades later, he was still alone. His wife—Mario's mother—had passed away shortly after he left Italy, leaving Mario and his sisters to be raised by their grandmother. Then the war came and Mario was conscripted into the army. His sisters, meanwhile, fled to the U.S. to join their father.

After the war, Mario married Rita Gallo and started a family. While he contented himself with making a life for his family in the village, he never stopped dreaming of the day he would reunite with his father and his sisters. Then, in the late 1950s, opportunity came. His father had bought a small grocery store in Lansing, Michigan, with the dollars he had saved repairing streets and working in the factories. He had the money. Mario could join him, and he could bring his family, too.

In 1960, Mena was twelve years old; her brother and sisters Gino, Silvana, Marianna, and Lori ranged from nine to under a year in age. No one spoke English. They were going to America, her parents said. They were flying on a Pan American plane from Rome to New York and then to Michigan. When they arrived in

Mena's Papá stayed in Italy with his mother and two sisters when his father Luigi Baldino went to America in the early 1920s. Pictured left to right: Assunta (Aunt Susie), Giovannina (Aunt Ginnina), Filomena Bozzo-Baldino (Mena's "Nonna"), and Mario.

Lansing, the grandfather she had never met was there to greet them. Luigi had been in the U.S. since he was twenty-nine. In thirty-nine years, the five-year-old son he had left in Italy had grown to be a man.

"We came in September," says Mena, recounting how they moved into a house next to her grandfather's store. "We had never seen snow or lived in a heated house, and we had only had a small amount of milk for breakfast. My brother and I were completely amazed by the refrigerator. We sometimes opened and shut it more than we should."

A Baldino family portrait taken in Italy, right before Mena's family came to Lansing. Pictured from left front row: Luigi or "Gino" (b. 1951), Silvana (b. 1954), Rita Gallo-Baldino or "Mamma," Loredana or "Lorie" (b. 1959), Marianna (b. 1956). Back row: Filomena or "Mena" (b. 1948).

LANSING'S LITTLE ITALY

Within days of arriving in Lansing, Mena's father went to work in her grandfather's grocery store. North Town Grocery was located at 807 E. Grand River Ave., a few blocks east of the river and in a neighborhood north of the Capitol. Like in Italy, Mario worked as a butcher. And like in Italy, too, he brought home delicious meats for special occasions. The difference, Mena says, was that he also brought home unheard-of treats and packaged foods—things like chocolate, gum and soft white flour she used to make cookies with her Mamma.

"For my whole life in Italy, all we knew was vegetables, fruit, fish, eggs, and lots of bread and sauces," says Mena. "Here in America, we had everything. Even desserts."

Mena's life changed, but not so much that she didn't still continue to help her mother cook and run the household. She did laundry, helped clean the little house at 813 E. Grand River Ave., and watched out for her brothers and sisters. Within a few years of arriving in Lansing, her Mamma and Papá had another girl, Julianna, and boy, Robert, adding to Mena's responsibilities as the eldest of seven children.

Mena also became her parent's translator, learning English with the help of her aunt and her teachers at St. Therese Catholic School and C.W. Otto Middle School. School, Mena recalls, was a place where she learned more than a new language: she learned about the customs and foods of her new land. Classrooms and schoolyards also became places where she could introduce new friends to her own customs, particularly when it came to food. Lunch times were filled with daily trades of her staple meatball sandwiches, cheeses or crusty breads for her peers'

Mario Baldino's sisters and father in the North Town Grocery at 807 E. Grand River in Lansing. Pictured left to right: Giovannina (Ginnina), Luigi and Assunta (Susie).

Mena as a young girl making her first communion in Italy. Religious events and holidays were often celebrated with special foods and meals.

peanut butter and jelly sandwiches made with soft white bread.

"The food was completely different," she says. "Hamburgers, hot dogs, potato chips. I loved trying it."

Her friends and neighbors loved sampling authentic Italian cuisine, too. Along with her Mamma, Mena began to cook meatballs and spaghetti for neighbors and friends, introducing homemade Italian food to families used to eating spaghetti out of a can.

"It was just like how we would get together and cook with neighbors in Italy," Mena says. "What's food if it's not for friends and family?"

The Baldino family's Christmas portrait in America in 1961. Pictured sitting front from left: Silvana, Julianna (Julie), Rita (Mamma). Pictured sitting middle from left: Loredana (Lori), Mario (Papá). Pictured standing: Luigi (Gino), Filomena (Mena), Grandpa Luigi, Marianna. Not pictured: Robert Baldino (not yet born).

INTRODUCTION

That sentiment strengthened as Mena and her family became more settled in Lansing. Her Mamma and Papá never forgot the traditions marked by special foods. The celebrations of saints, festivals, and major holidays like Christmas and Easter involved feasts—big or small, replete with pasta, fish or meats—or simply gifts of fruit, nuts or cookies made just for the occasion.

Mena's family continued to honor the saint days along with new friends and family from Lansing's Italian community. St. Joseph's Day on March 19 involved traditions from the old country including meatless feasts and zeppole—a deep-fried Italian pastry topped with sugar and filled with custard, jelly, pastry cream or a butter and honey mixture (see Desserts and Cookies for the recipe).

The mid-July celebration of Our Lady of Mount Carmel was always marked by Italian traditions that included baked goods, feasts, and delectable cheeses made into the shapes of animals. Among the holiest of saint days, this day-long celebration shows devotion to the Blessed Virgin Mary as well as to family and friends, and involves special foods, special preparations, and the wearing of special garments.

"Our gifts to each other were generally food," says Mena, who recalls just once, receiving a doll from her Papá on the Epiphany. "I still remember those times when Papá brought home flour for cookies, or a block of ice that we would shave and flavor with orzata (almond syrup), wine, or coffee. Things like that were our celebrations."

THE BAKERY AND DELI

As Mena grew, so did her passion for her cooking and her new home in America.

When she turned seventeen, a new love entered her life thanks to her cousin Carmela Bonofiglio Galletta. Carmela invited Mena to visit her in Hamilton, Ontario, so she could meet someone special. That someone special was Sostine Castriciano. He was the cousin of Carmela's husband Franco and had emigrated from Sicily just six months earlier to work in the bakery. Mena was skeptical of Carmela's matchmaking, but to her surprise, she discovered she and Sostine had a lot in common—including his love of baking that complemented her love of cooking.

Mena returned home after a short visit. Sostine called her every day for the next three weeks. Within a month, he came to Lansing to meet her family. He stayed with them about six weeks, baking up breads and cookies and cakes alongside her mother while Mena went to school. She was a junior in high school then, attending Lansing Eastern. Sostine was two years older wanted to get married.

While she wanted to marry Sostine, too, Mena was determined to be among the first in her family to get her high school diploma. She told him she could get married after she graduated. Sostine agreed and told her he would wait. While she finished school, Sostine went back to Canada, and kept in close touch through phone calls and letters.

Sostine Castriciano working at his cousin Franco Galletta's bakery in Hamilton, Ontario. Sostine was 19 when he emigrated from Sicily in 1965. He met Mena his first year in Canada and they were married three years later when she graduated from Lansing Eastern High School.

INTRODUCTION

Behind-the-scenes at the bakery owned by Sostine's cousin Franco Galletta in Hamilton, Ontario, circa 1965. Franco was married to Mena's cousin Carmela Bonofiglio. Sostine (pictured right) joins his best friend Nicola (far left) and Franco in making a cake.

Mena graduated in June of 1968 and became an American citizen that summer along with her Papá. She married Sostine in the fall, and they settled in a tiny apartment down the street from her family. All the while they dreamed of owning their own store or bakery and carrying on the traditions of their families.

Mena and Sostine were still newlyweds when big news stirred in the neighborhood. Frank Antonio's—a small Italian food store on Erie and Cedar Streets—was up for sale. Her Papá was a loyal customer of the store and came straight to their home to tell them.

That night, Mario encouraged Mena and Sostine to buy the store and open their own business. Sostine would be the baker, and Mena would tend and managed the store in between teaching everyone in the neighborhood about the wonders of Italian food. They were excited and smiled. But then, looking at each

Sostine and Mena on their way to their honeymoon on Mackinac Island. Mena and Sostine were married Oct. 26, 1968 at Lansing's St. Therese Catholic Parish.

First born daughter AnneMarie with Sostine at the Bakery. Mena's children enjoyed visiting their parents at the bakery in between being cared for by Mena's mother, Rita Gallo-Baldino.

other, their smiles faded and they shook their heads. No one, not one of them, had the money to buy the store.

With the financial help of Mario's sister—Mena's Aunt Giovannina—their dream came true. Mena and Sostine bought the store and went to work restocking the shelves and filling the aisles with groceries, meats, and imported foods like olive oil, pastas, olives, deli meats and cheeses. Sostine began baking, adding fresh breads, cookies, cakes and pastries to the store's local flavor. Three months after opening in 1969, they brought new life to the store by changing the name from Antonio's to Roma Bakery and Imported Foods.

Roma grew in popularity. Mena worked harder. She began making and selling the sauces she had perfected from the years of cooking with her mother, grandmother and aunts. Customers began asking for more. Their selections grew. And like before, when a parcel of land came up for sale just a few blocks away, they looked at each other and decided to make their move.

Mena and Sostine broke ground on the now familiar site of Roma Bakery and Deli in the mid-1970s. They constructed a 5,500 square foot store that stands today at 428 N. Cedar Street with cases and refrigerators for meat and cheeses, aisles for imported foods, groceries and olive oil, and a large in-house bakery and kitchen for Sostine and Mena.

"We worked very hard," says Mena. "We had nothing when we came here. Papá always told me, 'You're American now. Get your schooling. Lift yourself up.' We were just so very proud."

COOKING FOR TODAY

Although becoming a store owner and mother to three daughters—AnneMarie, Elisabeth, and Filomena ("Mena") Francesca—Mena never lost sight of her first love: cooking. She cooked at work and she catered. Customers asked her for tips. They asked her for guidance. She was always advising, educating people on the wonders of Italian breads, pastas and cheeses like Romano, Parmesan, ricotta and mozzarella. Sostine's cookies, cakes and pastries were the go-to items for satisfying Lansing's sweet tooth and for festive occasions. Every week, they imported different foods through Detroit, New York and Chicago. At one time, Mena says, they carried 20 kinds of olives—all fresh and in barrels. They also had 25 kinds of pasta, dozens of hard and soft cheeses, and meats with names like prosciutto, pancetta, mortadella and others that few in Lansing had ever heard.

Sostine and Mena at Roma Bakery and Deli in the late 1990s.

As busy as she was, Mena always took time to sit down with customers. She would answer questions about what kinds of foods went best together and how to prepare certain dishes. On occasion, she held cooking classes, setting up a special area in the store to demonstrate how to dice, slice, sauté or simmer your way to a savory Italian meal.

"It was my dream to show people recipes," she says. "And for people to share recipes with me."

Mena stirring the sauce at one her cooking classes at Roma Bakery and Deli in the 1980s and 1990s. Mena shared her knowledge of cooking with aspiring Italian cooks as the bakery and deli grew in popularity.

Throughout decades of business, Mena's genuine warmth and interest in every person who walked through the door made Roma a place where Lansing went to learn about food. It wasn't uncommon for Mena to take a break and talk over coffee about Italian foods or to tell stories about her early life in Italy.

INTRODUCTION

Her openness encouraged customers to tell stories, too, and to share their favorite family recipes. Soon, Mena became as skilled at cooking Mediterranean, Greek and American foods as she was at cooking Italian. She began carrying different cheeses, different spices, different oils and sauces, broadening the store's appeal to Lansing's diverse community.

"Here was the world," she says of the stories and recipes she shared with her customers. "I saw that here, in America, I could have any type of food."

This book, Mena says, is her gift to her family, friends, and customers. It's her legacy. It's her way of saying thank you for the opportunities afforded her and her family to live their dream.

The recipes featured throughout *Cooking with Mena* include those from her own family as well as those passed along from others just as proud of their family traditions. Since few recipes were ever written down, many of Mena's family recipes were gathered through conversations Mena had with her mother, grandmother, aunts, cousins and friends in Italy. Any recipes that were written came in the form of simple lists of ingredients on worn sheets of paper, many without instructions, some without quantities. After hours of talk, countless days, and working with friends to translate, write and type, Mena selected the recipes that represent the course of her life and the gift she wants to leave to others.

"I've just been so blessed," says Mena. "I love people and I love to cook. God has given me both."

❧ ❧ ❧

Mena learned many of her recipes from her mother's side of the family. Pictured here are her maternal grandparents in Italy: Luigi Gallo and Annunziata Bonofiglio-Gallo.

ANTIPASTI, SOUPS & DIPS

- Artichoke and Cheese Casserole 2
- Artichokes with Stuffing 6
- Artichoke Tapenade 4
- Asparagus Patties, Small 10
- Chicken Broth with Pasta and Eggs 8
- Chicken Soup with Little Meatballs 9
- Creamy Tomato Bisque 11
- Crispy Eggplant Flat Meatballs ("Meatless") 12
- Eggplant Appetizer 14
- Eggplant Rolls 16
- Eggplant (Spread) 18
- Flaming Cheese 22
- Fried Artichoke Hearts 5
- Fried Stuffed Zucchini Blossoms 19
- Fried Zucchini 20
- Italian Fish Soup 21
- Lentil Soup with Sausage & Pancetta 23
- Marinated Artichokes 24
- Mushrooms Stuffed with Ricotta 25
- Mushrooms Stuffed with Sausage 26
- Panini (Grilled) 27
- Pickled Zucchini, Sweet & Sour 28
- Potato Garlic Soup 29
- Ricotta Dumpling Soup 30
- Roasted Red Pepper and Sun-Dried Tomato Tapenade 31
- Sausage Soup with Minestrone 32
- Spinach and Olive Tapenade 33
- Spinach Pie 34
- Taramasalata Dip 37
- Tomato and Mozzarella Fondue 36

Artichoke and Cheese Casserole

Parmiggiana di Carciofi

I use to go to Italy every two years, and I stayed with Zia (Aunt) Emilia in Cosenza. I loved cooking with her. We had a picnic with my cousins in Sila and my aunt made Artichoke Casserole. I loved it so much, I asked her to give me her recipe. I hope you enjoy it as much as I do. We love eating it hot or cold.

BREAD CRUMB INGREDIENTS

Bread crumbs, ⅔ cup

Italian parsley, 2 tablespoon

Romano cheese, ½ cup

Mozzarella, 1 cup shredded

Oregano, ¼ teaspoon

Black pepper, ¼ teaspoon

Garlic, 1 clove chopped finely

Extra-Virgin Olive Oil, 3 tablespoon

BREAD CRUMBS DIRECTIONS:

In a medium bowl, pour bread crumbs, parsley, Romano cheese, shredded mozzarella, oregano, black pepper, and chopped garlic. Mix well with hands. Add the olive oil. Mix well with hands and set aside.

ARTICHOKE DIRECTIONS:

Preheat oven to 350°F.

Bring water to a boil in a medium pot. Pour in defrosted artichokes. Boil according to package directions or for 3–5 minutes on medium heat; let cool.

In a medium bowl, whisk 6 large eggs with a pinch of salt. Set aside.

In another medium bowl, add 1½ cup San Marzano tomatoes, parsley, garlic, 1 tablespoon olive oil, and pinch of salt and black pepper.

Remove boiled artichokes from pot and drain well. Pour artichokes in a medium sized bowl, and let it cool. Season artichokes with 2 tablespoon of oil, 1 tablespoon lemon juice and a pinch of salt. Mix well.

(recipe continues)

ANTIPASTI, SOUPS & DIPS

In an 8×11-inch casserole dish, pour 2 tablespoons olive oil, artichokes, half of the bread crumbs mixture, half of the San Marzano mixture and half of the egg mixture. Lightly press down with a fork. Pour remaining bread crumb mixture, San Marzano mixture, 2 tablespoons olive oil, and remaining egg mixture. Lightly press down with a fork, pour remaining oil and add salt to taste.

Place in a 350°F oven for 30 minutes. Increase oven to 375°F and cook for another 5–10 minutes until the eggs are set. Serve hot.

TIP: *Use stale bread to make bread crumbs. Let leftover bread dry out on a baking sheet in the oven on low heat. When the bread is hard and crisp, whirl it in a food processor. Put in a Ziplock bag and place in the refrigerator for later use.*

ARTICHOKE INGREDIENTS

Eggs, 6 large, whisked (add a Salt, a pinch)

San Marzano tomatoes, 1 ½ cup diced

Italian parsley, 2 tablespoons chopped

Extra-Virgin Olive Oil, 10 tablespoon

Artichoke hearts, 2 packages (12 oz. each) frozen, defrosted

Lemon juice, 1 tablespoon fresh

Garlic, 1 clove chopped

Oregano, ¼ teaspoon

Mozzarella, 1 cup shredded

Romano cheese, ½ cup grated

Salt, to taste

Black pepper, ½ teaspoon

INGREDIENTS

Lemon, ½ teaspoon lemon zest, 1 tablespoon lemon juice

Artichoke hearts in water, 1 can (14 oz.)

Fresh Parsley, ¼ cup loosely packed

Garlic, 1 clove, peeled

Green olives, ½ cup pitted

Capers, 1 tablespoon drained

Olive oil, 5 tablespoons

Artichoke Tapenade

Tapenade di carciofi

Serve with your favorite cracker or toasted baguette slices.

DIRECTIONS:

Grate ½ teaspoon lemon zest; juice 1 tablespoon of lemon.

Drain artichokes using small colander; pat dry using paper towels.

Combine parsley, garlic, lemon zest, juice, artichokes, olives, capers and oil in food processor.

Cover and process to desired consistency, removing lid and scraping down sides of bowl as necessary.

Makes 16 servings.

ANTIPASTI, SOUPS & DIPS

Fried Artichoke Hearts

Cuori di Carciofi Fritti

DIRECTIONS:

Rinse frozen artichoke hearts in a strainer under warm water to defrost.

Place flour in a shallow bowl. In another bowl, whisk eggs with a teaspoon of salt and pepper. In a third bowl, combine lemon zest with breadcrumbs and Romano cheese. Dredge artichoke hearts in flour and shake off excess. Lightly coat with eggs, letting excess drip off. Coat thoroughly in breadcrumb mixture. Arrange in a single layer on a platter lined with wax paper. Refrigerate for 1 hour to allow coating to set.

In a deep skillet, heat vegetable oil over medium-high heat on 350–375°F. Fry artichokes on both sides until lightly golden (do not crowd pan; fry in 2 or 3 batches to avoid crowding). Transfer with a slotted spoon to paper towels to drain. To serve, arrange on a large platter, and garnish with lemon wedges.

Makes 8 servings.

INGREDIENTS

Artichoke hearts, 2 packages (12 oz. each) frozen, defrosted

Wondra flour, ½ cup

Eggs, 3 large

Salt, 1 teaspoon

Black pepper, ½ teaspoon freshly milled

Lemon zest, 2 tablespoons grated

Dry breadcrumbs, 2 cups, fine

Romano cheese, ¼ cup

Vegetable oil, 2 cups (preferably corn)

Lemon, 1 medium, cut into thin wedges for garnish

Artichokes with Stuffing

Carciofi Ripieni

In Italy, my family loved the flavor of the stuffed artichokes. Even my daughters love the flavor of this dish. It's a holiday favorite!

INGREDIENTS

Artichokes, 6 medium (not large)

Lemon, 1

Fresh bread crumbs, 4 cups

Romano cheese, 1 ¼ cup

Garlic, 2 cloves, chopped very fine

Italian parsley, 3 tablespoons, chopped

Oregano, 1 teaspoon

Black pepper, ½ teaspoon

Eggs, 3 large, whisked with a pinch of salt and 2 tablespoons cold water

Water, 4 cups reserved from boiled artichoke water

Olive oil, 1 ½ cup (reserve ¼ cup for bottom of deep casserole dish)

DIRECTIONS:

Cut the tough stem off the bottom of the artichoke, remove hard outer leaves. Cut off top section of artichoke (about 1 inch) to make a flat surface. Cut off bottom so that it will set flat. Rub with lemon juice to prevent darkening.

In a large pot, boil the artichokes in salted water for 35 minutes, drain and let cool.

How to prepare seasoned bread crumbs: In a large bowl, add Romano cheese, garlic, parsley, oregano, and black pepper. Carefully fill artichokes with bread crumb mixture—½ cup seasoned mixture for each artichoke. If there is any leftover mixture, drizzle on top of each artichoke. Place in deep casserole dish so they fit tightly together.

Mix 2 cups water with ¾ cup olive oil (whisk together quickly). Drizzle mixture evenly over artichokes (to moisten). Take the other 2 cups of water mixed with ½ cup olive oil, and drizzle around the artichokes, filling the bottom of the casserole dish.

Cover with foil and bake at 375° for 30 minutes. Check after 15 minutes to make sure there is enough water in the bottom of the pan. (Take the remaining juice in

(recipe continues)

ANTIPASTI, SOUPS & DIPS

the bottom of the pan and distribute over top of the artichokes). If water has evaporated, add an additional 1 cup of water to the bottom of the pan.

After 30 minutes, take the foil off. Whisk the eggs; add pinch of salt, and 2 tablespoons water—take a fork and poke into each artichoke gently, making holes for the egg mixture to absorb. Drizzle egg mixture with water over each artichoke. Bake again, uncovered until crusty, about 15 minutes. Serve hot as a vegetable, or at room temperature as an appetizer.

Makes 16 servings.

TIP: *If artichokes are large, you may need more bread crumb mixture.*

ANTIPASTI, SOUPS & DIPS

INGREDIENTS

Chicken broth, 2 ½ quarts

Pastina, 1 ½ cups
(acini di pepe)

Salt, to taste

Butter, 1 tablespoon

Eggs, 5 large

Parmigiano or Romano cheese, ½ cup grated

Fresh parsley, 1 tablespoon, chopped

Chicken Broth with Pasta and Eggs

Pastina in brood con le uova

This pastina soup is usually for children. However, adults love it too. Sprinkle with chopped parsley, if desired.

DIRECTIONS:

Bring the chicken broth to a boil in a 4 quart pan. Stir in the pastina and cook for 7 minutes. Add butter.

Whisk the eggs and ¼ cup of cheese together, then drizzle slowly into the pot of broth, slowly stirring for 1 minute.

Ladle into serving bowls and add the remaining ¼ cup of cheese on top of each serving. Serve immediately.

ANTIPASTI, SOUPS & DIPS

Chicken Soup with Little Meatballs

Zuppa di Pollo con Polpettine

DIRECTIONS:

In a large soup pot add chicken pieces and thighs. Then add cold water so it covers just the top of the chicken; bring to a boil until foam comes to the surface. With a large spoon, skim the foam off the top and discard; lower heat. Add 3 sprigs parsley, 1 medium onion (quartered), 1 celery stalk (halved), 1 carrot (halved), and salt. Bring to a boil and lower heat; cover pot and cook for 1 ½ hour, until the chicken is tender.

Remove the chicken from the broth with a large slotted spoon, place on a platter and keep covered. Discard the vegetables from the broth (not going to eat—just for flavor). Add 2 carrots (peeled and cut into chunks) into the broth; cook for 10 minutes and lower heat.

To make the meatballs (use ½ Meatball recipe). Roll meatballs into the size of a hazelnut and place on platter (set aside). Add the tiny meatballs into the broth (gently pushing them off of the platter). Bring to a boil and cook for 10 minutes; lower heat. If too much fat comes to the surface, skim off with a large spoon and discard.

While the meatballs are cooking, remove bones from the chicken and cut into bite-sized pieces. Add chicken pieces to the broth; boil for an additional 3–4 minutes. Cover and set aside on stove.

Cook pasta orzo or rice (according to package). Place a small amount of cooked orzo in a bowl, ladle broth and meatballs over the orzo. Serve with Parmesan or Romano.

TIP: *Do not add pasta to soup. The pasta will swell too much and absorb all the broth.*

INGREDIENTS

Chicken, 3 ½ pounds (cut into serving pieces), plus 3 thighs washed well

Water, 6 quarts

Salt, 2 tablespoons

Carrots, 3 peeled

Celery, 1 stalk

Onion, 1 medium, quartered

Fresh Italian parsley, 3 sprigs

In Italy my mamma would serve the chicken pieces with broth ladled on top for flavor. This would be our second course. (Traditionally, in Italy we have a first and second course of your choice!)

ANTIPASTI, SOUPS & DIPS

INGREDIENTS

Asparagus, 4 bunches boiled, mashed, cooled

Eggs, 10 large

Bread crumbs, 1 cup (unseasoned)

Parmigiano cheese, ½ cup grated

Italian parsley, 2 tablespoons

Garlic, 2 cloves minced or put through press

Oregano, ½ teaspoon

Salt, 1 teaspoon

Pepper, to taste

Vegetable oil, 2 cups for frying

Asparagus Patties, Small

Fritelli di Asparagi

A wonderful dish anytime but springtime asparagus is best. We looked forward to the first new shoots after a long winter. So tender!

DIRECTIONS:

Beat eggs in a large bowl and add the mashed asparagus, bread crumbs, grated cheese, parsley, salt, oregano, pepper and garlic. Mix well. The texture should be thick like pancake batter; if necessary, add more crumbs, add salt and pepper to taste. Heat oil in large skillet and pour batter—about a tablespoonful for each patty into the pan. You should be able to fit about 4 patties at a time. Fry until golden on bottom and turn, only once, to brown the other side. Drain thoroughly on paper towels. Garnish with lemon wedges.

TIP: *Before boiling the asparagus, it's important to remove the tough ends.*

ANTIPASTI, SOUPS & DIPS

Creamy Tomato Bisque

Zuppa di Pomodori con Crema

This is very tasty with your favorite sandwich.

INGREDIENTS

Olive oil, 1 tablespoon

Butter, 1 tablespoon

Red onion, 1 medium, chopped

Garlic, 1 tablespoon chopped

Ripe red tomatoes, 8 large, peeled, seeded and chopped

Chicken stock, 4 cups

Sugar, 1 teaspoon

Mascarpone, 1 cup (8 oz.) softened

Coarse salt

Ground black pepper

Fresh basil, ¼ cup chopped

DIRECTIONS:

Heat olive oil and in butter in a large soup pot over medium-high heat. Add the onion and garlic; cook, stirring occasionally, until soft, about 5 minutes. Add the chopped tomatoes and cook for 5–6 minutes, stirring well. Then add the chicken stock and sugar and bring to a boil over high heat. Reduce the heat to medium-low and simmer until the liquid is reduced by one quarter, about 20 minutes. Cool for 10 minutes.

In a blender, puree the soup in several batches until smooth, 2–3 minutes per batch. Strain into a clean pot and bring to simmer over medium heat. Turn off the heat and stir in Mascarpone; whisk until smooth. Season to taste with salt and pepper.

TIP: *This can be made up to 2 days in advance, cover and refrigerate. When ready to serve, reheat gently over low heat, ladle the soup into bowls and garnish with fresh basil.*

ANTIPASTI, SOUPS & DIPS

INGREDIENTS

Eggplants, 1 large or 2 medium (unpeeled), cut into 1" cubes

Salt, 1 tablespoon

Fresh bread crumbs, 1 cup (cubed bread put into food processor)

Salt, ½ teaspoon

Ground black pepper, ¼ teaspoon

Dry bread crumbs, ¾ cup

Basil, 2–3 leaves chopped

Pecorino cheese, ⅓ cup grated

Fresh Italian parsley, 2 tablespoons minced

Garlic, 1 clove minced

Egg, 1 large, lightly whisked

Vegetable oil, ½ cup, for frying

Variation: Add a little crushed hot red pepper for heat if desired.

Crispy Eggplant Flat Meatballs ("Meatless")

Frittelle di Polpette di Melanzane—"Senza Carne"

As kids in Italy we only had meat on Sundays. My mom started this meatless recipe, made with eggplant. She would mix the eggplant into meatball patties when we didn't have meat, and we loved it!

DIRECTIONS:

Bring a pot of approximately 2 quarts of water and 1 tablespoon salt to a boil.

Add cubed eggplant and bring to a boil, leave uncovered until the eggplant is tender (about 2–3 minutes), stirring a few times.

Drain into colander and let cool. Press on the eggplant with the back of a wooden spoon to remove excess water. The eggplant should be as dry as possible.

Chop the eggplant very finely by hand. Place in a large bowl and combine with fresh breadcrumbs, salt, pepper, dry breadcrumbs, basil, cheese, parsley, and garlic. Blend a little with a fork, then season to taste with additional salt and pepper if desired.

Add 1 egg (whisked), and mix well with hands. Let stand for 1–5 minutes. Scoop mixture into ¼ cup sized balls and shape into patties.

Heat ½ cup oil in a large skillet over medium-high heat. When oil starts to simmer, drop patties into the skillet, spacing a couple inches apart. Fry patties, turning

(recipe continues)

ANTIPASTI, SOUPS & DIPS

them gently with a slotted spoon, until brown on each side; about 3–4 minutes. Transfer to a platter lined with paper towels.

Serve with marinara sauce on top, or plain.

TIP: *This recipe uses both fresh and dry bread crumbs to help retain some moisture as well as to provide texture and a filler.*

TIP: *Nonna (my grandma) would put the handle of the wooden spoon down in the heating oil. If it sizzles, the oil is ready to go.*

ANTIPASTI, SOUPS & DIPS

INGREDIENTS

Eggplants, 2 large or 4 medium, cubed into ¾-inch pieces

Bell peppers, one red and one yellow, cubed into ¾-inch pieces

Celery stalks, 2, cut thin on an angle

Olive oil, ¾ cup

Onion, 1 medium, cubed into ½-inch pieces

Garlic, 2 cloves, sliced

Green olives, 6 jumbo, pitted, sliced

Capers, 1 tablespoon

Fresh basil, 1 tablespoon finely chopped

Fresh Italian parsley, ¼ cup finely chopped

Sugar, 1 ½ tablespoons

Salt, 1 teaspoon

Black pepper, ½ teaspoon

Red wine vinegar, ¼ cup

San Marzano tomatoes, 16 ounces, chopped

Eggplant Appetizer

Caponata Siciliano

This delicious appetizer can be served either warm or cold with your favorite crusty bread

DIRECTIONS:

Place the cubed eggplant in a colander and lightly salt. Place a plate underneath the colander and another on top. Let sit for 15–20 minutes to help drain some of the water. Dry excess moisture off with a paper towel.

Place the cut peppers and celery in a bowl.

Place cut onion and garlic in another small bowl.

Place sliced olives, capers, basil and parsley in another small bowl.

Mix the sugar, salt, black pepper and vinegar in a bowl, then set aside.

Heat ½ cup olive oil, onion and garlic in a large skillet, stirring for 1 minute. Add the eggplant and sauté for 5 minutes while stirring. Remove from pan and place in bowl.

In the same pan, add ¼ cup olive oil, peppers, and celery. Sauté for 5 minutes and keep stirring. Remove from pan and place into bowl with eggplant mixture.

Add the tomatoes into the pan and cook for an additional 4–5 minutes. Return the eggplant, onion, and garlic mixture (all the ingredients) back into the skillet. Add olives and capers, mix well.

(recipe continues)

ANTIPASTI, SOUPS & DIPS

Add the sugar mixture while stirring. Cook gently for 10 minutes. Add toasted pine nuts to the mixture if desired.

Remove from skillet; taste and add salt and pepper if needed. Place into a bowl. Allow to cool to room temperature.

Cover and store overnight in the refrigerator to allow the flavors to blend.

TIP: *You can serve this as an antipasto, a side dish, or with a sandwich.*

ANTIPASTI, SOUPS & DIPS

INGREDIENTS

Eggplants, 2–3 pounds, small–medium

Olive oil, ¾ cup

Ricotta, 2 cups

Dried bread crumbs, 2 tablespoons

Provolone, ½ cup finely chopped or shredded

Egg, 1 large, lightly whisked

Parmigiano-Reggiano or Romano cheese, 1 cup freshly grated

Fresh Italian parsley, 2 tablespoons chopped

Salt, ½ teaspoon, for stuffing

Black pepper, ¼ teaspoon

Favorite marinara sauce, 3 cups

Eggplant Rolls

Rollatini di Melanzane

A wonderful appetizer, main dish or side dish. This recipe serves 4 as an entrée and 6–8 as a side dish.

DIRECTIONS:

Peel the eggplants and slice lengthwise into ¼-inch thick slices. Place into a large bowl and lightly sprinkle each layer with salt. Cover with a plate and let sit for 15–20 minutes.

Preheat oven to 400°F

Add 1 cup of water to the eggplant slices and use your hands to swirl around a little. Drain in a colander. Then remove slices one at a time and pat dry with paper towel. This process removes bitterness and extra moisture from the eggplant.

Brush both sides of eggplant slices with olive oil and place on large cookie sheet lined with parchment paper. Cook until light golden brown, just until soft, about 10–12 minutes. Set aside to cool.

Reduce oven temperature to 375°F.

In a large bowl, mix the ricotta, bread crumbs, provolone, egg, ½ cup Parmigiano-Reggiano, Italian parsley, salt and pepper. Mix together well with your hands.

To make the rolls, take a slice of eggplant and place 2 ½ tablespoons of the filling mixture at the wider end.

(recipe continues)

ANTIPASTI, SOUPS & DIPS

Spread along the length of the slice and roll from wide to narrow end. Repeat until all of the eggplant slices are filled and rolled.

Spread 1 cup of Marinara sauce into the bottom of a 9x13-inch baking pan (larger if needed). Arrange eggplant rolls, seam side down, in a single layer of rows. Spread remaining 2 cups of marinara sauce evenly over the top and sprinkle with remaining ½ cup Parmigiano-Reggiano.

Cover the dish with aluminum foil and bake for 25–30 minutes. Then, uncover and cook 5 minutes longer. The cheese should be melted and sauce bubbly.

TIP: *Serve with extra sauce and cheese on the table to add as desired.*

ANTIPASTI, SOUPS & DIPS

INGREDIENTS

Eggplant, 1 large, skinned and diced large

Olive oil, ⅓ cup

Onion, 1 small, chopped

Garlic, 2 medium cloves, peeled (or 1 large clove)

Salt, 1 ¼ teaspoon, divided use

Red or yellow peppers, 1 cup cubed large

Black pepper, ½ teaspoon

Lemon, 1, juiced

Fresh parsley, 2 tablespoons

Fresh oregano, 1 tablespoon (or 1 teaspoon dried)

Eggplant (Spread)

di Melanzane

Serve as an antipasto.

DIRECTIONS:

Preheat oven to 350° F.

Toss the eggplant, oil, onion, garlic, 1 teaspoon salt, red and yellow peppers, and black pepper in a bowl.

Pour onto a greased baking sheet.

Place the eggplant mixture in the oven and bake for 25–30 minutes until eggplant is soft.

Put the eggplant, lemon juice, parsley, oregano, and remaining salt and pepper in a food processor and blend well.

Adjust seasoning as you wish and serve with Italian or French bread or crackers.

ANTIPASTI, SOUPS & DIPS

Fried Stuffed Zucchini Blossoms

Fiori di Zucchini Fritti Ripieni

A beautiful summer treat. Just make sure you check the blossoms for bugs first! For variety, add a small pieces of anchovy fillet with the mozzarella cheese for the stuffing. Amazing!

BATTER INGREDIENTS

Eggs, 2 large
Water, 1 ¾ cups
All-purpose flour, 1 ¾ cups
Baking powder, ¼ teaspoon
Fresh Italian parsley, 1 teaspoon
Garlic salt, ¼ teaspoon
Salt, ½ teaspoon
Black pepper, ¼ teaspoon ground
Vegetable oil, 1 cup, for frying

INGREDIENTS

Zucchini flowers, 30, golden yellow color
Mozzarella, ¾ pound (30 pieces cut into ½ inch x 1 inch rectangles)
Romano cheese, ½ cup

DIRECTIONS:

In a mixing bowl, beat the eggs. Add the water, flour, baking powder, parsley, garlic salt, salt and pepper. Beat until smooth.

Stuff each zucchini flower with a small piece of mozzarella cheese. Wrap the flower back up and twist the tip of the flower to close the blossom and keep the filling inside. Dip the flower into the batter. Fry on medium heat, until golden on both sides. Lay on paper towel to absorb excess oil. Arrange on a serving platter and dust with Romano cheese. Add salt and pepper to taste.

TIP: *This can also be made without cheese. The petals of the flower become very light and crispy.*

ANTIPASTI, SOUPS & DIPS

BATTER INGREDIENTS

Eggs, 2 large
Water, 1 cup
Milk, ¾ cup
All-purpose flour, 1 ¾ cups
Butter, ¼ cup melted
Baking powder, ¼ teaspoon
Fresh Italian parsley, 1 teaspoon
Garlic salt, ¼ teaspoon
Salt, ¾ teaspoon
Black pepper, ¼ teaspoon
Vegetable oil, 1 cup, for frying

INGREDIENTS

Zucchini, 3 medium, thinly sliced
Zucchini flowers, 15, golden yellow color
Romano cheese, ½ cup

Fried Zucchini

Frittelle con Zucchine

What to do with all the zucchini in the summer and fall? Your family will never get tired of my crispy fried zucchini. Don't forget to check the flowers for bugs!

DIRECTIONS:

In a large mixing bowl, whisk the eggs. Add the water, milk, flour, melted butter, baking powder, parsley, garlic salt, salt and pepper. Beat until smooth.

Place the sliced zucchini in a bowl. Sprinkle 1 teaspoon salt to sweat the zucchini. After 10 minutes, put the zucchini on a thin towel (tea towel) and press to wring the water out of the zucchini. Add zucchini slices to the batter. Tear the zucchini flowers into pieces and add to the batter. Put a tablespoon of the zucchini and flower mixture into the frying pan. Fry on medium heat for 1–2 minutes on each side, until golden brown and crunchy. Use paper towel to absorb the oil. Serve on a platter and dust with Romano cheese.

ANTIPASTI, SOUPS & DIPS

Italian Fish Soup

Zuppa di Pesce

INGREDIENTS

Garlic, 5 large cloves, peeled

Onions, 2 chopped

Olive oil, ½ cup

Bay, 1 leaf

San Marzano tomatoes, 1 large can (28 oz.), crushed

Fresh Italian parsley, ½ cup, chopped (use ¼ cup to sprinkle)

Water, 2 quarts

Fish, 2 ½–3 pounds non-oily (such as cod, walleye, whiting, or red snapper).

Salt 2 teaspoons

Pepper, to taste

Spaghetti, ½–¾ pound, broken into 1-inch pieces, or petite pasta of choice.

DIRECTIONS:

In a large, 4-quart stockpot, sauté garlic and onions in olive oil until soft and translucent, but do not brown. Add ¼ cup parsley and cook for 1 minute. Mash the garlic cloves; add bay leaf and tomatoes. Simmer for 35 minutes. Add 2 quarts water and bring to boil.

Add fish and cook until tender (about 15–20 minutes). Add 2 teaspoons salt and pepper to taste. Cook spaghetti or petite pasta of choice in boiling water, al dente. Drain, add to soup and cook until tender. Remove bay leaf and sprinkle with ¼ cup parsley.

Makes 6 servings.

TIP: *If you want to add shrimp, add it the last 30 to 60 seconds.*

TIP: *Taste the broth, if you need more salt and pepper add if needed.*

TIP: *You can buy bags of "Spaghetti baby" at the store (pre-broken, 1-inch pieces) or break the pieces yourself.*

ANTIPASTI, SOUPS & DIPS

Flaming Cheese

Saganaki (Greek Recipe)

Kasseri is a medium-hard pale yellow Greek or Turkish cheese made from unpasteurized sheep milk with very little, if any, goat's milk mixed in. There is also a cow's milk version. It belongs to the pasta filata family of cheeses, like Provolone.

DIRECTIONS:

Beat egg and water. Mix the flour and cracker crumbs. Dip the cheese slices in egg then coat with the flour/cracker mixture. Fry in very hot oil, quickly on each side until golden in color. Drain with a slotted spatula and place on warm platter.

Transfer cheese to a preheated plate (plate must be oven proof to withstand the heating and flaming). Warm Brandy lightly and pour over cheese; ignite cheese with lighter. Extinguish flame with juice from the lemon. Reminder—stand back a good distance while igniting!

Makes 4–6 servings.

INGREDIENTS

Egg, 1 large

Water, 1 tablespoon

Flour, ½ cup

Cracker crumbs, ½ cup (fine ground Saltines)

Kasseri cheese, ¾ pound sliced ½ or ¼-inch thick

Vegetable oil, ¼ cup

Brandy, 2 tablespoons

Lemon, ½ lemon

TIP: *Serve with crusty bread.*

ANTIPASTI, SOUPS & DIPS

Lentil Soup with Sausage & Pancetta

Zuppa di Lenticchie Con Salsiccia

This is normally eaten as lentil soup, but we also like to eat it with ditalini pasta. You can also make this as a vegetarian soup. My friend Boni hates lentil soup but loves my version. I think you will too!

INGREDIENTS

- **Olive oil,** 2 tablespoons
- **Sweet or hot Italian sausage,** ½ pound
- **Pancetta,** ¼ pound chopped
- **Onions,** 2 cups chopped
- **Garlic,** 1 tablespoon chopped
- **Celery,** 1 cup chopped (2 stalks)
- **Diced tomatoes,** 1 can (28 oz.)
- **Lentils,** 1 pound dry, rinsed
- **Carrots,** 1 ½ cup large chunks
- **Water,** 8 cups
- **Chicken broth,** 4 cups (add more if needed)
- **Bay,** 1 leaf
- **Fresh basil,** ½ teaspoon chopped
- **Salt,** 1 teaspoon or to taste
- **Parsley,** 2 tablespoons chopped
- **Optional:** dry ditalini pasta, 1 cup

DIRECTIONS:

Heat oil in a large pot. Over medium high heat, add the sausage and pancetta; stirring occasionally. Cook until light brown for about 4–5 minutes. Add the onion, garlic, celery, and sauté until translucent. Add tomatoes, cook for about 3–4 minutes. Stir in lentils, carrot, water, chicken broth, bay leaf, basil, and salt. Bring to a boil. Reduce heat, cover and simmer for 1 ½ hours or until lentils are tender. Add parsley and salt to taste. Drizzle with olive oil and serve with Romano cheese sprinkled on top of each serving bowl.

TIP: *Add 1 cup ditalini pasta to make with lentil soup. Cook until tender. Delicious!*

ANTIPASTI, SOUPS & DIPS

INGREDIENTS

Artichokes, 1 can (14 ounces) halved in brine (drained)

Sweet red pepper, 1 sliced

Red pepper, ⅛ teaspoon crushed

Kalamata olives, ½ cup (no pit)

Italian red onion, ¼ thinly sliced

MARINADE SAUCE INGREDIENTS

Vegetable or light olive oil, ⅓ cup

Red wine vinegar, 2 tablespoons

Garlic, ½ teaspoon finely chopped

Paprika, ½ teaspoon

Salt, ¼ teaspoon

Black pepper, dash

Oregano, ½ teaspoon

Marinated Artichokes

Carciofi Marinati

Can be eaten with salad or as an antipasto.

DIRECTIONS:

Combine and whip the marinade sauce ingredients. Pour over the vegetables and marinate overnight.

ANTIPASTI, SOUPS & DIPS

Mushrooms Stuffed with Ricotta

Funghi Ripiene con Ricotta

Use a 9x12-inch baking dish, or size of your choice depending upon size of mushrooms.

INGREDIENTS

Mushrooms, 1 dozen caps (more if small)
Ricotta, 1 ½ cups well-drained
Breadcrumbs, ⅓ cup dried
Romano cheese, ⅓ cup grated
Fresh basil leaves, 2 teaspoons, chopped
Fresh Italian parsley, 2 teaspoons, chopped
Garlic salt, ¼ teaspoon
Ground black pepper, to taste

DIRECTIONS:

Preheat oven to 400°F.

Remove stems from mushrooms and quickly rinse caps under water. Drain well. Set aside.

In a large bowl, mix the ricotta, breadcrumbs, Romano cheese, basil leaves, parsley, garlic salt and pepper until well blended. Coat a baking dish (9x12-inch) with some olive oil. Sprinkle the mushroom caps with salt.

Stuff each cap with 1–2 tablespoons of ricotta filling, depending upon size. Place the stuffed mushroom caps inside the baking dish right next to each other. Drizzle with olive oil, or sprinkle with Romano. Bake at 400°F for 25 minutes for large caps, 15 minutes for small caps.

TIP: *Instead of getting rid of the mushroom stems, sauté them and enjoy!*

ANTIPASTI, SOUPS & DIPS

INGREDIENTS

Mushrooms, 1 pound fresh

Garlic, 2 cloves minced

Olive oil, ¼ cup

Italian sausage, ½ pound (fresh), plain or spicy

Bread crumbs, ½ cup

Fresh Italian parsley, 1 tablespoon chopped

Romano cheese, ¼ cup grated

Salt & Pepper, to taste

Mushrooms Stuffed with Sausage

Funghi ripieni con Salsiccia

DIRECTIONS:

Preheat oven to 350°F.

Wipe mushrooms with a damp cloth. Remove stems and set aside on a plate. Place caps in a shallow baking pan (9x13).

In a large skillet, sauté garlic in olive oil until light brown. Chop mushroom stems; add stems and Italian sausage into the large skillet with garlic. Cook until sausage is done (all the way through) and crumble with wooden spoon, let cool. Place sausage crumbles in a large bowl; add breadcrumbs, parsley, cheese, salt and pepper to taste.

Stuff each mushroom. Drizzle oil over mushrooms and bake in oven (350°F) until tender, about 15–20 minutes. Wonderful!

ANTIPASTI, SOUPS & DIPS

Panini (Grilled)

Panini

Great for lunch or dinner. Add your favorite soup as a side dish. Enjoy!

DIRECTIONS:

On each of four bread slices, layer prosciutto, mozzarella, capocollo, and basil. Top with remaining bread slices. Brush sandwich sides with olive oil. Grill each sandwich in a Panini or sandwich; grill according to manufacturer's directions.

Makes 4 sandwiches.

INGREDIENTS

Italian bread, 8 slices, soft-textured (Calabrese bread from Roma's Bakery)

Sliced prosciutto, 4 ounces

Mozzarella cheese, 4 ounces fresh or regular, sliced

Capocollo, 8 slices

Basil, 4–8 large leaves

Olive oil

INGREDIENTS

Zucchini, 8 small, quartered lengthwise

Salt, 1 teaspoon

Olive oil, ½ cup

Garlic, 2 cloves, sliced

Red wine vinegar, 3 tablespoons

Sugar, 1 teaspoon

Mint, 3–4 leaves, chopped

Pickled Zucchini, Sweet & Sour

Zucchine Agrodolci

DIRECTIONS:

Cut zucchini quarters in half, crosswise, and toss with salt. Let it sit for one-half hour then squeeze dry gently. Heat oil over medium-high heat and add zucchini in batches, cooking until just wilted slightly, for about 3 minutes. Remove zucchini and add garlic to skillet, stirring over medium heat until garlic is soft. Stir in vinegar and sugar and cook until sugar dissolves. Pour mixture over zucchini, toss mint gently, cover and refrigerate, mixing occasionally, for at least two days.

It will keep for 1–2 weeks.

ANTIPASTI, SOUPS & DIPS

Potato Garlic Soup

Zuppa di Aglio e Patate della Mamma

This was made by Mamma because it was economical and so delicious. In Italy we had it on Fridays because we couldn't eat meat.

DIRECTIONS:

Place 5 tablespoons olive oil in a deep pan. Add 2 cloves sliced garlic and sauté for about 2 minutes. Add potatoes, salt, pepper, and oregano. Stir well; add water and parsley. Bring to a boil and simmer for 30 minutes. Add salt to taste. Serve with Parmesan or Romano cheese. Enjoy!

INGREDIENTS

Garlic, 2 large cloves, sliced

Olive oil, 5 tablespoons

Russet potatoes (or Yukon Gold), 3 pounds cut into chunks

Salt, 1 teaspoon

Black pepper, pinch

Oregano, pinch

Water, 3 ½–4 cups (as needed)

Italian parsley, 2 tablespoons coarsely chipped

Parmesan or Romano cheese, on top

RICOTTA BALL INGREDIENTS

- **Ricotta cheese,** (regular) 1 ½ – 2 pounds
- **Fresh Italian parsley,** 3 tablespoons chopped
- **Romano cheese,** ½ cup
- **Bread crumbs,** ¾ cup unseasoned
- **Dried bread,** 3 slices, soaked in water and water squeezed out
- **Eggs,** 2 large
- **Salt,** ½ teaspoon
- **Black pepper,** pinch
- **Butter,** 1 tablespoon (softened)

CHICKEN BROTH INGREDIENTS

- **Chicken broth,** 2 quarts
- **Endive or escarole,** 2 heads (washed), chopped into 2-inch cubes

Ricotta Dumpling Soup

Pollpetti di Ricotta in Brodo

This simple yet delicious soup is my Mamma's recipe. Unbelievably good. Great on a cool fall day or for a light dinner.

DIRECTIONS:

Mix ricotta ball ingredients well with hands. Form into 1 ½ inch balls. Set aside on baking sheet or platter.

Bring broth to a boil and simmer until the endive or escarole is tender. Boil for 5 minutes.

Drop the ricotta balls into the broth and bring to a boil over medium heat. Cover and simmer slowly for 7–10 minutes. Turn off heat and let set for approximately 10 minutes. Taste; add salt if needed.

NOTE: *In Italy we eat Ricotta any time; especially in this dumpling soup. In Calabria, it is customary to eat this soup on St. Joseph's Day.*

ANTIPASTI, SOUPS & DIPS

Roasted Red Pepper and Sun-Dried Tomato Tapenade

Impasto di Peperoni Rossi arrostiti e Pomodori essicata al sole

This is a delicious variation of a traditional Tapenade, a paste or dip, made from black olives, capers, and anchovies.

DIRECTIONS:

Drain tomatoes using a small colander. Place tomatoes in prep bowl. Microwave on high 6–10 seconds or until tomatoes are slightly softened.

Combine parsley, garlic, olives and walnuts in food processor. Cover and process until coarsely chopped. Add tomatoes, oil and vinegar; process until coarsely chopped. Add peppers; process to desired consistency, removing lid and scraping down sides of bowl as necessary.

Makes 16 servings.

TIP: *Drizzle a little bit of olive oil over the top when finished.*

TIP: *Serve with crackers or toasted baguette slices (cut diagonally).*

INGREDIENTS

Sun-dried tomatoes, ½ cup in oil

Fresh parsley, ½ cup loosely packed

Garlic, 1 clove, peeled

Kalamata olives, ⅓ cup pitted, drained

Walnut halves, ¼ cup, toasted

Olive oil, 2 tablespoons

Balsamic vinegar, 1 tablespoon

Red peppers, (jarred) 1 cup roasted, drained and patted dry

ANTIPASTI, SOUPS & DIPS

INGREDIENTS

Extra-virgin olive oil, 3 tablespoons

Sweet Italian sausage, 1 pound (remove the casing and cut into small pieces)

Garlic, 1 large clove, minced

Onion, 1 cup, chopped

Tomatoes, 16 ounces stewed (with juice)

Beef bouillon, 2 cubes

Beef broth, 32 ounces

Water, 4 cups

Salt, 2 teaspoons

Black pepper, ½ teaspoon

Fresh Italian parsley, 1 tablespoon chopped

Celery, 2 stalks, chopped

Carrot, 1 large, chopped

Cabbage, 3 cups, chopped

Potato, 1 large, cubed

Tubettini pasta, 1 cup (dry)

Cannellini beans (or white northern), 20 ounces drained

Pecorino Romano cheese, ½ cup

Sausage Soup with Minestrone

Minestrone con Salsiccia

A Roma Bakery Specialty! Very tasty and delicious.

DIRECTIONS:

Place olive oil and sausage in a large pot and sauté about 3 minutes. Add the garlic and onion, stirring occasionally about 1–2 minutes until golden. Add tomatoes and cook about 1 minute. Add bouillon cubes, beef broth, water, salt, black pepper and bring to a boil. Add parsley, celery, carrot, and cabbage. Bring to a boil again then adjust the heat to medium, simmering. Cook covered about 15–20 minutes. Add potatoes and cook about 5 minutes. Add the dry Tubettini pasta and Cannellini beans and cook about 8–10 minutes stirring occasionally until pasta is tender. Remove the soup from heat and let it set 5 minutes. Taste the soup, and if too thick, add a little more broth.

Serve in individual bowls and top with grated Pecorino Romano or Parmesan-Reggiano cheese.

TIP: *If you have fresh pesto, add 1–2 tablespoons to the soup.*

ANTIPASTI, SOUPS & DIPS

Spinach and Olive Tapenade

Impasto di Spinaci e Olive

Serve with your favorite toasted baguette slices.

INGREDIENTS

Fresh baby spinach leaves, 1 package (6 oz.)

Garlic, 2 cloves, peeled

Capers, 2 tablespoons drained

Red bell pepper, ¼ medium, cut into 1-inch pieces

Green olives, ¾ cup pitted

Fresh basil, ¼ cup loosely packed leaves

Parmigiano-Reggiano cheese, ¼ cup

Olive oil, ¼ cup

Fresh lemon juice, 1 tablespoon

Salt, ¼ teaspoon

DIRECTIONS:

Place spinach in a large bowl. Microwave, covered, on high for 2 minutes or until spinach is wilted.

Carefully remove lid; press spinach to side of bowl. Blot excess moisture with paper towels (or use hands to wring out water) and set aside.

Place garlic, capers, bell pepper and olives in food processor; pulse until coarsely chopped. Add spinach, basil, cheese, oil, lemon juice and salt; process to desired consistency, removing lid and scraping down sides of bowl as necessary.

Makes 16 servings.

Spinach Pie

Spanakopita (Greek Recipe)

Filo (Filo Pastry) is a dough made of paper thin sheets of flour dough separated by a thin film of butter. It is used for making pastries in the Middle Eastern and Balkan cuisine. It can be found in the freezer section of Roma Bakery.

INGREDIENTS

Frozen spinach, 3 pounds, chopped (de-thawed and well-drained; squeeze water out with hands)

Eggs, 7 large

Feta cheese, 1 pound, crumbled

Ricotta cheese, ¾ pound, crumbled

Semolina flour, 2 tablespoons

Fresh Italian parsley, ¼ cup, chopped

Dill weed, 1 tablespoon

Fresh green onions, 2 bunches, chopped

Lemon juice, 1 tablespoon

Salt, 1 teaspoon

Black pepper, ½ teaspoon (add additional Salt and pepper, to taste)

Filo dough, 1 pound package

Clarified butter, 1 pound

DIRECTIONS:

In a large bowl, thoroughly mix the first 11 ingredients with hands and set aside.

Make clarified butter* and set aside. Set 1 pound of filo dough aside.

Start with ½ package of filo dough. In a 12x18-inch cookie sheet, create the following layers: first brush melted butter on the cookie sheet, next place one sheet of the filo dough, then lightly brush it with more melted

(recipe continues)

butter. Continue layering filo dough lightly brushing butter on each sheet until ½ package of filo is used up.

Once ½ package of filo dough is used up, add the spinach mixture (spread evenly with hands) and top with the remaining filo dough. Create the same layers (alternating butter and filo dough). On the last two layers, brush the dough with a little bit of water and butter (mixed). Tuck in the sides with a knife.

Score the surface into serving size pieces to make 24 pieces (4 x 6). Bake in a 350°F oven for 20 minutes then bake at 375°F for another 25–35 minutes until golden brown. Let set about 5–6 minutes then cut all the way through the pieces (to the bottom of pan). Serve hot. I suggest serving with a fresh green salad and fresh fruit with the spinach pie for a perfect lunch or dinner.

* **How to clarify butter:** Cut the butter into small pieces for quick melting. Bring it to a slow boil in a saucepan. Watch for several minutes until the crackling and bubbling almost cease, meaning that the milky liquid has evaporated and the clarification is complete. Watch that the butter does not burn and darken. Pour the clear yellow butter through a tea strainer. It will turn a yellowish white when cold. This will keep in the refrigerator for months.

TIP: *To keep Filo dough from drying out while using it, keep it wrapped in a towel.*

TIP: *It is best to defrost the package of filo dough in the refrigerator overnight before using. It dries very quickly so have everything ready before you open the plastic bag that it comes in.*

TIP: *If there is extra clarified butter, store in the refrigerator.*

ANTIPASTI, SOUPS & DIPS

INGREDIENTS

Fresh basil, 1 bunch of large leaves, cleaned

Bocconcini mozzarella, 1 pint (small, cherry size mozzarella balls)

QUICK TOMATO SAUCE INGREDIENTS

Tomatoes, 1 (28-ounce) can whole peeled or San Marzano tomatoes (crushed)

Extra-virgin olive oil, 3 tablespoons

Garlic, 1 tablespoon minced

Salt, to taste,

Freshly ground black pepper, to taste

Tomato and Mozzarella Fondue

Pomadore e Mozzarella Fonduta

DIRECTIONS:

Open the can of tomatoes, pour off the juice. Squeeze the whole tomatoes to pulp into a bowl. Set aside.

Heat olive oil in a heavy saucepan. Add garlic and cook until golden and fragrant; do not overcook. Add tomato pulp, stir to combine, and reduce the heat to a simmer. Simmer for about 5 minutes. Season, to taste, with salt and pepper. Serve as a dipping sauce for bocconcini. Serves 6 to 10.

Dip fresh large basil leaves in boiling water for just a second and then remove and place into a large bowl of ice water. Drain the basil, carefully squeezing out the excess water, but keeping the leaves whole. Wrap 1 basil leaf around each bocconcini. Skewer the wrapped bocconcini onto the end of a wooden skewer. Dip in the tomato sauce and enjoy!

Makes 6–10 servings.

Taramasalata Dip

A Greek recipe from my friend Sophia.

Enjoy with raw vegetables or sliced bread as a dip.

DIRECTIONS:

Combine the vegetable and olive oils. In a blender or food processor, combine tarama, and onion. Mix until creamy. Add the moistened bread a little at a time, alternating with combined oil until both are used up. After well blended or pulsated, add the lemon juice slowly. Beat until smooth. If it is too thick, add a little more oil. Add salt to taste. Refrigerate.

INGREDIENTS

Vegetable oil, ½ cup

Olive oil, 1 cup

Tarama, 5 ounces (caviar-carp roe)

Onion, ½ cup chopped

White bread, 9 slices, cut off crust, moisten in water, wring out

Lemon Juice, 2 squeezed lemons

ANTIPASTI, SOUPS & DIPS

EGG DISHES

Eggs Poached in Tomato Sauce   40

Eggs with Tomatoes   41

Frittata (Easter Omelet)   42

Frittata – Ham and Cheese   45

Frittata (Mamma's Spaghetti)   44

Frittata with Artichokes   45

INGREDIENTS

Marinara tomato sauce, 2 cups

Butter, 2 tablespoons

Olive oil, 2 tablespoon

Eggs, 8 large

Romano cheese, 4 tablespoons

Italian parsley, 1 tablespoon, chopped

Eggs Poached in Tomato Sauce

Uova in Purgatorio

Eggs in Purgatory! Italians can be so dramatic!

DIRECTIONS:

Pour the marinara tomato sauce into a medium frying pan. Add butter and olive oil; stir together. Heat until it starts to gently bubble, reduce to medium heat. Break the eggs into the liquid very gently (don't touch or beat the eggs). Cover the pan with a lid and simmer on low heat for 5 minutes or until the whites get firm. Remove the eggs and place on a slice of Italian bread. Pour the sauce on top, sprinkle with Romano cheese and parsley and serve immediately. Sprinkle with salt to taste.

NOTE: *My mother served the egg with sauce on a plate; this way we could eat more bread and dip it in the egg sauce. In Italy, we did not have breakfast (our breakfast was coffee, milk, biscotti, or brioche). Instead would have this for lunch or in the evening for dinner!*

EGG DISHES

Eggs with Tomatoes

Uova alla Diavola

Great with Italian crusty bread!

INGREDIENTS

Butter, 3 tablespoons

Olive oil, 1 tablespoon

Onions, 2 medium, thinly sliced

Marinara tomato sauce, 2 cups (fresh)

Salt and freshly ground Pepper, to taste

Hot pepper, ¼ teaspoon

Eggs, 6 large

Parmigiano cheese, 8 tablespoons, freshly grated

DIRECTIONS:

Melt butter with oil in a large skillet. When butter foams, add onions. Sauté over medium heat until pale yellow. Add tomato sauce and season with salt and hot pepper. Cook for 10 minutes. Break eggs into skillet and cook about 1 minute. Spoon a generous tablespoon Parmesan cheese over each egg. Cover skillet and reduce heat. Simmer 3 to 4 minutes or until eggs are firm and cheese is melted. Spoon tomato sauce around eggs. Serve immediately.

Frittata (Easter Omelet)

Frittata

A tradition at Easter but welcome any time of year. What makes this one different is the meat and cheese which makes it Calabrese. The beauty of a Frittata is that no matter what you put in it…It's delicious!

INGREDIENTS

Eggs, 6 large

Salt, ¼ teaspoon

Water, ½ cup

Ricotta, ½ cup, crumbled

Flour, 1 cup

Provolone cheese, 6 ounces, cubed

Mozzarella, 6 ounces, cubed

Pancetta, 2 ounces, thinly chopped

Prosciutto or ham, 2 ounces, in thin strips

Salami or sopressata, 2 ounces, in thin strips

Italian pork sausage, 2 ounces, cooked (or dry cured)

Oil, ¼ cup

DIRECTIONS:

Preheat oven to 325°F.

In a large mixing bowl lightly whisk the eggs and salt. Add the water and flour and whisk or use a mixer to blend until smooth, like pancake batter. Add the remaining ingredients and mix well with a spatula.

In a 10-inch, non-stick frying pan, add half of the oil, saving the rest for later. Pour the egg mixture into the pan and cook over medium heat. Use a fork or small spatula to separate clumps of meat or cheese. Pull the edges in toward the middle.

Center the edge of the pan over the burner, holding about ¼ of the pan over direct heat for about 1 minute. Then rotate clockwise around the burner applying heat to each quarter of the pan for about 1 minute. This method will prevent the center of the frittata from burning. Cook until set on bottom and golden brown.

Use a small amount of the reserved oil to grease a large plate. Place the plate on the frying pan and flip over to place the omelet on the plate. Place the frying pan back on medium heat, adding the remaining oil. Slide

(recipe continues)

the omelet back into the pan and use a fork or small spatula to lift the edges to see when golden brown and poke center to check if eggs still runny. Again, rotate the pan ¼ at a time over the center of the burner, about 1 minute for each ¼ of the pan. When set, place the frying pan into the oven for about 10 minutes or until edges sizzle and a fork comes out clean when poked in the center.

Remove from oven to set for couple minutes while you place a couple sheets of paper towel on a large plate. Slide the omelet from the pan onto the paper towel covered plate. Let rest for a minute to absorb excess oil. Then flip the omelet over onto a serving platter. Let set for a few minutes before slicing into 6 portions. Serve with a tossed salad.

NOTE: *Pepperoni could also be used as a substitution for cooked pork sausage. It will add a spicier flavor.*

Rotate pan around burner to prevent center from burning.

EGG DISHES

Frittata (Mamma's Spaghetti)

Frittata di spaghetti della Mamma

Making leftover spaghetti into a frittata was done all the time in Italian kitchens. Leftover vegetables or meats, such as sausage, can be used, but our preference was plain.

INGREDIENTS

Eggs, 6 large

Fresh parsley, 2 tablespoons, minced

Salt, ¼ teaspoon

Romano cheese, 2 tablespoons, finely grated

Provolone or mozzarella, ¾ cup, diced

Leftover spaghetti, 2 ½ cups, sauced (can cut if preferred)

Extra virgin olive oil, 4 tablespoons

DIRECTIONS:

Preheat oven to 325°F

Whisk the eggs in a medium sized bowl, just until foamy. Stir in the parsley, salt and cheese. Stir in the spaghetti. Set aside. Heat the olive oil in a 10-inch, non-stick frying pan, over medium heat. When the oil is hot, carefully pour in the spaghetti mixture and smooth with a rubber spatula. Cover the pan and cook until the mixture begins to firm up and the frittata moves in one piece when the pan is shaken. Lift up one end of the frittata with the spatula and when it's light golden brown, slide out onto a lightly oiled, large plate. Turn it over and slip back into the pan to cook the other side, until lifted edges are golden brown.

Place the frying pan into the oven on the bottom rack for about 10 minutes, until the edges sizzle and a form poked into the middle comes out clean. Let cool for a few minutes, then slide onto serving platter. Let set for couples minutes longer before slicing into 6 portions. Serve with desired amount of marinara sauce poured over slices.

EGG DISHES

Frittata with Artichokes

Frittata di Carciofi

DIRECTIONS:

In a bowl, whisk the eggs. Add garlic salt, black pepper, parsley, and Romano cheese, mix well. Add artichoke hearts, bread crumbs, and mozzarella. Mix together well.

Heat the oil in a large (10-inch), non-stick frying pan. Pour in the batter and fry on medium heat until set on one side. Use a large plate (lightly oiled) to flip the frittata. Place the plate over the frying pan, flip over so frittata is on the plate, and slide the frittata back into the pan. Be careful not to burn yourself. Flip the frittata two or three times until the center is set. To check, pull the center apart a little with a fork; it should be set like custard in the center.

INGREDIENTS

Eggs, 5 large
Garlic salt, ½ teaspoon
Dash of black pepper
Fresh parsley, 1 tablespoon, chopped
Romano cheese, ¼ cup
Artichoke hearts, 14 ounces (canned), drained and cut into quarters
Bread crumbs, ½ cup
Mozzarella, ½ cup, cubed
Vegetable oil, ½ cup

Frittata — Ham and Cheese

Frittata Contadina

DIRECTIONS:

Sauté onions in 1 tablespoon olive oil, over medium-heat, until soft. Add mushrooms and cook until lightly browned. Mix together the eggs, salt, pepper, parsley and cheese. Stir in the ham, mozzarella, onions and mushrooms.

Heat the remaining oil, 10-inch skillet, until very hot. Pour in egg mixture and lower heat immediately. Cover and cook until eggs are no longer runny. Turn the frittata onto a large plate and slip back into pan. Return to heat and cook until lightly browned on bottom. May be served warm or at room temperature.

INGREDIENTS

Onion, ½ cup, chopped
Mushrooms, ½ cup, sliced
Eggs, 5 large, whisked
Salt and pepper, to taste
Fresh Italian parsley, 1 tablespoon, chopped
Parmesan cheese, 1 tablespoon, grated
Ham or prosciutto, ½ cup, chopped
Mozzarella cheese, ½ cup, cubed
Olive oil, 4 tablespoons

EGG DISHES

FISH

Baked Halibut   48

Baked Swordfish Steaks   49

Codfish Salad (Sicilian Style)   51

Codfish Stew (Baccalá)   52

Codfish Stew (Fresh)   54

Cod Sautéed with Shrimp Sauce   50

Deep-Fried Squid   55

Halibut and Onions   48

Mixed Fried Fish   56

Mussels Marinara   57

Salmon with White Bean Salad   58

Scallop Kabobs   61

Scallops and Mushrooms   60

Shrimp Scampi with Artichokes   62

Spicy Shrimp   63

Tiella (Casserole)   59

Baked Halibut

Ippoglosso al forno

INGREDIENTS

Halibut steaks, 1 ½ pounds
Salt and pepper (to taste)
Butter, 5 tablespoons
Worcestershire sauce, 1 teaspoon
Scallions, 3, chopped with green tops
Italian parsley, 2 tablespoons, finely chopped

GARNISH

Lemon wedges
Paprika, sprinkled

DIRECTIONS:

Preheat the oven to 375°F. Wash and dry your steaks with paper towel. Salt and pepper both sides. Place the steaks in a greased shallow baking dish. In a saucepan, melt the butter and Worcestershire sauce. Pour over the steaks. Arrange chopped scallions on top. Sprinkle with parsley and bake for 20–25 minutes. Cut and place lemon wedges around edges of platter. Sprinkle with paprika

Halibut and Onions

Ippoglosso e Cipolle

INGREDIENTS

Salt, ½ teaspoon
Pepper, ½ teaspoon
Garlic salt, ½ teaspoon (mix together)
Halibut steaks, 2 pounds
Onions, 2 medium, thinly sliced
Butter, 4 tablespoons, melted
Heavy cream, ½ cup
Fresh Italian parsley, 2 tablespoons, finely chopped
Paprika, ½ teaspoon

DIRECTIONS:

Preheat the oven to 350°F. Wash and dry your fish. Sprinkle both sides with salt, pepper, and garlic salt mixture. Place half the onions in a greased baking dish. Put the fish on top, and then put the remaining onions on top of the fish. Melt the butter and pour over fish; then pour on the cream. Bake 20–25 minutes. Before serving, sprinkle with parsley and paprika.

TIP: *Serve with lemon wedges*

FISH

Baked Swordfish Steaks

Pesce Spada al Forno

DIRECTIONS:

First, preheat oven to 375°F and adjust rack to center of oven.

Melt butter in a large skillet over low heat. Add onion and sauté, stirring constantly, until soft but not brown; approximately 5 minutes. Add carrot, celery, lemon zest, and juice. Increase heat to medium-high and sauté, stirring constantly, until mixture is soft and slightly glazed; about 10 minutes. Stir in thyme, 1 teaspoon salt, ½ teaspoon pepper and remove from heat. Spread half of the vegetable mixture evenly in bottom of 9x13-inch baking dish.

Rinse steaks and blot dry with paper towel. Cut steaks into 6 servings.

In a shallow bowl, combine flour with remaining salt and pepper. Dredge steaks on both sides and shake off excess (dredge immediately before sautéing or flour coating will get gummy).

In a large skillet, heat oil over medium-high heat until hot. Add steaks and quickly sauté on both sides to seal in juices; about 30 seconds on each side.

Arrange steaks in a single layer on top of the vegetable mixture. Spread remaining vegetable mixture evenly over each steak. Pour wine over vegetable mixture.

Cover dish tightly with foil and bake for 15 minutes. Remove foil and spoon some of the pan juices over vegetable mixture. Bake uncovered until fish barely flakes when tested with a fork, about 5 to 10 minutes. Serve immediately. Drizzle a little bit of Salmoriglio (lemon oil dressing) on each steak.

INGREDIENTS

Unsalted butter, 6 tablespoons

Onion, 1 cup finely chopped

Carrot, 2 cups, cut into ¼-inch cubes

Celery, 2 cups (strings removed), cut into ¼-inch cubes

Lemon zest, 1 teaspoon grated

Fresh lemon juice, 2 tablespoons

Fresh thyme, 1 tablespoons minced or 1 teaspoon crumbled dried thyme

Salt, 1 teaspoon

Black pepper, ½ teaspoon

Swordfish steaks, 2 ½ pounds, about 1-inch thick

Wondra flour, ½ cup

Salt, ½ teaspoon

Light olive oil, ½ cup

Dry white wine, ½ cup

INGREDIENTS FOR COD

Cod steaks, 3 pounds (fresh or frozen), cut into large pieces (3x5 inches)

Milk, 1 cup

Cornmeal, 1 cup

Butter, ¼ pound

Garlic salt, ½ teaspoon

Pepper, ¼ teaspoon

Italian parsley, 1 tablespoon, chopped

INGREDIENTS FOR COD

Shrimp, 1 cup cooked, chopped

Milk, 1 ½ cups

Butter, 3 tablespoons

Flour, 3 tablespoons

Paprika, ⅛ teaspoon

Salt and pepper, to taste

Cod Sautéed with Shrimp Sauce

Merluzzo salato in padella con salsa di gamberi

DIRECTIONS:

Prepare the shrimp sauce first. In a small saucepan, melt the butter over very low heat. Remove from the heat and stir in the flour, paprika, salt and pepper; stir 1 minute with a wooden spoon. Return to heat and add the milk all at once; Stir until smooth and the heat has thickened the sauce. Add the shrimp.

Dip the cod steaks in milk, then in cornmeal, salt and pepper. Melt the butter. Sauté the cod in butter for 4 minutes on each side. Serve steaming with hot shrimp sauce. Garnish with Italian parsley.

TIP: *Add salt and pepper to taste*

FISH

Codfish Salad (Sicilian Style)

Insalata di Merluzzo-Baccalá

INGREDIENTS

Dried salted cod, 1 pound

Milk, 3 cups

Red skin potatoes, 2 medium, cooked, peeled and diced

Celery, ½ cup, diced

Sweet red pepper, ½ cup diced

Capers in brine, 2 tablespoons, drained

Fresh Italian parsley, ¼ cup minced

Extra virgin olive oil, ½ cup

Red wine vinegar, 2 tablespoons

Sea salt, to taste

Ground black pepper, to taste

DIRECTIONS:

Rinse the salted cod in cold water. Place in a large container (1–2 gallons). Cut the cod into 2x4-inch pieces. Store in refrigerator to soak and de-salt for 2–3 days, changing the water at least 2 times per day. Cod will taste salty if the water is not changed.

Place the fish in a sauté pan and add the milk; bring to a boil then lower the heat and simmer the fish until it begins to flake for 8–10 minutes. Lift the fish out of the pan with a serrated spatula and place it on a cutting board. Let it cool then flake fish into bite size pieces and place in a large bowl. Discard the milk.

Add the potatoes, celery, red pepper, capers and fresh Italian parsley and toss the mixture gently. Add the olive oil and vinegar; toss again to combine. Add salt and pepper to taste.

Place on a serving platter and serve at room temperature. Add a few slices of lemon.

FISH

INGREDIENTS

Dried salted cod, 2 ½ pounds, cut into 2x3-inch pieces (plus 2 quarts water for soaking)

Flour, 1 cup

Olive oil, 1 cup

Onion, 1 ½ cups, chopped

Celery, 1 stalk, cubed

Dry Vermouth, ½ cup (or dry white wine)

Water, 4 cups

Fresh chopped parsley, 1 tablespoons

Oregano, ¼ teaspoon

Salt, ½–1 teaspoon (taste first then add salt)

Potatoes (Yukon Gold), 6 medium–large, peeled and cut into chunks

Capers, 1 ½ –2 tablespoons

Green Italian olives, ½–¾ cup (or Kalamata olives, pitted)

INGREDIENTS FOR THICKENING

Water, ¼ cup

Flour, 1 tablespoon

Codfish Stew (Baccalá)

Stufato di Merluzzo alla Calabrese

This recipe is from the Calabria region. My family loves Baccala stew, especially for Christmas Eve or for Lent.

DIRECTIONS:

Rinse the salted cod in cold water. Place in a large container (1–2 gallons). Cut the cod into 2x4-inch pieces. Store in refrigerator to soak and de-salt for 2–3 days, changing the water at least 2 times per day. Cod will taste salty if the water is not changed.

Rinse cod fish, drain and pat dry.

Cut into desired pieces and dredge in flour.

Heat 1 cup oil in a large skillet (12-inch); fry cod, in batches, until golden brown on all sides. Remove and place cod in bowl; keep warm.

Reserve remaining fried oil and set aside in a bowl; In the same large skillet, add ⅓ cup of the reserved oil (scooping only the clear oil from surface of the bowl); heat oil on high-heat. Add onion and celery; sauté for 5 minutes then lower heat. Add wine and cook slowly uncovered 2–3 minutes until alcohol is evaporated. Add 4 cups of water. Add parsley, oregano, ½–1 teaspoon salt (taste water prior to adding desired amount of salt), potatoes and enough water to barely cover them.

(recipe continues)

FISH

Dissolve 1 tablespoon of flour in a little cold water and stir into the potato mixture. Cook until potatoes are tender but still firm. Lay pieces of fried cod fish on top of potatoes then add olives and capers on top of cod. Spoon some of the juices on top of cod to moisten. Cover and steam slowly for about 7 to 10 minutes.

TIP: *If stew becomes too thick, dilute with a little more water. After cooking and before serving, taste the broth to see if more salt is needed. Ladle the stew fish into the soup bowl. Serve with a crusty loaf of Italian bread and enjoy!*

TIP: *Variation: If a red sauce is preferred add 28oz. can of Italian plum tomatoes (crushed) after adding the wine (in addition to the stew ingredients listed). Cook for 20 minutes before adding the potatoes, water, and remaining ingredients (follow exact recipe above).*

FISH

INGREDIENTS

Extra-virgin olive oil, ½ cup

White onion, 1 large, thinly sliced

Italian parsley, ½ cup, minced (use 1 teaspoon on top)

Potatoes, 4 large, peeled and cut into chunks

Hot water, 3 cups

Fresh cod filets, 3 pounds, cut into chunks (2x3 inches)

Pine nuts, ¼ cup

Raisins, ¼ cup

Salt, 1 ½ teaspoons, to taste

Grinding black pepper, to taste

Codfish Stew (Fresh)

Stufato di Merluzzo—Baccala all Siciliana

This recipe comes from Sicily.

DIRECTIONS:

In a Dutch oven, heat the olive oil. Stir in onions and cook over medium heat until they are wilted down but not browned. Stir in the parsley and potatoes; cook for 5 minutes, stirring occasionally.

Add water and stir with the onion and potatoes mixture. Place the codfish chunks on top of the mixture. Sprinkle pine nuts and raisins on top. Cover the Dutch oven and allow to cook for 12 minutes. Uncover the Dutch oven and stir carefully. Season to taste with salt and pepper. Ladle the fish into soup bowls.

Serves 4–6.

TIP: *Sprinkle with parsley.*

FISH

Deep-Fried Squid

Calamari Fritti

INGREDIENTS

Squid, 2 pounds fresh or frozen, cleaned & washed

Flour, 1 cup, seasoned with ¼ tablespoon black pepper, ½ teaspoon paprika, and ½ teaspoon garlic salt

Vegetable or Peanut oil, for deep-frying

Salt, to taste

Lemon, 2 to 3, cut into wedges

DIRECTIONS:

Clean and wash squid in cold water. Cut the bodies into ½-inch rings, and tentacles in half. Drain well in colander. Coat the squid in the seasoned flour by shaking them in a study plastic bag (place a little bit of squid in the bag at a time). After shaking in flour; gently submerge them into the deep fryer or skillet in batches. Make sure not to over crowd the fryer or skillet.

Use vegetable or peanut oil to fry at 375°F (using a deep fryer or a frying pan) for 2–3 minutes, until golden brown. Drain well. Remove with slotted spoon. Add salt to taste.

TIP: *Use paper towel to drain the oil. Put on a plate and serve with lemon wedges.*

TIP: *Do not overcook or the squid will be tough and chewy! Be careful when placing the fish in the fryer, the hot oil could splash.*

INGREDIENTS

Squid (small), 1 ½ pounds fresh or frozen, cleaned

Shrimp (medium), 1 pound fresh or frozen, peeled and deveined

Smelt, 1 pound fresh or frozen (or other tiny cleaned fish, ie: perch)

Flour, 2 cups, seasoned with ½ tablespoon black pepper, ½ tablespoon paprika, and ⅛ teaspoon garlic granulated

Vegetable oil, for deep-frying

Salt, to taste

Lemons, 2, cut into wedges

Mixed Fried Fish

Fritto Misto di Pesce

DIRECTIONS:

Defrost fish if necessary. Clean and wash squid. Cut bodies into rings and tentacles in half. Shell and devein shrimp. Clean the smelt. Drain all fish well in colander. Dredge all pieces by shaking them in a study bag with seasoned flour (or in a bowl), 1 cup at a time.

In a pan or deep skillet, bring oil to a high heat for frying (375°F). Drop the fish in a few at a time, so that the pan is full but not overcrowded. Keep turning the pieces as they become golden and remove them with a slotted spoon when crispy and golden throughout. Drain on a cookie sheet layered with paper towels and sprinkle with salt. Place on platter with lemon wedges.

Mussels Marinara

Cozze alla Marinara

Serve with Fresh Italian Crusty Bread!

INGREDIENTS

Garlic, 3 cloves, minced

Olive oil, ½ cup

Tomatoes, 1 can (16 oz.), crushed (or 6 fresh Roma tomatoes, cut into quarters/chunks)

Oregano, ½ teaspoon

Fresh Italian parsley, 2 tablespoon, chopped

Salt, ½ teaspoon (or to taste)

Hot red pepper flakes, a pinch

Dry white wine, ½ cup

Mussels, 4 dozen, scrubbed, soaked and de-bearded

DIRECTIONS:

Sauté garlic in olive oil until golden. Add tomatoes, oregano, parsley, salt and red pepper. Cook sauce over medium high heat for 5 minutes. Add wine and cook for about 5 minutes. Add mussels and cook over medium high heat, shaking pan and stirring until all mussels are opened. Serve hot in bowl with the sauce.

Serves 4–6.

TIP: *If mussels do not open, discard*

WHITE BEAN SALAD INGREDIENTS

Extra-virgin olive oil, 3 tablespoons

Celery, ½ cup, chopped

Carrots, ½ cup, chopped

Shallots, ½ cup, chopped

Garlic, 2 cloves, minced

Fresh lemon juice, 3 tablespoons

Fresh Italian parsley, 2 teaspoons, chopped

Fresh mint, 2 teaspoons, chopped

Water, 2 tablespoons

Cannellini beans (white kidney beans), 1 can (20 oz.), drained

SALMON INGREDIENTS

Fresh Italian parsley, 1 tablespoon, chopped

Salt, ½ teaspoon

Black pepper, ⅛ teaspoon

Extra-virgin olive oil, 2 tablespoons

Salmon, 4 fillets, 1-inch thick

Fresh lemon juice, 3 tablespoons

Salmon with White Bean Salad

Salmone con Insalata di Cannellini

WHITE BEAN SALAD DIRECTIONS:

Heat oil in a medium nonstick skillet. Add the celery, carrots, shallots, and garlic. Cook 4 minutes or until tender. Add remaining ingredients. Cook until heated through, stirring constantly. Remove from heat.

SALMON DIRECTIONS:

Combine parsley, salt, black pepper, and olive oil in a small bowl. Sprinkle over the salmon fillets. Place the fillets on a baking sheet. Bake at 375°F for 15 minutes or until the fish flakes easily when tested with a fork. Remove from the oven and sprinkle with lemon juice. Serve salmon with White Bean Salad and fresh Italian bread.

Serves 4.

Tiella (Casserole)

"Tiella" or "Tiedda" Calabrese

DIRECTIONS:

Wash the sole and drain in colander. Lightly sprinkle with salt. Grease the bottom of a 2-quart, 9x13-inch casserole dish with 2 tablespoons oil. In a bowl, make the sauce by mixing together the tomato juice, water, vinegar, and lemon juice. In another bowl, mix together the bread crumbs, Romano cheese, garlic, black pepper, oregano, and parsley.

Proceed to make your layers:
1. A layer of sole
2. Sprinkle a handful of crumb mixture
3. Drizzle a little bit of the sauce to moisten the bread crumbs
4. Chopped tomatoes (⅓ cup per layer)
5. 3 tablespoons olive oil

Repeat layers (3 total). Use the back of a fork to press layers together. Cover with foil. Bake at 375°F for 35 minutes. Remove foil and bake 10 more minutes to get a crispy golden brown top. Let rest 10–15 minutes before serving.

INGREDIENTS

Sole fish, 2 ¼ pound
Salt, for sprinkling
Olive oil, 11 tablespoons
Tomato juice, ¾ cup
Water, ¼ cup
Vinegar, 1 tablespoon
Lemon juice, 1 tablespoon
Dry bread crumbs, 2 cups
Romano cheese, ½ cup
Garlic, 1 teaspoon, finely chopped
Black pepper, ½ teaspoon
Oregano, ½ teaspoon
Fresh Italian parsley, 2 tablespoons, chopped
Tomato, 1 cup, chopped

INGREDIENTS

Water, ½ cup

Dry white wine, ½ cup (or dry vermouth)

Sea scallops, 1 ½ pounds (washed)

Butter, 4 tablespoons

Olive oil, 1 tablespoon

Onion, 1 large, chopped

Mushrooms, ½ pound, sliced

Flour, 3 tablespoons

Milk, ¾ cup

Tabasco sauce, 3 dashes

Swiss cheese, ½ cup, grated

Ketchup, 1 tablespoon

Scallops and Mushrooms

Cappa Santa con Funghi

DIRECTIONS:

Combine water and wine in a bowl. Place ½ cup of the mixture in a medium pan.

Simmer scallops (sliced if thick) 1–2 minutes in the water and wine mixture.

Melt butter and olive oil in the same pan over medium heat. Stir in the onion and mushrooms and simmer for 2–3 minutes. Add the flour and cook for another 1–2 minutes. Add remaining ½ cup water and wine mixture and milk; stir until you have a nice saucy look. Add Tabasco and Swiss cheese; stir over heat until the cheese melts. Add ketchup for color. This is scrumptious served over rice.

Scallop Kabobs

Cappa Santa Kabob

A customer gave me this recipe. Thank you!

DIRECTIONS:

Place the pineapple, mushrooms, red pepper and scallops in a bowl. Combine oil, lemon juice, salt, parsley, Worcestershire sauce, and black pepper. Pour over scallop mixture.

Fry the bacon, 2 minutes on each side (just enough so it is easy to manipulate), and cut in half. Using a skewer, alternate scallops, pineapple, mushrooms, red peppers, and bacon. Cook for 4 minutes, on each side, under the broiler.

TIP: *Serve kabobs on a bed of basic risotto. This is delicious! Enjoy.*

TIP: *Good with orzo pasta!*

INGREDIENTS

Pineapple chunks, 16 ounces, fresh or canned

Fresh button mushrooms, 1 pound

Red pepper, 1, cut in 1-inch squares

Sea scallops, 1 pound (washed)

Oil, ¼ cup

Lemon juice, ¼ cup

Salt, ¼ teaspoon

Fresh Italian parsley, ¼ cup, chopped

Worcestershire sauce, ¼ cup

Black pepper, to taste

Bacon, 12 slices

Skewers

INGREDIENTS

Olive oil, ½ cup

Garlic, 4 large cloves, minced (about 4 teaspoons)

Shallots, 2 medium, thinly sliced (about ⅓ cup)

Shrimp (large), 1 ½ pounds, peeled and de-veined

Artichoke hearts, 12 ounces frozen, thawed and quartered

Dry white wine, ⅓ cup

Fresh lemon juice, 1 tablespoon

Fresh Italian parsley, 2 tablespoons, chopped

Salt, ½ teaspoon

Fresh ground black pepper, ¼ teaspoon

Paprika, ½ teaspoon

Shrimp Scampi with Artichokes

Gamberi con Carciofi

This is my Cousin Carmela's recipe.

DIRECTIONS:

Heat the oil in a large skillet over medium heat. Add garlic and shallots and cook, stirring until softened but not browned; about 2–3 minutes. Add artichoke hearts, wine, and lemon juice; cook for about 3–4 minutes. Add shrimp and cook for an additional 2 minutes until shrimp is pink (add a little bit of chicken broth if needed to keep the shrimp moist). Stir in parsley, salt, pepper, and paprika. Divide among 4 plates; garnish with additional parsley and serve.

TIP: *You can serve this dish with a nice side salad of your choice (try Green Beans with Mint). It is a tasty spring dish!*

FISH

Spicy Shrimp

Gamberi Arrabbiati

DIRECTIONS:

Melt butter in a heavy skillet over high heat. Add flour and stir until it is light golden brown in color. Lower heat; add garlic, onion, parsley, and red pepper. Cook an additional 2 minutes. Raise heat; gradually add water and tomato sauce, stirring constantly until smooth, then add salt, bay leaf, cayenne pepper, and black pepper. Bring to a boil, then simmer and cover for 20–25 minutes. Add shrimp and cook for 2–3 minutes. Do not overcook shrimp. Serve hot over fluffy rice, or Italian Arborio rice.

INGREDIENTS

Butter, ½ cup

Flour, ¼ cup

Garlic, 4 cloves, minced

Onion, 1 medium, sliced

Fresh Italian parsley, 1 tablespoon, minced

Fresh red pepper, ½ cup, chopped

Water, 1 cup

Tomato sauce, 1 cup

Salt, 2 teaspoons

Bay leaf, 1 leaf

Cayenne pepper, ¼ teaspoon

Ground black pepper, to taste (optional)

Shrimp, 1 package (16 oz.) raw (or fresh), peeled and deveined

MEAT

Braciole — Rolled Sirloin Tip   66

Broccoli Rabe with Sausage   80

Grandma's Beef Pizzaiola   67

Lamb Shanks in Tomato Sauce with Orecchiette   68

Leg of Lamb   70

Meatballs   73

Oxtail Style Sauce   74

Pan-Roasted Rabbit with Marsala   75

Papá's Pork Rolls in Tomato Sauce   76

Sausage with Sweet Red Pepper   79

Stuffed Beef Roll   82

Stuffed Eggplant   84

Tripe with Sauce   72

Veal Scaloppine with Marsala Wine Sauce   69

Veal Stuffed Jumbo Shells with Mushroom Béchamel   86

Braciole — Rolled Sirloin Tip

Braciole

There are as many braciole recipes as there are regions in Italy. This braciole is a classic Sicilian dish consisting of a very thin rolled sirloin filled with ham, mozzarella, and breadcrumbs. The cheese oozes from the braciole when cut. Delicious!

INGREDIENTS

Beef (round tip or sirloin), 2 pounds, sliced very thin for best results

Mozzarella cheese (2%), ½ pound, ½-inch thick cubes

Deli ham, ½ pound thinly sliced, cut into quarters

Salted butter, 2 sticks softened

Garlic powder, 1 teaspoon

FILLING INGREDIENTS*

Dried bread crumbs, 2 cups

Romano cheese, ½ cup, grated

Garlic powder, ½ teaspoon

Freshly ground black pepper, 1 teaspoon

Italian parsley, 2 tablespoon, chopped

*Mix ingredients together in a small bowl and set aside

DIRECTIONS:

Microwave butter and garlic in a small bowl, until very soft but not melted (10 seconds). Spread thin amount of butter mixture on top of beef (doesn't have to be perfect, it will melt during cooking; do not cover entire slice of beef with butter — that would be too much).

Top with about 1 teaspoon bread crumb mixture. Place ham slices on top and then cubes of cheese. Roll up, tucking sides in as you roll; put two pieces on each skewer (with loose ends together — that way meat will not turn up while cooking). Sprinkle breadcrumb mixture on top of each roll.

Heat 3–4 teaspoons vegetable oil (as needed), over medium heat, in bottom of large skillet; coat the entire bottom of the pan with oil.

Place 6–7 meat skewers in the oil at a time; cook for 2–3 minutes on each side for medium-rare (cook longer if preferred).

Makes 45 rolls (using small wooden skewers)

TIP: *Dust a clean counter top with bread crumbs then lay a row of sliced meat over the crumbs.*

TIP: *If you prefer to cook the braciole on the grill, make sure to soak the wooden skewers in water for about ½ hour prior to assembling meat skewers.*

MEAT

Grandma's Beef Pizzaiola

Manzo Pizzaiola della Nonna

This was my grandmother's recipe. She served it with spaghettini or mashed potatoes.

DIRECTIONS:

Place the sliced beef in a large, deep, 12-inch frying pan; add the rest of the ingredients. Cover and cook on low heat for 1 ½ hours until tender. Remove parsley springs before serving.

TIP: *Add ½ cup extra water if needed.*

INGREDIENTS

Sirloin tip or top round, 1 ½ pound, sliced ⅛-inch thick

Olive oil, 4 tablespoons

Garlic, 1 large clove, chopped

Roma tomatoes, 2 cups (fresh), peeled and crushed

Fresh Italian parsley, 2 sprigs (leave whole)

Oregano, 1 teaspoon

Salt, 1 ½ teaspoons

Black pepper, ½ teaspoon

Water, ½ cup

MEAT

INGREDIENTS

San Marzano plum tomatoes, 2 cans (28 oz.), crushed

Extra virgin olive oil, ½ cup

Meaty lamb shanks, 1 ½–2 pounds (about 4), washed and drained

Garlic, 4 cloves, peeled and cut in half

Onion, 1 large, peeled and chopped

Dry red wine, ¾ cup

Tomato puree, 1 cup

Water, ½ cup

Salt, 1 teaspoon

Dried red pepper flakes, to taste

Oregano, ½ teaspoon

Fresh basil, 5 large leaves

Orecchiette, 1 pound (or Ziti cut)

Salt, 1 tablespoon

Water, 2 tablespoons

Romano cheese, ¾ cup, grated for sprinkling

Lamb Shanks in Tomato Sauce with Orecchiette

Agnello con Orecchiette in Salsa di Pomodoro

DIRECTIONS:

Place the San Marzano tomatoes in a food processor or blender and pulse until smooth. Transfer tomatoes to a pot (large enough to hold the lamb shanks). Bring the tomatoes to a boil and reduce heat; let simmer while preparing the lamb shanks.

Heat the olive oil in a sauté pan (large enough to hold the lamb shanks). When the oil is hot, add the shanks and brown them evenly on all sides. Transfer the lamb shanks to the pot with the tomatoes. Discard all but ⅓ cup of the oil remaining in the sauté pan.

Add the garlic to the sauté pan and cook over medium-low heat until the garlic is medium golden brown. With a slotted spoon, remove the garlic and add it to the pot with tomatoes and lamb shanks. Add the onion to the oil and cook over medium-low heat until the onions are soft, about 8 minutes. Increase the heat to medium, pour in the wine, and allow it to evaporate (about 2 minutes). Stir in the tomato puree and water with a wooden spoon and scrape up any bits of meat that are stuck to the bottom of the pan.

Add the onion mixture to the tomatoes and lamb; stir in the salt and red pepper flakes and oregano; cover the pot and allow the ingredients to simmer gently. Stir occasionally. When the meat is fork-tender but not falling from the bones, remove it to a dish, cover and keep warm. Stir the basil into the tomato sauce for about 2 minutes. Set aside.

(recipe continues)

MEAT

Cook the orecchiette in 4 to 6 quarts of rapidly boiling water (to which 1 tablespoon of salt has been added). Orecchiette take a little longer to cook than other types of dried pasta because of their shape. The orecchiette should retain their shape and be al dente, firm but cooked.

Drain the orecchiette, reserving ¼ cup of the cooking water. Transfer the orecchiette to a serving dish. Mix 2 cups of the tomato sauce with the 3 tablespoons of water and pour it over the orecchiette. Mix well. Serve the pasta immediately as a first course with a sprinkling of grated Romano cheese. Serve the lamb shanks as a second course. Serves 4. Serve with salad and enjoy!

TIP: *If the sauce gets too thick, add a little bit of water.*

Veal Scaloppine with Marsala Wine Sauce

Scaloppine alla Marsala

DIRECTIONS:

Flour the veal by pressing it in the seasoned flour and patting gently. Heat oil and butter in large frying pan. Add the veal slices; turn them as soon as the edges turn white. When both sides are done, remove and cover to keep warm. With a little more oil (if needed) sauté the onion. Add wine, cook for 8 minutes on low heat. Add mushrooms and chicken broth; then add the veal. Cook for 15 to 20 minutes. If juices start evaporating, add a little more chicken broth. Add parsley, salt and black pepper before serving. Serve hot.

TIP: *If you cannot get ⅛-inch thick slices, pound veal with a mallet to ⅛-inch thick between plastic wrap.*

INGREDIENTS

Veal, 1 ½ pound, sliced ⅛-inch thick

Flour, 1 cup seasoned with salt and black pepper

Olive oil, ¼ cup

Unsalted butter, 2 tablespoons

Onion, 1 small, chopped or shallots

Marsala dry wine, ¾ cup

Fresh mushrooms, 1 cup, sliced

Chicken broth, 6 tablespoons

Fresh Italian parsley, 2 tablespoons, chopped

Salt and pepper, to taste

MEAT

INGREDIENTS FOR BATTUTO OR PESTATA*

Pancetta, ½ pound, sliced or in chunks

Garlic, 5 large cloves, cut

Fresh Italian parsley, ½ cup (5 or 6 sprigs)

Olive oil, 2 tablespoons

Black pepper, ½ teaspoon

*Pulse in food processor (5–10 times) until finely minced (pancetta should be finely chopped).

INGREDIENTS

Leg of lamb or lamb shoulder, 4–5 pounds (no bigger than 5–6 pounds)

Olive oil, 3 tablespoons (for rubbing)

Oregano, 1 teaspoon, dry

Flour, ½ cup

Salt, 1 tablespoon

Black pepper, 1 teaspoon

Dry white wine or Vermouth, 1 cup

Olive oil, ½ cup, for browning

Leg of Lamb

Cosciotto di Agnello

This recipe was given to me as a child by Papá in Italy. I still I love to make this dish (especially with a spring lamb).

DIRECTIONS:

Preheat oven to 375°F

Place the lamb on a 12x18-inch baking pan to prepare.

Wipe the meat with a damp kitchen cloth. With a sharp knife, make small pockets in lamb, about 1 ½-inch wide and 1 ½-inch deep, approximately 8–10 slits on the lamb. When making the slits; insert the Battuto seasoning at that time so you can identify where the slits are (use a teaspoon to fill the slit). Put any leftover seasoning on the side.

Leaving the lamb on the baking sheet, rub 3 tablespoons of olive oil around the outside of lamb (covering the lamb completely); sprinkle the entire lamb with 1 tablespoon salt, 1 teaspoon black pepper, and oregano. Sprinkle flour over all sides of the lamb and pat with hands.

In a large roaster: heat ½ cup olive oil and brown lamb on all sides (cooking lamb on each side for approximately 5–10 minutes). Add 1 cup wine (cook for 1 minute to allow alcohol to evaporate).

(recipe continues)

MEAT

Bake, covered, at 375°F for about 1 hour. Check the lamb—spoon the juices over the meat—then cover and bake for another ½ hour. Remove the cover and check the lamb with a fork to see if the lamb is tender (lamb should pull away from the bone when tender). If lamb is not tender, cover and bake for another ½ hour. When lamb is tender, uncover, and bake for 10–15 minutes until golden brown. If the juices evaporate, add 1 cup of water to retain moisture.

TIP: *If you have any leftover Batutto seasoning, smear on top of lamb before baking.*

TIP: *If you have a spring lamb you need 4 pounds or bigger (between 5–6 pounds).*

TIP: *You can substitute baby goat (Capretto) as well.*

MEAT

INGREDIENTS

Raw beef honeycomb tripe, 3 pounds
White vinegar, ¼ cup
Bay, 5 leaves
Extra-virgin olive oil, ⅓ cup
Onion, 1 large, chopped
Garlic, 2 cloves, chopped
Carrots, 2, chopped
Celery, 2 stalks, chopped
Salt, 1 ½ teaspoons
Black pepper, ¼ teaspoon
Crushed hot pepper flakes, ¼ teaspoon
Oregano, ½ teaspoon
Dry white wine, ⅔ cup
San Marzano tomatoes, 2 cans (28 oz.) crushed
Cold water, 3 cups
Fresh basil, 6 leaves, chopped
Salt and pepper, to taste
Cannellini beans, 1 can, drained
Garnish: Pecorino Romano and chopped basil

Tripe with Sauce

Spezzatini di Trippa alla Calabrese

It is a lot of work but worth the effort!

DIRECTIONS:

Depending on the size and quantity of tripe you are able to get, cut tripe into chunks (2 × 1 inch). Rinse in cold water. Remove any visible fat and discard.

Soak tripe in cold water filled to the top, with ¼ cup white vinegar and 1 bay leaf. Soak for 1 hour, then drain.

In an 8-quart pot with cold water, place tripe and 2 bay leaves. Cover pot and bring to a boil for 5 minutes, then drain, rinse and discard the bay leaves.

In the same 8-quart pot, add the tripe, 2 bay leaves and cold water. Cover and bring to boil; then reduce heat to a simmer, uncovered, stirring tripe occasionally. Add additional hot water to pot as necessary to keep tripe fully covered. Cook 2 hours until a little chewy, then drain.

SAUCE:

Heat olive oil in 6-quart sauce pan over moderate heat, add onions, garlic, carrots, and celery, stirring frequently, about 5 minutes. Add prepared tripe, salt, black pepper, hot pepper, oregano and wine. Bring to a boil for 2 minutes. Pour in crushed tomatoes, 3 cups cold water, and basil. Return to a simmer for 30 minutes. Add 1 can cannellini beans and simmer for 15 minutes.

Serve in a bowl garnished with Pecorino Romano and chopped basil.

Meatballs

Polpette di Carne

Everyone knows and loves the classic meatball. Here is my version. Meatballs are my grandson Matthew's favorite dish. Remember, you can freeze meatballs for future use.

DIRECTIONS:

Mix the ground chuck and pork in a large bowl; add salt, pepper, garlic, cheese, parsley, and eggs. Mix well with hands. Wet the slices of Italian bread, squeeze out water, and combine into meat mixture. Add dried bread crumbs, marinara sauce, and mix with hands, folding in all ingredients. Don't over mix. Shape mixture into 2-inch balls; fry in oil. Cook in batches until lightly browned (3–5 minutes); drain on paper towels. When the sauce is almost cooked, add the meatballs and cook 20–25 minutes longer.

TIP: *For soup: roll mixture into small, hazelnut-sized meatballs and cook in chicken broth until tender.*

TIP: *You will need half of the meatball mixture to make mini-meatballs from the chicken broth soup recipe; use the remaining mixture (half) and roll into 2-inch sized meatballs, fry in batches, and save in freezer. For lasagna, make small size meatballs and fry about 3 minutes. Drain and will be ready to add to lasagna.*

TIP: *You could also bake the meatballs instead of frying them. Place meatballs on a greased cookie sheet. Bake at 375° F for 20–25 minutes. They won't be as crispy, but they are just as delicious and you can cook more at once.*

TIP: *Enjoy meatballs with my tasty marinara sauce.*

INGREDIENTS

Ground chuck, 1 ½ pound
Ground pork, ½ pound
Salt, 2 teaspoon
Black pepper, to taste
Garlic, 1–2 teaspoons, crushed
Romano cheese, ⅓ cup, finely grated
Fresh Italian parsley, 3 tablespoons, chopped
Eggs, 2 large
Day-old Italian bread, 6 slices
Water, ½ cup
Unseasoned bread crumbs, 1 cup
Marinara sauce, ½ cup
Vegetable oil, 1 cup, for frying

INGREDIENTS (OXTAIL TO BOIL)

Oxtail, 3 pounds (pieces)
Water, 3–4 quarts
Bay, 1 leaf
Celery, 1 stalk
Salt, 2 teaspoons

INGREDIENTS (SAUCE)

Olive oil, 4 tablespoons
Oxtail, 3 pounds (prepared)
Pancetta, 2 ounces, sliced (cut into pieces)
Oregano, ½ teaspoon
Red wine, 1 ½ cups
Onion, 1 medium, sliced
Garlic, 2 cloves, sliced
Carrot, 1 medium, diced
Celery, 4 stalks (cut into ½-inch pieces)
Crushed tomatoes, 2 cans (28-oz), Italian style
Tomato paste, 6 ounces
Water, 4 cups
Italian parsley, 1 ½ teaspoons, chopped
Fresh basil, 5 leaves
Salt, 1 ½ teaspoons (add more if desired)
Black pepper, ½ teaspoon
Hot pepper, ¼ teaspoon

Oxtail Style Sauce

Coda di Bue

This recipe is from my cousin Nella, from Cosenza, Calabria, Italy. You don't really think of making Oxtail these days, but once you try it, you will understand how delicious it really is.

PREPARING THE OXTAIL:

Place 3 pounds Oxtail in a large pot filled with water (3–4 quarts); enough to accommodate the Oxtail meat. Add 1 bay leaf, 1 stalk of celery, 2 teaspoons salt, cover and cook over medium-high heat for 45–50 minutes. Drain in a colander; put Oxtail in a bowl.

DIRECTIONS (MAKING THE SAUCE):

To make the sauce, heat the olive oil in a large, deep saucepan. Add the Oxtail, Pancetta, and Oregano; fry until the Oxtail is golden brown; add the red wine and cook for 5 minutes (until the alcohol has evaporated). Add onion, garlic, carrots, and celery; cook until wilted (about 5–6 minutes). Add crushed tomatoes, tomato paste, water, parsley, fresh basil, salt, black pepper, and hot pepper. Simmer on medium-low for 2 hours until the meat is tender. Stir occasionally to prevent scorching. Season to taste. If the sauce gets too thick, add a little bit of water.

TIP: *Skim the excess fat from the sauce.*

TIP: *The sauce is for any cut of pasta (Penne, Rigatoni, or Spaghetti) with Romano cheese. Enjoy!*

MEAT

Pan-Roasted Rabbit with Marsala

Coniglio Arrosto al Marsala

DIRECTIONS:

Heat oil in large skillet.

Add the rabbit to the hot oil, and cook until golden brown, about 5 minutes.

Add onion, garlic, rosemary, salt, and black pepper. Cook another 5 minutes.

Add wine and cook another 5 minutes. Add water, gently simmer with lid on for another 40 minutes, until tender. Remove lid, cook about 5–10 minutes, until remaining liquid is reduced. Fry until golden brown.

Serve with salad and enjoy!

Oxtail Style Sauce

INGREDIENTS

Olive oil, ¾ cup

Rabbit, 3 ½ pounds (washed and drained), cut into 8 pieces

Onion, 1 large, chopped

Garlic, 2 cloves, sliced

Fresh rosemary, 1 sprig

Salt, 1 teaspoon

Black pepper, ½ teaspoon

White wine or marsala, ¾ cup

Water, 1 ½ cup

Papá's Pork Rolls in Tomato Sauce

Papá's Pork Rolls in Tomato Sauce

This was my Papá's recipe. The little pork rolls are tender and delicious, with creamy filling. He loved the taste of this sauce with Bucatini, Romano cheese, and Bracioline.

BATTUTO PASTE INGREDIENTS

Pancetta, ⅓ pound, sliced and cut into pieces

Garlic, 3 cloves

Onion, ¼ cup, chopped

Fresh Italian parsley, ½ cup, chopped

Olive oil, 3 tablespoons

Bread crumbs, ½ cup

Romano cheese, 1 tablespoon

Pork tenderloin, 2 ½– 3 pounds, cut into ½-inch thick strips

Fontinella, ½ cup fine, crumbly

Eggs, 1 or 2 hardboiled, peeled and coarsely chopped

Salt and freshly ground black pepper, to taste

DIRECTIONS:

In a food processor, chop the pancetta, garlic, onion, and parsley. Add 3 tablespoons olive oil to form the Battuto paste and set aside in a small bowl.

In a small bowl, add bread crumbs and Romano, mix well with hands and set aside.

Now, take the pork tender loin and cut into ½-inch thick strips. Place strips between two pieces of plastic wrap. Gently pound strips down to ¼-inch thick using the plate side of a heavy meat mallet.

Add 1 tablespoon Battuto paste on top of the pork loin slices (smearing it on with the backside of a spoon). Sprinkle the crumbly bread mixture on top of pork, then add the Fontinella with your hands over all of the slices. Leave ½–1-inch border around the edge of slices. Sprinkle each bracioline with chopped hard cooked eggs.

DIRECTIONS FOR ROLLS:

Begin rolling the bracioline, starting with the end closest to you. Tightly roll the bracioline like a jelly roll, gently folding in the sides as you roll. Once you have finished rolling, secure the ends of the bracioline with a toothpick and use kitchen twine to wrap the entire roll and hold it together while cooking. Remove the tooth picks. Add salt and pepper on the outside.

(recipe continues)

In a large, deep, frying pan, add 4–5 tablespoons olive oil. Fry the bracioline for 5–8 minutes, stirring occasionally, until golden brown Add red wine and cook for another 2 minutes, to evaporate the alcohol, turning the bracioline a few times. Transfer the bracioline with a large spoon into a bowl. Set aside.

DIRECTIONS FOR SAUCE:

In the bottom of the same pan used to fry the bracioline, there should be a nice left over crust formed; be sure to save this (leave in bottom of pan).

In this same pan, add an additional 4 tablespoons olive oil on top of the reserved crust. Sauté 1 cup onions in this reserved mixture (with additional olive oil), for 3–4 minutes, until softened. Add 2 (28 oz.) cans crushed San Marzano tomatoes, 2 cups water, 4–5 leaves fresh basil, 1 teaspoon salt, and 1 teaspoon sugar (optional). Cook for approximately 10 minutes.

Add the bracioline into the sauce. Taste sauce, season lightly with salt and pepper. Adjust heat to simmering. Cook about 45 minutes, simmering slowly and stirring occasionally. Take a fork and poke it into the bracioline (to see if it's tender). If needed, cook an additional 10 minutes.

Add a little more water if needed to thin the sauce. Put bracioline on a platter to cool for 15 minutes before removing the twine. Put a little sauce on the bracioline and cover to keep warm.

Prepare spaghetti or bucatini pasta per package directions. Drain and place pasta in a large bowl. Mix with tomato sauce (you may have extra sauce). Sprinkle with Romano cheese. Serve 2–3 bracioline on a dinner plate with a side of pasta.

SAUCE INGREDIENTS

Olive oil, 9 tablespoons

Red wine, ½ cup

Onion, 1 cup, chopped

San Marzano tomatoes, 2 cans (28 oz.), crushed

Water, 2 cups

Fresh basil, 4–5 leaves

Salt, 1 teaspoon

Sugar, 1 teaspoon (optional)

PORK SAUSAGE INGREDIENTS

Pork shoulder, 5 pounds

Sea salt, 1 ½ tablespoons

Black pepper, 1 tablespoon

Fennel or Paprika, (optional, see below)

MENA'S FENNEL SAUSAGE

Pork shoulder, 5 pounds

Fennel, 1 tablespoon

Crushed hot pepper flakes, 1 tablespoon (or to taste)

Paprika, 1 tablespoon

Sea salt, 1 ½ tablespoons

Black pepper, 1 tablespoon

MENA'S LIVER SAUSAGE

Pork shoulder, 4 pounds

Pork liver, 1 pound

Garlic, 2 cloves, chopped

Italian parsley, 2 tablespoons, chopped

Crushed hot pepper flakes, 1 tablespoon (or to taste)

Sea salt, 1 ½ tablespoons

Black pepper, 1 tablespoon

Papá's Sausage Recipes

Ricette per Salsicce

These are my Papá's recipes which I have tweaked a bit. Enjoy!

DIRECTIONS:

Trim the pork. Remove bone if it has not already been removed and cut into 2-inch cubes. Medium grind the pork and place in a large bowl with the seasonings. Use your hands to mix well until a piece of it sticks to your palm when held upside down. Make into patties. Fry until tender, about 20 minutes. It should reach an internal temperature of 150°F.

These recipes may also be used to make link sausages, stuffing the pork and seasoning mixture into sausage casings which are available at Roma Bakery.

HOW TO COOK ITALIAN SAUSAGE LINKS:

In a frying pan add about 1 cup of water and a drizzle of oil (if needed). Add the sausages to the pan; cover and cook for ½ hour. For the first 20 minutes, cook sausage on medium heat, keep covered, let sausage steam in pan. Remove lid, stir on high heat until water has evaporated; fry until golden brown.

NOTE: *You can make links with an old-fashioned machine or KitchenAid® attachments (food grinder and sausage stuffer).*

MEAT

Sausage with Sweet Red Pepper

Salsiccie con Peperoni Rossi

This is a recipe from Calabria, Italy.

Sausage Patties

INGREDIENTS

Fresh sausage, 2 pounds (links or patties)
Water, 1 cup
Olive oil, ¼ cup
Red peppers, 3, sliced
Onion, 1 large
Fresh basil, 1 teaspoon
Oregano, a pinch
Salt and pepper, to taste

DIRECTIONS:

Place the sausage links in a large frying pan with 1 cup water on the bottom. Cook covered over medium heat until the water has evaporated. Add the oil and fry for a few minutes until the outside has browned.

Remove the sausage and set aside. Then put in the red pepper and onion. Season with the spices (basil, oregano, salt and pepper); fry over medium heat for a few minutes, then add the sausage again. Continue to cook for 2–3 minutes and then place everything on a serving platter. Serve immediately.

TIP: *Sausage should reach an internal temperature of 150°F.*

TIP: *If you don't have sausage links, you can make sausage patties.*

MEAT

INGREDIENTS

Broccoli rabe, 2 bunches (about 2 pounds)

Extra virgin olive oil, ½ cup

Garlic, 3 cloves, crushed

Cooking water, 1 ½ cup (water the Broccoli Rabe was cooked in)

Black pepper, ¼ teaspoon

Crushed hot pepper flakes, a pinch

Salt, 2 teaspoons

ITALIAN SAUSAGE
SWEET OR HOT

Water, 1 cup

Olive oil, 2 tablespoons

Italian sausage, 1 ½–2 pounds (about 8 links)

Broccoli Rabe with Sausage
Broccoli Rabe con Salsiccia

This recipe is from my hometown of Calabria, Italy.

Broccoli rabe are naturally bitter. But, if blanched, much of the bitterness is reduced. Do not overcook. When I first came to America in the 60's, "Rapini", as they are called in Italy, were not available. My family and I used to go to Canada to get some. Today, they're made this way and they're now called "Broccoli Rabe".

DIRECTIONS:

Start by trimming the tough ends of the Broccoli Rabe. Cut the rest of it into 2 to 3 inch pieces. Clean Broccoli Rabe in a large amount of cold water, until all dirt is removed, then drain in a colander. Bring a large pot of water to boil. Add the Broccoli Rabe and boil for 1 to 2 minutes. Drain in a colander, reserving 1 ½ cups of the cooking water.

Heat olive oil in a large skillet on medium heat. Add the crushed garlic. Sauté garlic until golden. Add the Broccoli Rabe and the 1 ½ cups of the reserved cooking water. Add black pepper, a pinch of hot pepper flakes, and salt. Cover with a lid and cook at medium heat for about 5 minutes. With the lid removed, stir on high heat for 5–6 minutes until the liquid is evaporated and the Broccoli Rabe is tender. Check tenderness occasionally while stirring. Check for seasoning and taste then set aside.

SAUSAGE DIRECTIONS:

Place the water and oil in a large frying pan. Poke the sausage links with a fork 4–5 times, then add to the

(recipe continues)

MEAT

frying pan. On medium heat, cook the sausage about 5 minutes. Cover with a lid and cook on medium-to-low heat for about 20–25 minutes. Check occasionally and add a little water as needed if sausage looks dry. After about 20 minutes, turn on high heat and remove the lid, turning sausages continually until water is evaporated and the sausage is golden brown on all sides. Add sausage to the Broccoli Rabe pan and warm for a few minutes. Place in a serving dish and serve hot.

TIP: *We love this! This could be a sandwich: on sub bread, add a link of sausage and some Broccoli Rabe, and it is delicious!*

TIP: *If you like pasta, cook pasta as usual (about 1 pound). Cut the sausage into about ¼-inch pieces and add, with the Broccoli Rabe, to the pasta. Top with sprinkled Romano or Parmesan cheese. Finally, add a drizzle of Extra-virgin olive oil.*

MEAT

Stuffed Beef Roll

Falsomagro o Braciolone Calabrese

This is a classic large Braciolone that you serve sliced.

INGREDIENTS FOR MIXTURE

Top round steak, 2 pounds, butterfly cut about ½-inch thick

Butter, 3 tablespoons (soft)

Salt, ½ teaspoon

Black pepper, ½ teaspoon

Garlic, 3 cloves, chopped

Fresh Italian parsley, 2 tablespoons, chopped

Celery, ½ cup chopped

Pine nuts, 1 tablespoon

Thin salami or sopresata, 8 slices

Ham, 8 slices, thinly sliced

Pancetta, 6 slices

Fontinalla cheese, ½ pound, crumbled

Eggs, 4 hardboiled

DIRECTIONS:

To make the Braciolone: lay the meat out flat, place between plastic wrap and pound with a meat mallet to flatten it slightly to a uniform thickness (about ¼–½ inch thick). Be careful not to tear the meat. Pat the meat dry with paper towels. First spread the butter and sprinkle with salt and black pepper; add minced garlic and parsley; then add celery and pine nuts. Add salami, ham, pancetta, fontinella (crumbled), and hardboiled eggs (cover the surface of the meat and cheese except for the edges). Tie the roll with cotton twin at 1-inch intervals. Set aside.

To make the sauce: heat the olive oil in a large deep saucepan, add the beef roll to the pan and brown it on all sides. Add onions and cook until softened. Add wine, cook one minute. Cook the crushed San Marzano tomatoes, pureed tomatoes, and water. Stir; add 1 whole bay leaf and 4–5 basil leaves; add salt & black pepper. Cook and simmer on medium-low for 2 ½ hours—stirring occasionally, making sure the sauce does not stick.

(recipe continues)

Remove the meat from the sauce and let rest 10–15 minutes. Remove the cotton twine and cut the Braciolone into 1-inch thick slices. Arrange the slices on a serving platter. Spoon some sauce on platter and a little on top and serve.

INGREDIENTS FOR SAUCE

Olive oil, ½ cup

Onion, 1 chopped

Dry red wine, ½ cup

San Marzano tomatoes, 1 can (28 oz.) crushed (use food processor or use your hands)

Pureed tomatoes, 1 can (28 oz.)

Water, 1 cup

Bay, 1 whole leaf

Fresh basil, 5 leaves

1 Salt, ½ teaspoon (add more salt if desired)

Black pepper, ½ teaspoon

TIP: *This sauce is very good with pasta (penne, rigatoni or spaghetti). Top with Romano cheese.*

MEAT

INGREDIENTS

Eggplant, 6 small (makes 12 halves) or 4 medium (makes 8 halves), about 5–6 inches long

Olive oil, ½ cup

Ground chuck, 1 pound

Italian sausage, ½ pound (bulk) or 2 links (remove casings)

Olive oil, 1 tablespoon (drained from the meat)

Onion, 1 cup chopped

Garlic, 2 cloves, chopped

Dry white wine, ½ cup

Salt, 1 ½ teaspoons

Black pepper, 1 teaspoon

Fresh Italian parsley, 2 tablespoons, chopped

Day-old Italian or French bread, 2 cups of cubed

Milk, ¾ cup

Romano cheese, 1 cup

Dry bread crumbs, ½ cup

Eggs, 2 large, whisked

Marinara sauce, 5 ¾ cups

Stuffed Eggplant

Melanzane Ripiene

This is a Calabrese recipe.

DIRECTIONS:

Cut eggplant lengthwise in half. Place in a bowl, face up, and sprinkle with salt. Cover with a plate (to keep eggplant from turning brown), set for 30 minutes. Pour 2 cups of cold water over eggplant and drain well. Place eggplant face down on paper towel, pat dry with your hands to remove excess moisture. Scoop out the majority of the pulp leaving about ¼ pulp inside the shell. Put pulp in bowl and chop; set aside. Blanch the eggplant shell in boiling water with a pinch of salt for 1–2 minutes. Remove and place on a baking sheet to cool.

In a large skillet, put ¼ cup olive oil over medium high heat. Add beef and sausage. Use a wooden spoon to break up and cook for 10 minutes. Using a colander, strain fat into a small bowl. Add 1 tablespoon of oil (you strained) into pan; add onion and garlic then cook for 5 minutes. Return meat to the pan with the sautéed onion and garlic. Stir until meat releases its juices. Add ½ cup wine, salt and pepper, and 2 tablespoons chopped parsley. Stir and cook 2–3 minutes. Add the chopped pulp, cook and stir for another 5 minutes. Strain through a colander. Put in a large bowl, let cool.

Preheat oven to 375°F.

In another small bowl, add 2 cups cubed dry bread and ¾ cup milk. Let it sit for 2 minutes. When bread has softened, squeeze out excess milk with your hands. Put

(recipe continues)

MEAT

the bread mixture into the meat mixture. Take ½ cup Romano cheese (reserving the other ½ cup), ½ cup bread crumbs, 2 beaten eggs, and ¾ cups marinara sauce. Mix well with hands. Stuff the eggplant with the filling. Distribute any excess filling over each eggplant.

Take a large square casserole dish, add 1 cup of marinara sauce in bottom. Drizzle ¼ cup olive oil over sauce. Place stuffed eggplant shells on top of sauce. Pour the remaining 4 cups of sauce over the stuffed shells, and sprinkle with the other ½ cup of Romano cheese.

Cover with foil and bake for 30 minutes. Uncover and bake for another 10 minutes until golden brown. Place on serving platter and enjoy!

TIP: *The larger the eggplant, the longer the cooking time. These are served hot from the oven or can be served at room temperature as an antipasto.*

INGREDIENTS

Jumbo pasta shells, 24

INGREDIENTS (SHELL STUFFING)

Olive oil, 1 tablespoon

Onion, ½ cup, finely chopped

Garlic, 2 teaspoons, minced

Veal, 1 pound (ground)

Pork, ½ pound (ground)

Fresh Marjoram leaves, 2 teaspoons, finely chopped

Salt, 1 ½ teaspoons

Black pepper, ¾ teaspoon

Fresh Italian parsley, 2 tablespoons, chopped

Heavy cream, ¼ cup

Egg, 1 large

Veal Stuffed Jumbo Shells with Mushroom Béchamel

Conchiglioni Ripieni di Vitello con Besciamella di Funghi

DIRECTIONS:

Fill a large, 4–6-quart stockpot with water and bring to a boil over high heat. Season with salt and add the dried shells to the pot. Cook the pasta until pliable for about 6–8 minutes. Remove the shells from the water and lay out on a sheet pan to cool. Be sure to lay each shell directly on a lightly oiled pan without touching any of the other shells so that they will not stick.

While the shells cool, make the shell stuffing. Set a large sauté pan (or large frying pan) over medium heat and add the olive oil to the pan. Once the oil is hot, add the onions and garlic to the pan. Cook until the onions are softened about 3 minutes. Remove from heat and set aside to cool. In a medium bowl, combine the ground veal, pork, marjoram, salt, black pepper, cooled onions, garlic, and parsley. In a separate bowl (smaller), combine the cream and egg and whisk to combine. Add the cream and egg mixture to the veal mixture and mix until thoroughly blended without over-mixing.

(recipe continues)

When the shells have cooled, place 2 tablespoons of stuffing into each of the 24 shells, and place the open-end up in a 9 x 13 by 2-inch deep, large casserole dish. When completed, wrap the casserole with plastic wrap and set aside in the refrigerator as you prepare the mushroom béchamel.

Preheat oven to 350°F.

Set a 1-quart saucepan over medium-high heat and add the butter. Once melted, add the mushrooms and thyme leaves to the pan and cook, stirring often, until most of the liquid has evaporated, about 5 minutes. Add the onions and garlic to the pan and cook for 3–4 minutes, stirring occasionally. Sprinkle the flour into the pan, stir to combine, and cook the roux, stirring, for 2 minutes. Whisk the milk into the saucepan. Season the béchamel with the salt, pepper, and nutmeg and stir to combine. Bring the béchamel to a boil, reduce the heat to a simmer, and cook, stirring frequently, until sauce is smooth and any floury taste is gone, about 5 minutes.

Add Béchamel to the stuffed shells, pouring over top. Bake 30–35 minutes at 350°F. Sprinkle with Parmigiano-Reggiano & chopped parsley for color and flavor.

TIP: *If sauce gets too thick, add a little bit of chicken broth.*

INGREDIENTS (MUSHROOM BÉCHAMEL SAUCE):

Unsalted butter, 4 tablespoons

Button mushrooms, 1 pound, cleaned and thinly sliced

Fresh thyme leaves, 1 teaspoon

Onion, ½ cup, finely chopped

Garlic, 2 teaspoons, minced

All-purpose flour, 4 tablespoons

Whole milk, 3 cups

Salt, ½ teaspoon

White pepper, ¼ teaspoon

Nutmeg, just a pinch

Parmigiano-Reggiano, ½ cup freshly grated

Fresh Italian parsley, 1 tablespoon, chopped

MEAT

POULTRY

Baked Chicken and Potato with Rosemary   90

Chicken Breast Saltimbocca   92

Chicken Cacciatore   93

Chicken or Veal Cutlets   94

Chicken Piccata   95

Chicken Tetrazzini   96

Linetta's Chicken   98

Skillet Chicken Breasts   99

Turkey Breast with Lemon Sauce   100

Turkey Cutlets with Spinach, Crab, and Asiago Cheese Sauce   101

INGREDIENTS

Chicken, 6 thighs, washed

Chicken, 6 drumsticks, washed

Potatoes, 6–8 large (red skin or Yukon gold), peeled and cut into wedges

Sweet onion, 1 whole (large), cut in ¼ inch slices

Italian plum tomatoes, 1 ½ –2 cups canned or fresh with seeds and juice removed, diced

Fresh rosemary, 1 tablespoon chopped

Olive oil, ½ cup

Salt, 3 teaspoons, to taste

Black pepper, 1 teaspoon

Olive oil, 2 tablespoons reserved

Baked Chicken and Potato with Rosemary

Pollo al forno con patate e Rosmarino

I was vacationing in Sicily, staying with my sister-in-law, Pina. One evening there was a deliciously irresistible aroma wafting from the kitchen. "Madonna Mia, what is cooking Pina?" I hope you enjoy this recipe as much as I did that night in Sicily.

We love to take crusty Italian bread, soak up the extra juice and eat it that way. In Italian that is called "Scarpetta". It means taking a piece of bread, pinching the bread together as if to form a little shoe (scarpetta). And with that you clean the dish.

DIRECTIONS:

Pre-heat oven to 375° F

Pour 2 tablespoons olive oil in the bottom of a large roasting pan (deep).

In a large bowl add potato, onion, ½ tomatoes, 1 ½ teaspoon salt, ½ teaspoon black pepper, 1 teaspoon rosemary, and ¼ cup olive oil; mix well with spoon and set aside.

In a separate large bowl, add the chicken (drained), ½ tomatoes, 1 ½ teaspoon salt, ½ teaspoon black pepper, ¼ cup olive oil, and 1 teaspoon rosemary; mix together well.

Add the bowl with potato and onion mixture into the large roasting pan.

(recipe continues)

Add the chicken to the roasting pan; arranging nicely on top of the potato mixture (pour remaining juices over top of chicken). Cook, uncovered, in oven for ½ hour.

Cover the roasting pan (with lid or tin foil) and place in oven for 30 minutes; check and distribute juices over top of chicken with a large spoon. Check chicken with fork for tenderness—if tender, remove lid and cook for additional 15–20 minutes. Remove from oven, let sit about 10 minutes allowing flavors to absorb.

INGREDIENTS

Chicken, 6 whole breasts, skinned and split in ½ to make 12 pieces

Sage, 12 leaves

Fontina cheese, 12 slices

Flour, ½ cup

Eggs, 3 large

Water, 3 tablespoons

Italian bread crumbs, 1 cup seasoned (homemade)

Butter, ½ cup

Olive oil, 2 tablespoon

Dry white wine, ½ cup or sherry

Chicken broth, ½ cup

Corn starch, 1 tablespoon

Cold water, 1 tablespoon

Salt and Pepper, to taste

Chicken Breast Saltimbocca

Petti di Pollo Saltimbocca

DIRECTIONS:

Flatten chicken breasts evenly with a meat mallet and place 1 leaf of sage on each breast, a slice of cheese and prosciutto on each. Roll up from narrower end and skewer with toothpicks. Dip each roll in flour, whisked eggs in 1 tablespoon of cold water, and then in bread crumbs, coating completely. Brown rolls in butter and oil and place in baking dish. Mix chicken broth and wine and pour over rolls. Bake at 375°F for 20–25 minutes. Drain off juices into small saucepan and, if not enough to measure 1 cup, add chicken broth to make up the difference. Mix cornstarch with cold water and stir until smooth. Bring to boil and slowly add cornstarch and water mixture, stirring constantly, until thickened. Spoon sauce over chicken and serve.

Serves 10–12.

Chicken Cacciatore

Pollo alla Cacciatora di Papá Cacciatore

A familiar classic but this is my Father's favorite chicken recipe. Cacciatore in Italian means hunter.

DIRECTIONS:

In a large sauté pan, brown chicken pieces in 4 tablespoons of olive oil over medium-high heat. Salt and pepper chicken and add oregano as it cooks; fry until brown. Add dry white wine, cook for 2–3 minutes (until alcohol is evaporated). Add onion and garlic; sauté a few minutes. Add carrots, celery, yellow or red peppers, tomatoes, salt and pepper to taste, and fresh basil and parsley; bring to a boil and lower the heat; stir well. Slowly simmer with the lid on the pan for 45–1 hour until tender. When chicken is cooked through and liquids reduced to a slightly thick sauce, remove from heat and serve.

INGREDIENTS

- **Chicken,** 3 ½ pounds (8 pieces)
- **Extra-virgin olive oil,** 4 tablespoons
- **Oregano,** ½ teaspoon
- **Dry white wine,** ⅔ cup
- **Onion,** 1 medium-large size, thinly sliced
- **Garlic,** 3 cloves, diced
- **Carrots,** 2, peeled and sliced on the diagonal
- **Celery,** 2 stalks, sliced on the diagonal
- **Bell pepper,** 1 (yellow or red), cut into thin julienne strips
- **Fresh plum tomatoes,** 4–6 or 1 can (28 oz.) diced Italian tomatoes in their juice (In the summer, use fresh plum tomatoes from the garden. Peeled, seeded, and diced)
- **Salt,** 2 ½ teaspoons
- **Pepper,** to taste
- **Fresh basil and parsley,** 2 sprigs

Chicken or Veal Cutlets

Cotoletta

Another of Mamma's recipes. To this day I still love her Chicken Cutlets.

BREAD CRUMBS INGREDIENTS

Bread crumbs, 2 cups
Romano cheese, ¼ cup
Black pepper, to taste

INGREDIENTS

Chicken, 1 ½ pound skinless breasts (or Veal, ¼" thick, pound with mallet if needed)
Eggs, 3 large
Garlic, 1 clove, crushed
Salt, to taste
Fresh parsley, 1 teaspoon, chopped
Vegetable oil, 1 cup

BREAD CRUMBS DIRECTIONS:

You can make your own bread crumbs for this recipe. Take dry Italian or French bread and let it dry out completely. Remove the crust and grate either by hand or food processor. The bread crumbs may be stored in the freezer until ready to use. Combine the bread crumbs, Romano cheese, and black pepper.

DIRECTIONS:

Take the chicken breasts and slice ¼–½ inch thick. Place the chicken between sheets of plastic wrap (this keeps juices from splattering) and pound with a mallet. What you are trying to achieve is uniform thickness. Add salt to taste. Beat the eggs and add garlic and parsley. Dip the chicken cutlets in egg and then in bread crumbs. Fry in ¼–½ inch vegetable oil until the chicken is golden brown on both sides (oil may have to be changed while frying). Remove cutlet and place on plate with paper towel.

TIP: *If you have time, marinate the chicken in the egg mixture (if you marinate a day before, it tastes better). Cover and refrigerate overnight. When ready, coat the chicken breast with the bread crumb mixture. Then fry in ¼–½ inch vegetable oil until chicken is golden brown. After frying a few cutlets place them in a warm oven at 150°F (this will stay warm till you're ready to serve).*

TIP: *Place any leftover bread crumbs in the refrigerator.*

TIP: *Substitute veal or turkey for the chicken in this recipe if you prefer! All are delicious.*

POULTRY

Chicken Piccata

Pollo Piccata

In the United States, it is usually served with pasta, polenta, or rice. In Italy, chicken or veal piccata is a secondo and would be served after the pasta course.

DIRECTIONS:

Combine coating mixture together, and set aside. Add chicken base and water together, and set aside.

Cut chicken into slices (½-inch thick). Place the chicken between sheets of clear plastic wrap (this keeps juice from spilling) and pound with a flat mallet. Dip chicken into coating mixture covering both sides and set aside.

In a large frying pan, on high heat, add olive oil, and butter. Once the oil becomes hot, reduce to medium temperature and add chicken pieces. Cook for 3 minutes on each side. Remove chicken from frying pan and place on a platter. Drain off the remaining oil. There should be a nice left over crust formed in the bottom of the pan, be sure to save this. Use this same pan later.

On high heat add the wine to the pan, cooking approximately 1 minute to burn off the alcohol. Add chicken base with water, lemon juice, salt, and pepper, and bring to a boil. Add chicken into the pan and top with mushrooms and fresh chopped parsley. Cover and reduce heat to medium, continue cooking for 6 minutes, turning chicken occasionally. Add capers, and transfer your meat to the serving platter and you're ready to eat. Enjoy.

TIP: *Sauté with mushrooms in frying pan, then set aside in a bowl.*

INGREDIENTS

Minor's chicken base or chicken stock, 1 tablespoon

Water, 1 cup (mixed with base)

Chicken, 3 breasts, cut into ½-inch slices, flattened

Olive oil, 6 tablespoon

Butter, 2 tablespoons

Dry white wine or Vermouth, ¼ cup

Fresh lemon juice, 2 tablespoon

Salt and pepper, to taste

Fresh mushrooms, 1 cup, sliced

Fresh Italian parsley, 2 tablespoons, minced

Capers, 1 tablespoon

INGREDIENTS (COATING MIXTURE)

Garlic powder, ½ teaspoon

Pepper, ¼ teaspoon

Flour, 1 cup

Salt, ½ teaspoon

INGREDIENTS

Butter, 10 tablespoons

Olive oil, 2 tablespoons

Chicken, 4 boneless skinless breasts

Salt, 2 ¼ teaspoons

Black pepper, 1 ¼ teaspoons

White mushrooms, 1 pound, sliced

Onion, 1 large, finely chopped

Garlic, 5 cloves, minced

Fresh thyme leaves, 1 tablespoon chopped

Dry white wine, ½ cup

All-purpose flour, ⅓ cup

Whole milk, 4 cups, room temperature

Chicken broth, 1 ½ cups

Linguine, 1 pound

Peas, ¾ cup frozen

Fresh Italian parsley leaves, ¼ cup chopped

Dried Italian-style breadcrumbs, ¼ cup

Parmigiano-Reggiano, 1 ¼ cup grated

Chicken Tetrazzini

Pollo alla Mena

DIRECTIONS:

Preheat the oven to 450°F.

Spread 1 tablespoon of butter over a 13 x 9 by 3-inch deep baking dish.

Melt 1 tablespoon butter and 1 tablespoon oil in a large, deep, nonstick frying pan over medium-high heat. Sprinkle the chicken with ½ teaspoon salt and ½ teaspoon pepper. Add the chicken to the hot pan and cook until pale golden and just cooked through, about 4 minutes per side. Transfer the chicken to a plate to cool slightly. Coarsely chop the chicken into bite-size pieces and place into a bowl.

Meanwhile, add 2 tablespoon each of butter and oil to the same pan. Add the mushrooms and sauté over medium-high heat until the liquid from the mushrooms evaporates and the mushrooms become pale golden, about 12 minutes. Add the onion, garlic, and thyme, and sauté until the onion is translucent, about 8 minutes. Add the wine and simmer until it evaporates, about 2 minutes. Transfer the mushroom mixture to the bowl with the chicken.

(recipe continues)

POULTRY

Melt 3 more tablespoons butter in the same pan over medium-low heat. Add the flour and whisk for 2 minutes. Whisk in the milk, cream well; add chicken broth, remaining 1 ¾ teaspoons salt and remaining ¾ teaspoon pepper. Increase the heat to high. Cover and bring to a boil. Simmer, uncovered, until the sauce thickens slightly, whisking often, about 10 minutes.

Bring a large pot of salted water to a boil. Add the linguine and cook until tender but still firm, al dente, stirring occasionally, about 8–9 minutes. Drain. Add the linguine, sauce, peas, and parsley to the chicken mixture. Toss until the sauce coats the pasta and the mixture is well blended. Transfer the pasta mixture to the prepared baking dish. Stir the cheese and breadcrumbs in a small bowl to blend. Sprinkle the cheese mixture over the pasta. Dot with the remaining 3 tablespoons of butter. Bake, uncovered, until golden brown on top and the sauce bubbles, about 25 minutes.

INGREDIENTS

Rigatoni pasta, 1 pound

Virgin olive oil, ¼ cup

Onion, 2 cups, chopped

Garlic, 2 tablespoons, minced

Spicy Italian sausage, 1 pound, casings removed

Chicken, 1 pound boneless skinless breast, cut into 1-inch cubes

Chicken stock, ½ cup

Fresh Italian parsley, ¼ cup, chopped

Salt and pepper, to taste

Red pepper, 1, cut into strips

Hot cherry peppers, 2 pickled, with seeds removed, and sliced ¼ inch thick

Seasoned bread crumbs, 2 tablespoons

Linetta's Chicken

Pollo di Linetta

This recipe is from my friend Linetta, one of my best friends from Cosenza, Calabria region, Italy.

DIRECTIONS:

Heat oil in a large skillet over medium-high heat. Add onion and garlic; cook until onion is tender. Add sausage, cook, and stir to break up meat. Cook until sausage is browned. Add chicken, chicken stock and parsley. Cook, stirring until chicken is almost cooked through. Season with salt and pepper. Stir in roasted red pepper strips and cherry peppers. Cook briefly to finish chicken. Stir in bread crumbs. Cook pasta in boiling, salted water until al dente, then drain. When pasta is cooked, drain and toss into the skillet with the chicken and sausage. Serve immediately.

Serves 4–6.

TIP: *Reserve 1 cup of boiled pasta water to thin the sauce if it is sticking together.*

POULTRY

Skillet Chicken Breasts

Petti di Pollo con Aglio e Olio

DIRECTIONS:

Trim the chicken of all fat, skin, and connective tissue. Butterfly the breast. Sprinkle both sides of each breast with salt, using about ½ teaspoon in all. Place chicken between sheets of plastic wrap and flatten with a mallet. Then dredge chicken in flour to coat all surfaces.

In a 14-inch skillet heat 2 tablespoons of olive oil. Sauté sliced garlic, red pepper flakes and drained capers for 1 min. Remove sauté and keep on a plate.

In the same hot skillet add 2 tablespoon olive oil and 2 tablespoons of butter. Sauté the butterflied breast on one side until lightly brown, flip over and lightly brown the other side. Next, put about 1 tablespoon of garlic mixture on one side of breast and fold over to close.

Increase the temperature of the burner. When everything is sizzling loudly, pour the vinegar into open spaces and shake pan to spread it. Let vinegar sizzle and reduce for 30 minutes, then pour in the broth.

Cook on high, quickly bringing the liquid to a boil; drizzle with the remaining 2 tablespoons oil, and sprinkle on ¼ teaspoon salt. Let sauce bubble and reduce for a couple of minutes (shake skillet frequently). Then, sprinkle breadcrumbs into the sauce (not on the chicken) and stir and shake to mix. Cook, while shaking skillet, until the sauce has the consistency you prefer. Turn off the heat, sprinkle with parsley, and shake skillet again.

Serves 4–6.

TIP: *In a 12-inch skillet, cook chicken in batches, half at a time.*

TIP: *To butterfly the breast, cut the thick part of the breast almost through; open it up and flatten it with a mallet.*

INGREDIENTS

Chicken, 6 skinless, boneless breast halves (about 2 pounds)

Salt, ¾ teaspoon, or to taste

All-purpose flour, ½ cup

Extra-virgin olive oil, 6 tablespoons

Garlic, 8 large cloves, sliced

Red pepper flakes, ¼ teaspoon

Capers, 3 tablespoons in brine, drained

Butter, 2 tablespoons

Red wine vinegar, 2 tablespoons

Chicken broth, 1 cup

Fine dry bread crumbs, 1 tablespoon

Fresh Italian parsley, 3 tablespoons chopped

INGREDIENTS

Turkey breast, 1 ½ pounds, cut in thin slices

Flour, 1 cup, seasoned with
  Salt, 1 teaspoon,
  Black pepper, ¼ teaspoon
  Garlic powder, ¼ teaspoon

Butter, 2 tablespoons

Olive oil, ⅓ cup

Marsala dry wine, ½ cup

Chicken broth, ½ cup

Lemon juice, 1 lemon

Fresh Italian parsley, 2 tablespoons, chopped

Capers, 2 teaspoons, drained

Turkey Breast with Lemon Sauce

Petto di Tacchino al Limone

DIRECTIONS:

Dredge the turkey slices with seasoned flour and shake off excess. Melt butter in a big frying pan with oil. Add the turkey and sauté on each side about 2 minutes. If you don't have a large enough frying pan, fry the turkey in two batches and keep warm. If you don't have a large enough frying pan, fry the turkey in two batches and keep warm. Set the turkey slices aside on a plate. Pour the wine into the frying pan and stir, cooking for a minute to reduce the alcohol. Then add the chicken broth into the pan with the wine. Stir and cook for another minute. Return the cooked turkey slices and any collected juices, to the frying pan. Add the lemon juice and stir again, cooking for 2–3 minutes. Add the parsley and capers. Serve immediately with the sauce poured over the slices.

TIP: *You can substitute chicken or veal in this recipe if preferred.*

POULTRY

Turkey Cutlets with Spinach, Crab, and Asiago Cheese Sauce

Cotolette di Tacchino con salsa di spinaci, granchio e formaggio Asiago

INGREDIENTS

Turkey breast cutlets, 1 pound (thin-sliced raw turkey breast)
Flour, for dredging
Butter, 6 tablespoons, divided
Olive oil, 2 tablespoons
Salt and pepper, to taste
Shallots or onions, 4 teaspoons, minced
Fresh spinach, 10 oz. coarsely chopped
Crab meat, 8 ounces
Chicken stock, ¼ cup
Cream, ¾ cup
Asiago cheese, ½ cup grated

DIRECTIONS:

Dredge turkey cutlets in flour and shake off excess. Heat 2 tablespoons of butter and 2 tablespoons olive oil in a large sauté pan. Add turkey cutlets, but do not crowd cutlets in the pan; work in two batches if necessary. Sauté on one side and season with salt and pepper, turn to lightly brown on the other side; remove and keep warm. Repeat process with the remaining cutlets. When cutlets are done, place back in frying pan (set aside and keep warm).

In a separate frying pan, add 4 tablespoons butter to the pan and sauté the shallots until translucent. Add spinach, stir and season with salt and pepper. When spinach wilts add crab meat, chicken stock and cream. Simmer and reduce liquid (about 2 minutes), add Asiago cheese, bring back to a simmer. Place cutlets into the frying pan with the cream mixture; simmer for another minute. Pour turkey on a platter, and serve!

VEGETABLES

Eggplant Parmesan 104

Green Beans with Mint 106

Green Beans with Tomatoes 107

Mamma's Potato Cassarole 110

Mamma's Vegetable Zucchini Stew 105

Pasta with Peas and Onions 108

Peppers & Eggplant 109

Rosemary Potato Gratin 111

INGREDIENTS

Eggplants, 2 large (or 3 medium)

Olive oil, 1 cup

Eggs 2, whisked

Salt, a pinch

Water, 2 tablespoons

Eggs, 2 large, hardboiled then chopped

BREAD CRUMB MIXTURE
(COMBINE TOGETHER)

Dried bread crumbs, 1 ½ cup

Reggiano-Parmesan, ⅔ cup (or grated Romano cheese)

Italian parsley, 2 tablespoons, chopped

Black pepper, ¼ teaspoon

Garlic, 1 large clove, finely chopped

Mozzarella, ¾ pound, shredded or thinly sliced

Marinara sauce, 2 cups, mixed with ½ cup water (reserved)

Eggplant Parmesan

Melanzane alla Parmigiana

"Cosenza" Calabrese style

DIRECTIONS:

Preheat oven to 450°F.

Wash eggplant. Cut into ¼ inch thick slices. Put slices in large bowl and sprinkle lightly with salt. Cover for 30 minutes; this will make sure the eggplant does not turn dark.

Add cold water and rinse off salt from eggplant. Drain, and dry excess moisture off with paper towel. Brush both sides of eggplant with oil.

Cover 2 baking sheets with parchment paper. Arrange slices of eggplant in a single layer, just touching, but not over lapping on the sheet.

Place in oven for 10–15 minutes. Turn slices and continue baking until they are lightly golden and tender.

ASSEMBLY:

Put ½ cup of marinara sauce in bottom of 9x13-inch pan.

(recipe continues)

VEGETABLES

Combine 2 eggs (whisked) with 2 tablespoons water and pinch of salt.

Per layer (in 9x13-inch pan): add eggplant slices in a single layer over sauce. Sprinkle ½ cup bread crumb mixture over slices. Sprinkle with chopped hardboiled eggs, and then some beaten egg mixture. Top with approximately ½ cup shredded mozzarella, add more if you prefer.

Continue layering as above (3 layers). Pour a little bit of marinara sauce over the top of the last layer.

Cover with non-stick aluminum foil, bake at 375°F for 25–30 minutes. Remove foil and bake another 5–6 minutes. Let rest about 15–20 minutes before serving. Enjoy!

Mamma's Vegetable Zucchini Stew

Stufato di verdure di Mamma

This is very delicious and can be eaten with Romano cheese and crusty Italian bread. This can also be eaten with cooked pasta (about 1 pound), mixed together and topped with Romano cheese. You can also eat it as a side vegetable dish. Enjoy!

DIRECTIONS:

Heat the oil in a medium stock pot. Add the onions and cook until lightly golden. Add the zucchini, potatoes, peas, water, salt, black pepper, oregano, and crushed hot pepper flakes.

Cook on medium heat. Stir once, put the lid on top (covering half-way). Cook for 20–30 minutes until it is tender. Taste for salt (add more if necessary). Add the parsley and cook for a one minute or until well done.

INGREDIENTS

Olive oil, ½ cup

Onion, 1 medium, chopped

Zucchini, 4–5 small (cut into 1 ½-inch chunks)

Yukon gold potatoes, 4 medium (cut into 1 ½-inch chunks)

Petite peas, 2 cups fresh or frozen

Water, 2 ¾ cups

Salt, 1 ½ teaspoon

Black pepper, ½ teaspoon

Oregano, ½ teaspoon

Crushed Hot Pepper Flakes, to taste

Parsley, 1 teaspoon, chopped

VEGETABLES

Green Beans with Mint

Fagiolini all Menta

INGREDIENTS

Roman green beans, 2 pounds (flat or regular green beans)

Salt, 2 teaspoons

Garlic, 1 clove, chopped

Fresh mint, 8 leaves, chopped

INGREDIENTS (DRESSING)

Olive oil, 4 ounces

Red wine vinegar, 2 ounces

Salt and Black pepper, to taste

DIRECTIONS:

Prepare the beans (washed) and cook in boiling water (lightly salted with 2 teaspoons salt) for 6–9 minutes, until tender. Cool in cold water, drain well and add the rest of the ingredients in a large bowl. Toss well (taste and add salt if needed); place in refrigerator to marinate for at least one hour. Serve cold.

Serves 4–6.

TIP: *You can serve this cold or at room temperature (my favorite!).*

Green Beans with Tomatoes

Fagiolini con Pomodoro

We Italians love the flavor of Roman green beans but they are to find; sometimes you can find them fresh, at the market, in the summertime.

DIRECTIONS:

Sauté onions in oil until golden. Add garlic and stir for 1 minute. Add tomatoes, basil, salt and pepper. Simmer for about 15 minutes, or until sauce thickens. Add the cleaned beans, which have had the ends snapped off and string removed; add about 3 cups of water, stir the beans, cover and simmer over medium-low heat for about 20–30 minutes, or until beans are tender (if liquid cooks off before beans are done, add more water during cooking). Taste; add additional seasonings of your choice.

Serves 5–6.

INGREDIENTS

Onion, 1 medium or large, thinly sliced

Garlic, 1 clove, thinly sliced

Canned tomatoes, 1 ½ cup (crushed) or fresh tomatoes (peeled and chopped with their juices)

Fresh basil, 1 tablespoon chopped

Salt, 2 teaspoons

Pepper, to taste

Water, 3 cups (approximately)

Roman green beans, 1 pound (or regular green beans)

Olive oil, ½ cup

TIP: *You may add diced cooked bacon or cooked pancetta.*

VEGETABLES

INGREDIENTS

Petite spring peas, 1 pound, shelled (fresh or frozen)

Olive oil, ½ cup

Onion, 1 cup, chopped

Salt, 1 teaspoon

Black pepper, ¼ teaspoon

Butter, 2 tablespoons

Water, 1 ½–2 cups

Pasta, 1 lb. box (medium shells or tubettini)

Romano cheese, ½ cup

Pasta with Peas and Onions

Piselli e Cipolle Pasta

This works well as a side dish or you can serve over cooked pasta shells or tubettini. My husband, Sostine, likes this pasta and peas with Reggiano or Romano cheese. My son-in-law, Chad, loves this dish so much he made up a song about it!

DIRECTIONS:

Wash and drain the peas. Heat the oil in a 2-quart sauce pan and sauté the onion for 2–3 minutes. Add the peas, salt, pepper, butter and 1 ½ – 2 cups of water (make sure you can still see the peaks of the peas coming out of the water). Cook over medium heat for 15–20 minutes until tender.

Boil pasta according to package directions (medium-sized pasta shells or tubettini). Approximately 1 pound pasta will serve 4–6 people. Drain pasta and toss with peas.

TIP: *Top with your choice of Romano or Parmigiano-Reggiano cheese. Delicious!*

VEGETABLES

Peppers & Eggplant

Peperonata di Zia Rosina Baldino

I like this a lot, especially with my sub sandwich or as a side dish with steak, chicken or fish. This recipes comes from my Aunt Rosina.

INGREDIENTS

Olive oil, ¼ cup

Potatoes, 2 medium-large, peeled, sliced in half, then cut into wedges (½-inch thick)

Onions, 2 medium, sliced ½-inch thick

Yellow pepper, 1, sliced ½-inch thick

Red pepper, 1, sliced ½-inch thick

Eggplant, 1 peeled and sliced ¼-inch thick

Mushrooms, 10 small, quartered

Tomato, 1, peeled and chopped (remove seeds)

Hot pepper, ½ teaspoon

Fresh basil, 1 teaspoon, chopped

Salt, 1 teaspoon

Ground black pepper, ½ teaspoon

DIRECTIONS:

Heat the oil in a large fry pan. Add potatoes and stir for 5 minutes; then add onions, peppers, eggplant, and mushrooms. Stir or sauté over high-heat for about 5–6 minutes. Lower to medium-heat, add tomatoes, and spices, stir 3–4 minutes. Then place on low heat, stirring, and cook for another 8–10 minutes. Serve hot or room temperature.

INGREDIENTS

Yukon Gold or Russet potatoes, 2 ½–3 pounds (washed)

Butter, 1 stick and 2 tablespoons for the top

Philadelphia cream cheese, 3 ounces

Egg, 1 large (whisked)

Parmigiano-Reggiano cheese, ¾ cup grated

Salt, 1 ½ teaspoon

Black pepper, ¼ teaspoon

Italian parsley, 2 tablespoons, chopped

Milk, ½ cup (or half-and-half)

Mozzarella cheese, ½ pound, cubed

Eggs, 4 hardboiled, sliced

Mamma's Potato Cassarole

Spauma di Patate

This is another one of my Mamma's recipes. She was such a good cook!

DIRECTIONS:

Place the potatoes in a large pot filled with water. Bring to a boil and simmer 35–45 minutes or more depending on the size of the potatoes, until tender. Drain and set aside until cool enough to handle. Preheat oven to 350°F. Remove skins from potatoes. Place a potato ricer or a food mill over a large bowl and rice the potatoes.

Add butter and cream cheese (room temperature). With an electric mixer beat for 2 minutes. Add 1 egg, grated Parmigiano-Reggiano cheese, salt, black pepper, parsley and milk; beat 2–3 more minutes.

Grease the bottom of 8x11-inch (2-quart) baking dish. Take half the potato mixture and spread the mixture flat. Add the mozzarella, top with the hardboiled eggs. Add the rest of the potato mixture. Swirl top of potatoes (like a meringue). Dot the top with the 2 tablespoons of butter. Bake at 350°F for 30 minutes. Raise oven temperature to 375°F for 10–15 minutes until golden brown.

Rosemary Potato Gratin

Tortino di Patate al Rosmarino

This recipe is from a customer at Roma Bakery—it is great! Thank you so much!

DIRECTIONS:

In a small saucepan, bring the half-and-half, garlic cloves and fresh Rosemary to a simmer. Season, to taste, with salt and pepper. Remove and discard the garlic cloves. Set aside.

Peel and wash the potatoes and peel the onion; thinly slice the potatoes and the onion. Generously butter a 12-inch oven-safe baking dish (3-quarts).

Arrange the potatoes and a little onion in an overlapping layer on the bottom of the dish. Season the layer generously with salt and pepper. Lightly sprinkle with some of the grated mixed cheese. Make another potato-onion cheese layer, finishing with a generous amount of cheese.

Press the layers down gently (use a fork or your hands). Pour the half-and-half mixture over the potato-onion layers and fill the dish up to the top of the potatoes. Cover the dish loosely with foil so it doesn't touch the cheese on top and bake 30 minutes. Uncover and bake another 10–15 minutes until the cheese is bubbly and golden brown (potatoes should be tender).

Let it cool for 15–20 minutes before serving.

Serves 6–8.

TIP: *Place a cooking sheet underneath the pan to prevent spillage to the oven floor.*

INGREDIENTS

- **Half-and-half,** 2 cups
- **Garlic,** 2 cloves, smashed
- **Fresh Rosemary,** 1 tablespoon, chopped
- **Russet potatoes (Idaho),** 3 pounds, peeled
- **Butter,** 2 tablespoons, softened
- **Onion,** 1 medium
- **Salt and freshly ground black pepper,** to taste
- **Gruyère cheese,** 2 cups grated, packed
- **Parmigiano cheese,** ½ cup

VEGETABLES

PASTA & RICE

Baked Lasagna with Meat Sauce   114
Baked Pasta with Eggplant   115
Cannelloni Filling   116
Fettuccine Alfredo   120
Fettuccine with Artichokes   121
Fried Rice Balls   130
Homemade Egg Pasta   122
Jumbo Stuffed Shells   124
Linguine Carbonara   125
Mamma's Pasta & Anchovy Sauce   126
Mediterranean Pasta   127
Mena's Gnocchi   128
Mena's Manicotti Crêpes   118
Orzo Pasta or Rice Pilaf   133
Rice Croquettes   132
Rice with Tuna   134
Risotto — Basic   135
Sausage with Potato Lasagna   137
Spaghetti with Anchovies and Tomato Sauce   138
Spaghetti with Asparagus   139
Spicy Gemelli with Cauliflower   136

Baked Lasagna with Meat Sauce

Lasagna con Salsa di Carne

This is my Mamma's Calabria lasagna that the whole family will love

DIRECTIONS:

Make little meatballs, fry and set aside.

Prepare meat sauce.

In a small bowl, add chopped hardboiled eggs and set aside.

Cook pasta according to package directions and drain. Set on lightly oiled sheet pan. In a large bowl, mix the ricotta and with the egg, parsley, and Romano. Add salt and pepper to mixture to taste (if needed). Set aside.

Preheat oven to 350°F.

Pour about 1 cup of meat sauce in the bottom of a deep 9x13-inch pan. Layer the noodles, meat sauce, Romano, ricotta filling, meatballs, the chopped hardboiled egg, and mozzarella. Repeat, alternating noodle directions, for each layer, until all noodles are used (about 4–5 layers). Use only meat sauce and mozzarella on the top layer of noodles.

Cover with foil and bake for 45 minutes. Remove the foil and bake at 375°F for 5 more minutes. Let sit for 10 minutes before cutting to serve.

TIP: *You may use a different sized casserole dish, but may alter cooking time. Also, if you work quickly and sauce and noodles are warm, may only need 30–35 minutes to bake. If made ahead and refrigerated, you may need to cook 45–60 minutes. It's done when it's bubbly on top.*

INGREDIENTS

Fried little meatballs, 2 cups, if desired, make ½ batch for this recipe

Tomato meat sauce, 1 recipe from Sauces

Lasagna noodles, 1 lb. box

Mozzarella, 1 pound, shredded or sliced

INGREDIENTS (FILLING)

Ricotta cheese, 1 pound

Egg, 1 large

Fresh Italian parsley, 1 tablespoons, chopped

Romano cheese, 2 cups, finely grated, (½ cup for filling and 1 ½ cup to sprinkle on layers)

Eggs, 2 hardboiled, chopped

Salt and Black pepper, to taste

PASTA & RICE

Baked Pasta with Eggplant

Pasta al Forno con Melanzane

This is a picture of me teaching a cooking class at Roma Bakery. Baked pasta with eggplant, yum!

DIRECTIONS:

Make meat sauce first.

Put the diced, unpeeled eggplant in a bowl. Lightly salt. Put in a colander and cover with small plate. Drain and rinse with water. Pat dry with paper towels to remove as much moisture as possible.

In a large frying pan, heat the oil. Add the eggplant, stirring with a wooden spoon until tender and golden. Drain excess oil and set aside.

Preheat oven to 375°F. Boil water and cook pasta according to package directions, until al dente. Drain the pasta, put in a large bowl and toss with 3 cups meat sauce and half the Romano cheese, stir. Add the mozzarella, peas, eggs and eggplant; combine.

In a deep, 9×13 pan (or shallower 10x15 pan), pour 1 ½ cup of the meat sauce and top with eggplant mixture. Add more meat sauce on top and more of the Romano cheese. Cover with foil and bake for 25–30 minutes. Remove foil and bake for an additional 10 minutes until topping is crispy.

TIP: *Save the rest of the meat sauce to use later or add to casserole if you desire.*

INGREDIENTS

Eggplant, 1 large or 2 medium-sized eggplants, fried and cut into 1-inch cubes (do not peel)

Mostaccioli or cut Ziti, 1 pound (cooked)

Tomato Meat Sauce, 1 recipe from Sauces

Romano cheese, ¾ cup

Mozzarella, ¾ pound cheese (small cubes)

Frozen peas, 1 cup, boil 2 minutes and drain

Eggs, 2 hardboiled, chopped

Vegetable oil, ¾ cup, for frying

PASTA & RICE

INGREDIENTS

Cannelloni pasta, 1 box (12 oz.) for stuffing, cooked according to package directions. May also use the crêpes recipe.

Olive oil, 2 tablespoons

Onion, ¾ cup, chopped

Garlic, 1 tablespoon, chopped

Ground chuck, 1 pound

Ground pork, ½ pound

Frozen chopped spinach, 10 oz. package

Fresh Italian parsley, 2 tablespoon, chopped

Romano cheese, 1 ¼ cup (½ cup in filling and ¾ cup for sprinkling on top)

Ricotta cheese, ¾ pound

Mozzarella, 1 cup shredded

Egg, 1 large

Salt and pepper, to taste

Marinara sauce

Béchamel sauce

Cannelloni Filling

Ripieno per Cannelloni

In Italy tube pasta with cheese filling is called Manicotti. If filled with meat mixtures it's called cannelloni. When you buy dried stuffing tubes pasta, the box may label as manicotti or cannelloni.

DIRECTIONS:

First prepare the cannelloni pasta from a box or use crêpes. Set on lightly oiled pan, not touching so don't stick together.

In a large skillet, heat oil and sauté the onion and garlic. Add the ground chuck and pork stirring well until browned. Remove from stove and drain (place in a large bowl). Let cool before adding remaining ingredients.

Meanwhile, in a small or medium pot, cook the frozen spinach for 1 minute, drain and let it cool. Squeeze well with hands to remove all moisture. Add the spinach, parsley, Romano, ricotta, mozzarella, and 1 egg to the meat mixture. Add salt and pepper to taste.

Preheat oven to 350°F

Use mixture to fill cannelloni shells, diving equally between them. If using crêpes, place the filling along the center and roll up.

Pour 1 cup marinara sauce in the bottom of a large baking dish (10x15).

(recipe continues)

Arrange the cannelloni in the bottom of the dish, seam side down. Pour marinara sauce and béchamel sauce over cannelloni. Cover with foil and bake for 25 minutes (cover with foil). Uncover, add Romano cheese on top and bake for another 5 minutes.

TIP: *If the marinara sauce is thick, add ¼ cup water to dilute so sauce can be absorbed into the cannelloni.*

TIP: *If you do not have a 10x15 baking dish, use a casserole dish of your choice.*

PASTA & RICE

CRÊPE INGREDIENTS

Flour, 1 cup
Water, 1 cup
Salt, ¼ teaspoon
Eggs, 4 large

FILLING INGREDIENTS

Ricotta cheese, 2 pounds
Salt, ½ teaspoon
Eggs, 3 large
Parmigino-Reggiano cheese, 1 ¼ cup (½ cup for filling, ¾ cup for topping)
Black pepper, to taste
Mozzarella, 1 pound, cut in strips
Marinara sauce, 5–6 cups

Mena's Manicotti Crêpes
Manicotti di Mena con Crêpes

CRÊPE DIRECTIONS:

Combine flour, water and salt. Whisk until smooth. Beat in the eggs one at a time, until blended (about 1 minute), should look like pancake batter. Heat a 5 to 6 inch skillet and grease with a few drops of oil. Put about 3 tablespoons batter in hot skillet and roll around pan to distribute evenly. Cook over low heat until firm. Do not brown. Turn and cook lightly on other side. Do not grease skillet a second time. Place each on crepe on a large Platter. Makes 12 to 14 crêpes.

(recipe continues)

DIRECTIONS:

Preheat oven to 350°F.

In a large bowl add ricotta cheese, salt, eggs, ½ cup Parmigiano-Reggiano cheese and black pepper together for the filling. Mix well with hands until blended.

Cut mozzarella into strips and set aside.

Put about 2 tablespoons of the filling mixture and a strip of mozzarella on each crêpe and roll up. Pour 1 ½ cups marinara sauce in the bottom of a large shallow baking dish (10x15) (just to cover). Put crêpes seam side down in the dish.

Cover with more sauce (about 3 cups) and sprinkle with additional grated Parmigiano-Reggiano cheese. Cover baking dish with tin foil. Bake for 35–45 minutes. Uncover and bake for additional 5 minutes until bubbly (just like lasagna). Remove and let sit for additional 5–7 minutes. Serve with additional marinara sauce as needed and grated Parmigiano-Reggiano cheese. Add according to individual taste.

Serves 6–8.

TIP: *These crêpes shells can also be eaten with cannelloni filling.*

INGREDIENTS

Fettuccine, 1 pound (do not use egg pasta)

Butter, 1 stick

Heavy cream, 1 cup

Parmigiano cheese, 1 cup fresh grated

Fresh Italian parsley, chopped

Salt, 1 tablespoon

Pepper, to taste

Optional Version:

Olive oil, 2 tablespoons

Onion, ½ cup, chopped

Pancetta or boiled ham, ½ cup, finely chopped

Fresh mushrooms, 2 cups, thinly sliced

Fresh or frozen peas, 1 cup, blanched

Salt and pepper, to taste

Fettuccine Alfredo

Fettuccine Alfredo

DIRECTIONS:

In a large pot, cook Fettuccine in 6 quarts of boiling water with 1 tablespoon salt according to package directions.

Meanwhile, in a large frying pan add the butter, whipping cream, and ½ cup Parmigiano cheese. Heat the mixture on low heat until the butter is melted (set aside).

Drain the hot Fettuccine pasta and pour into the large frying pan; mix well with sauce. Serve with remaining ½ cup of Parmigiano cheese, parsley, salt and pepper to taste, and the recipe below if desired.

OPTIONAL DIRECTIONS:

In a frying pan, add the olive oil and onion. Sauté until the onion is translucent. Add the Pancetta or ham and cook for 2 minutes. Add the mushrooms and cook for 5 minutes. Add the cooked peas and stir. Mix with the Fettuccine and Alfredo sauce.

TIP: *Reserve 1 cup of boiled pasta water and add a tablespoon or two at a time to thin the sauce if pasta is sticking together.*

PASTA & RICE

Fettuccine with Artichokes

Fettuccine con Carciofi

INGREDIENTS

Frozen artichoke hearts, 1 package (12 oz.) (more if desired)

Garlic, 2 cloves, finely minced

Olive oil, ½ cup

Butter, 2 tablespoon

Fresh Italian parsley, 2–3 tablespoons, chopped

Water, ¾ cup

Salt, ½ teaspoon (or to taste)

Black pepper, to taste

Whipping cream, 1 cup

Parmigiano cheese, ¾ cup freshly grated

Fettuccine, 1 pound

DIRECTIONS:

Thaw the artichokes and slice into desired pieces.

In a frying pan place the olive oil and butter with the minced garlic and chopped parsley. Sauté lightly for a few minutes; do not brown.

Add the artichokes to the same frying pan with ¾ cup of water and salt and pepper. Cover the pan.

Simmer for 20–30 minutes or until the artichokes are desired tenderness and some of the water has evaporated. Remove from heat. Add the whipping cream and a couple of tablespoons of parmigiano cheese, set aside.

Boil the pasta according to package directions. Drain and place in a serving bowl or platter. Toss with the artichoke mixture and top with additional Parmigiano or Romano. Serve immediately.

Serves 6.

TIP: *Reserve 1 cup of boiled pasta water and add a tablespoon or two at a time to thin the sauce if pasta is sticking together.*

PASTA & RICE

INGREDIENTS

2–3 SERVINGS

All-purpose flour, 1 ½ cups

Eggs, 2 large (room temperature)

Salt, a pinch

Olive oil, ½ teaspoon

INGREDIENTS

4–6 SERVINGS

All-purpose flour, 3 cups

Eggs, 4 large (room temperature)

Salt, a pinch

Olive oil, 1 teaspoon

Homemade Egg Pasta

Pasta all Uovo Fatta in Casa

Making homemade pasta is easier than you think. Plus, you have never tasted pasta so tender. Roll it out very thin and cut into strips if you don't have a pasta machine.

DIRECTIONS:

On a large cutting board or counter, place mound of flour. Make a hole in the center (like a well). Crack the egg into the center of the well and beat gently with a fork. Add salt and oil; mix well with your hands, bringing the flour from inside the flour wall into the egg mixture. Continue with your hands until there is a small ring of flour around the egg mixture and the dough is firm, like bread dough. It will take 10–15 minutes to knead until consistency is obtained. Let the dough set, covered with a bowl or plastic wrap for 15 minutes. Then cut into 3–4 pieces, use one piece at a time, cover the rest so they do not dry out.

Using a rolling pin, sprinkle clean work surface with flour. Flatten the dough until ½-inch thick. Using a hand-crank pasta machine, set the roller setting, to "widest" setting. Pass one of the pasta rectangles through the roller 2–3 times. Keep the dough lightly floured to prevent the dough from sticking to rollers. You can adjust the machine depending on the thickness that you like for fettuccine, linguine, or to make lasagna

(recipe continues)

PASTA & RICE

sheets. The lasagna sheet you can cut down the middle of the sheet—length wise. Place the pasta (single layer) on a cookie sheet that is lightly floured and cover with clean towel.

When you are ready to cook pasta, bring 4 quarts of water to a rolling boil in a large pot with 1 tablespoon salt. Add the pasta and cook no longer than 3–4 minutes. If the pasta is a little thicker, cook for 5 minutes. Drain the pasta, add sauce as you wish.

TIP: *Depending on egg size, you may need to add 1 or 2 tablespoons of water to the dough.*

PASTA & RICE

INGREDIENTS

Jumbo shells, 2 boxes (12 oz.)

Ground chuck, 1 pound (cooked)

Garlic salt, 1 teaspoon

Black pepper, ¼ teaspoon

Ricotta cheese, 1 ½ pounds

Cream cheese, 8 ounces (room temperature)

Fontina cheese, 8 ounces, cut into very small chunks

Romano cheese, 1 ½ cups (save 1 cup for topping the pans, ½ cup goes into the mixture)

Mozzarella cheese, ½ cup shredded

Eggs, 2 large, whisked

Dried bread crumbs, 2 tablespoons

Fresh Italian parsley, 2 tablespoons, chopped

Marinara sauce, 8–10 cups homemade

This recipes makes enough for two 9x13-inch baking pans. If you don't have two 9x13 baking dishes, use any kind of casserole dish such as a 10x15 Pyrex.

Jumbo Stuffed Shells

Conchiglioni Ripieni

This is a special recipe from my friend Rose.

DIRECTIONS:

Preheat oven to 350°F.

Cook pasta according to package directions.

Place on lightly oiled sheets, not touching, so do not stick to each other or pans. Thoroughly cook the ground chuck in frying pan, then drain. Let cool. Add garlic salt and pepper to taste. Pour meat into large bowl. Add ricotta, cream cheese, Fontina, ½ cup Romano, mozzarella, eggs, breadcrumbs, and parsley. Mix well with your hands. Fill the cooked shells evenly with 3–4 tablespoons of meat mixture. Pout ¼ of marinara sauce into each baking pan, spreading evenly. Arrange the filled shells in the pans. Top the shells using half of remaining sauce for each pan. Sprinkle remaining 1 cup of Romano cheese over the tops (½ cup for each pan). Cover with foil and bake for 30 minutes. Uncover and bake for an additional 10 minutes. The sauce should be bubbling and cheese melted.

TIP: *Each box makes about 38 shells, which equals about 78 shells using the full recipe. For a smaller group, cut the recipe in half and it should fit in one 9x13 pan.*

PASTA & RICE

Linguine Carbonara

Linguine Carbonara

DIRECTIONS:

In a large skillet heat butter and olive oil. Add bacon or pancetta and fry for 3 minutes until medium brown and crispy. In the same skillet, add onions; sauté and stir over medium heat for 3 minutes until onions are golden. Slowly add stock. Bring to a boil then reduce heat and simmer, uncovered, for 5 minutes. Add 4 tablespoons cream and simmer an additional minute. Set aside.

Mix eggs, remaining whipping cream, and black pepper together in a bowl.

Meanwhile, in a 4-quart pot, cook pasta according to package directions. Remove from heat. Drain pasta; return to pot (reserve 1 cup of water, if needed, to loosen pasta at the end). Stir in egg mixture. Toss to coat by pulling up pasta and letting it fall back into pot. Stir in bacon and onion mixture. Cook and stir over medium heat for 2 minutes until mixture begins to thicken. Stir in half of the cheese. Season to taste with salt and pepper. Add a little bit of water for moisture, if needed. Garnish with the remaining cheese and parsley. Serve immediately.

Serves 6–8.

INGREDIENTS

Butter, 1 tablespoon

Olive oil, 2 tablespoons

Pancetta or bacon, 6 ounces, cut into ¼-inch pieces

Onion, 1 medium, thinly sliced

Chicken stock, 1 ½ cups

Whipping cream, 8 tablespoons

Eggs, 3 large, whisked

Black pepper, ½ teaspoon

Salt and pepper, to taste

Linguine, 1 pound

Parmigiano-Reggiano cheese, 1 cup freshly grated

Parsley, 1 tablespoon chopped (garnish)

INGREDIENTS

Vegetable or olive oil, ¾–1 cup

Anchovies, 4 ounces (2, 2 oz. cans) in oil

Walnuts, 1 cup, coarsely chopped

Fresh bread crumbs, 2 cups, coarse and crumbled (not fine; day old bread—remove crust and put into food processor)

Spaghetti or spaghettini, 1 ½ pounds

Mamma's Pasta & Anchovy Sauce
Pasta Alici

This is another of my Mamma's recipes. She taught me so much about cooking!

DIRECTIONS:

Heat the oil in a large pan. Add the anchovies with oil; anchovies will disintegrate and break up with a fork. Add walnuts and bread crumbs and toast until golden brown; keep stirring so it does not burn (bread crumbs may absorb oil as your frying; drizzle a little more oil if needed). Set aside.

In a large pot, boil pasta, lightly salted (because the anchovies will be salty). Cook until al dente. Reserve 2–3 cups pasta water. Drain then stir the pasta together with anchovy mixture. Add a little water to loosen the pasta and distribute flavor. Serve immediately. Add salt to taste.

TIP: *We Calabrese are known for making this pasta with anchovies on Christmas Eve, but it is delicious anytime of the year. Typically, we do not use grated cheese with this recipe. You may use it if you prefer!*

PASTA & RICE

Mediterranean Pasta

Pasta Mediterraneo

This is a wonderfully light and healthy pasta dish.

DIRECTIONS:

Sauté garlic in olive oil for a few minutes—do not brown or overcook. Add wine and cook for 2–3 minutes; bring to a boil. Combine chicken soup base with hot water and add to wine/garlic mixture. Lower temperature, cover and simmer for about 5 minutes. Add tomatoes and simmer for another 5 minutes until tomatoes are tender. Add salt to taste.

In a large pot, cook pasta according to package directions. Drain and toss with tomato, garlic, and wine mixture. Add spinach to the pasta pot and stir lightly. Spinach will wilt quickly. You only need to cook for 1 minute. Finish with butter; toss in feta and parsley, then top with pine nuts and serve. Serves 8–10.

TIP: *Reserve 1 cup of boiled pasta water to thin the sauce if it is sticking together.*

TIP: *You can cut this recipe in half and serve 5–6 people.*

INGREDIENTS

Pasta, 2 pounds (penne rigate, be sure to get the ribbed pasta—holds the sauce/flavor better)

Fresh baby spinach, 12 ounces

Sun dried tomatoes, ½ cup (about 15), roughly chopped

Garlic, 6 cloves, coarsely chopped

Olive oil, ¾ cup

Hot water, 2 cups

Chicken soup base (Minor's), 1 rounded tablespoon (or 2 cups chicken broth)

Dry white wine, 1 ½ cups

Butter, 2 tablespoons

Feta cheese, ¾–1 pound, crumbled

Pine nuts, 2 tablespoons (small handful) toasted

Fresh parsley, 2 tablespoons chopped

Salt, 1 tablespoon (or to taste)

PASTA & RICE

INGREDIENTS

Russet or Yukon Gold Potatoes, 6–7 medium

Italian flour, 2 cups (tipo "00") or unbleached all-purpose flour

Salt, 1 tablespoon, for the cooking water

Mena's Gnocchi

Gnocchi di Mena

DIRECTIONS:

Wash potatoes then individually wrap in tin foil. Place on 12x18-inch cookie sheet.

Bake potatoes at 350°F for about 1 hour until tender. Cool and peel.

While the potatoes are cooling, fill a large stockpot with 6 quarts of water and 1 tablespoon of salt. Bring to a boil over medium heat.

Pass the potatoes through a food mill or a potato ricer. Allow the potatoes to cool slightly.

Put a little bit of flour on a clean kitchen counter (set aside ½ cup of flour to work with dough).

Add 1 cup of flour and fluff dough with your hands. Mix gently. Add the remaining flour and mix to make soft dough (knead gently). The dough should be pliable and slightly sticky. If it's too sticky, add another ½ cup of flour.

Divide the dough into 6 pieces. Shape pieces into a long rope about the thickness of your thumb. Cut each rope into 1-inch pieces to make individual gnocchi's (sprinkle with flour to make it easier to work with). Take one piece of gnocchi (cut side down) and place it on the tines of fork; with a floured finger, gently press into it as you roll it off the end of the fork onto a

(recipe continues)

PASTA & RICE

This is a Gnocchi with meat sauce.

floured board. The gnocchi should have an indentation from the tines of the fork. Repeat this process with remaining pieces.

Place the gnocchi on a floured baking sheet to keep them from sticking to one another. Use a slotted spoon to add the gnocchi to the pot of boiling water. When the gnocchi rises to the surface of the water, cook for another 3–4 minutes. Use a strainer or slotted spoon to remove.

Put in a serving dish. Add marinara sauce, meat sauce, pesto, or your favorite pasta sauce. Add Romano cheese and mix gently. Sprinkle with Romano cheese. Serves 4–6.

TIP: *If you don't want to bake the potatoes, you can boil it with the skin. Boil for approximately 45–50 minutes. Cool and peel and put into the food mill or potato ricer. Then continue to the next step.*

TIP: *Press and roll with your index finger against the inside curve of the fork, from the handle to the tip end. You may also use a board or Italian paddle with ridges.*

PASTA & RICE

Fried Rice Balls

Arancine Sicilian Style

I especially loved the large platters of fried food that my cousin Maria prepared. I can remember the street vendor on the beach near Messina, singing out, "Arancine, sfincionelle, pizze, crochetta!" hoping to attract us with his delicacies. I love this! Enjoy. These are my daughter Elisabeth's favorite.

STUFFING INGREDIENTS

Extra-virgin olive oil, 2 tablespoons

Ground meat, 12 ounces, half beef and half pork

Carrot, 1, finely chopped

Celery, 1 stalk, finely chopped

Onion, 1, finely chopped

Tomato sauce, 2 cups

Water, ½ cup

Peas, ½ cup

Tomato paste, 2 tablespoons

Salt and black pepper

Mozzarella, ½ – ¾ pound, cubed (small cubes)

DIRECTIONS:

Make the stuffing: Combine the olive oil, meat, carrot, celery, and onion in a medium saucepan and cook over medium-high heat until browned. Stir in the tomato sauce, water, peas, and tomato paste. Reduce the heat to low, and cook until thickened, about 30 minutes. Season with salt and pepper to taste. Remove from the heat and set aside to cool.

Meanwhile, **make the rice:** Combine the olive oil and onion in a medium sauce-pan and cook over medium heat until softened, about 5 minutes. Add the rice and stir to coat with oil; stir in the saffron. Add the broth, and as soon as it comes to a boil (cook for about 10 minutes; stirring occasionally), cover and remove from heat. Let stand 20–25 minutes, until the water is absorbed and the rice is tender. Stir in the Parmigiano-Reggiano, salt and pepper to taste, and then spread out onto a large plate to cool.

Make the batter: Whisk together the flour, water, and eggs in a large shallow bowl until the batter is smooth and creamy. Fill another shallow bowl with the breadcrumbs. Put a bowl of cold water next to you—to wet your hands now and then; this will help the rice stick together.

(recipe continues)

To assemble the rice balls, wet your hands in the cold water and fill the palm of one hand with a spoonful of rice. Cup your hand and make a deep indentation in the middle of the rice mixture—making sure all sides of the rice are equally thick. Fill the hole with one small spoonful of stuffing and one small cube of mozzarella and close your hand—enclosing the meat sauce and the mozzarella with the rice (add more rice if you need to round out the ball). Keep the hand with which you are spreading the rice wet. The ball should be no bigger than a very small orange, from which it takes its name.

Roll the rice balls in the batter to coat, compacting with your hands. Then roll the rice balls in the breadcrumbs and coat again, patting them thoroughly with your hands. Place them on a baking sheet that is sprinkled with breadcrumbs. Put in the refrigerator for 1 hour.

Heat 5–6 inches of vegetable oil in a large 4–6 quart pan (use a thermometer to attain a temperature of 350–370 degrees) or (use a deep fryer at 350–375 degrees). Add the rice balls in batches and fry (3–4 at a time), turning occasionally, until crisp and golden for 3 to 4 minutes. Drain on paper towels and serve warm. Makes about 14 arancine.

TIP: *Keep arancine warm in a 225 degree oven.*

RICE INGREDIENTS

Extra-virgin olive oil, 2 tablespoons

Onion, 1 small, finely chopped

Arborio rice, 1 ½ cups

Chicken broth, 2 ½ quarts

Saffron threads, a pinch

Parmigiano-Reggiano cheese, 4 tablespoons finely grated

Salt and black pepper

BATTER INGREDIENTS

All-purpose flour, ½ cup

Water, ½ cup

Eggs, 2 large

Unseasoned dried breadcrumbs, 3 cups, plus more for lining the tray

Mozzarella, ½–¾ pound, cubed (small cubes)

Vegetable oil, for frying

Rice Croquettes

Crocchetti di Riso

My cousin Anna in Rome calls them telephone wire Croquettes. Because when eaten the cheese stretches into long threads.

INGREDIENTS

Arborio or rice, 2 cups

Chicken broth, 8 cups

Butter, 3 tablespoons

Unseasoned bread crumbs, 3 tablespoons

Parmesan, 1 cup grated

Eggs, 4 large, whisked (2 eggs for rice mixture, 2 eggs for coating)

Italian parsley, 1 tablespoon, finely chopped

Flour, 1 cup

Salt and pepper, to taste

Mozzarella cheese, 1 pound, cut into small cubes

DIRECTIONS:

In a 3–4 quart sauce pan; add rice and chicken broth. Stir well and bring to a boil over medium-heat (stirring well for about 5 minutes). Lower heat and cover until liquid has been absorbed; add butter and stir. Let cool. (We do not want the rice to be al dente; it has to be cooked until slightly sticky to make the croquettes).

TO ASSEMBLE RICE CROQUETTE:

In a large bowl, add rice, bread crumbs, Parmesan, 2 eggs, parsley, salt and pepper; mix well with hands. Scoop out 1 ½–2 heaping tablespoons of the mixture and roll into the size of a golf ball. Take your thumb and press a deep hole in the center of the ball; place 2 small cubes of mozzarella in the center. Close the rice around the cheese so that it is completely incased. Form into an American football shape with your hands; roll and coat croquettes in the flour, 2 eggs (whisked), and then the breadcrumbs (if egg absorbs into the croquettes quickly, whisk more eggs). After you coat the croquettes, I suggest you place them on a platter in the refrigerator for about 10–15 minutes. This allows the outside of the croquette to dry.

(recipe continues)

PASTA & RICE

In a large pot, deep frying pan, or fryer: heat 1 quart of vegetable oil over medium-heat (350°-375°F); fry croquettes in batches (depending on size of pot) until nicely golden brown. Do not crowd the croquettes in the pan/fryer. Drain on an absorbent paper and keep warm until all have been fried.

Makes about 15–20+ Croquettes, depending on size. Buon Appetito!

Orzo Pasta or Rice Pilaf

Orzo o Riso Pilaf

INGREDIENTS

Onion, 1 medium diced

Bell peppers (red or green), ½ cup diced

Butter, 2 tablespoons

Orzo, 8 ounces (about 1 ½ cup uncooked)

Chicken broth, 4 cups

Lemon juice, 1 teaspoon

Olive oil, 1 tablespoon

Parmigiano-Reggiano cheese, 4 tablespoons grated

Salt, to taste

DIRECTIONS:

Sauté onion and bell peppers in hot butter in a saucepan, stirring frequently until softened, for about 3 minutes. Add orzo, chicken broth, and lemon juice; continuously stir and bring to a boil. Reduce heat, cover and simmer for 7 to 10 minutes stirring occasionally, until orzo is tender. Add olive oil and stir again lightly. Top with grated cheese. Serve promptly. Select colorful vegetables or fresh sliced tomatoes for side dishes.

Serves 4.

TIP: *If you need more broth, add another cup.*

PASTA & RICE

INGREDIENTS

Garlic, 1 large clove, chopped

Onion, ½ cup chopped

Olive oil, ¼ cup

San Marzano tomatoes, 1 can (28. oz), crushed

Fresh basil, 4 leaves, chopped

Light tuna or Italian tuna, 6 ½–7 ½ ounce can, packed in olive oil

Salt, to taste

Arborio or long-grain rice, 2 cups

Water, 4 cups (add more water if needed)

Unsalted butter, 2 tablespoons

Salt, 2 teaspoons

Capers, 2 teaspoons (if preferred)

Rice with Tuna

Risotto con Tonno

DIRECTIONS:

Using a medium-large sized frying pan, sauté the chopped garlic and onion in the olive oil over medium heat until the garlic and onion are lightly golden. Add the tomatoes, basil, and tuna fish. (If you cannot get tuna packed in olive oil, purchase tuna packed in vegetable oil. Tuna in water is not the right consistency or taste for this dish). Simmer about 15 minutes (mashing tuna and tomatoes with a fork occasionally) or until juices are reduced, the color darkened, and the flavors blended. Add capers (if preferred). Taste for salt, add some if needed.

Put the rice, water, butter, and salt in another pan, bring to a boil, stir, cover, and reduce the heat. Cook about 10 minutes (18 for Arborio) stirring a couple of times. By this time the rice is practically dry, almost cooked. Add the tuna sauce, and continue stirring and cooking uncovered until the rice is tendered and done.

TIP: *This tastes better with Italian tuna. Also very taste on Pasta Orzo.*

PASTA & RICE

Risotto — Basic

Risotto

The beautiful thing about Risotto is that you can put just about anything you want in it. Just continue to cook until rice is al dente.

DIRECTIONS:

In a heavy, wide 3–4 quart Dutch oven or pot, heat olive oil and butter over medium heat. Add the scallions and shallot and cook until translucent, stirring often, about 3–4 minutes. Add the rice; stir to coat with the oil. Toast the rice until the edges become translucent, 2 minutes.

Pour in the wine and stir mixture well until evaporated. Add ½ cup of the hot stock and ½ teaspoon of the salt. Cook, stirring constantly, until all the stock has been absorbed. Continue to add hot stock in small batches (just enough to completely moisten the rice) and cook until each successive batch has been absorbed. Stir constantly and adjust the level of heat so the rice is simmering gently, until the rice mixture is creamy but al dente. This will take about 18–20 minutes from the first addition of stock.

Remove from heat and stir in the olive oil or butter until melted, then stir the grated cheese. Adjust the seasoning with salt, if necessary, and pepper.

TIP: *Add stock/broth as needed if rice is too sticky.*

INGREDIENTS

- **Extra-virgin olive oil,** 3 tablespoons
- **Butter,** 1 tablespoon
- **Scallions,** ½ cup minced (about 6)
- **Shallot,** 1 tablespoon minced
- **Arborio or Carnaroli rice,** 2 ½ cups
- **Dry white wine,** ½ cup
- **Hot chicken stock or canned broth,** 6 ½ cups
- **Salt,** ½ teaspoon, or as needed
- **Extra-virgin olive oil,** 2 tablespoons or butter
- **Parmigiano-Reggiano cheese,** ½ cup fresh grated
- **Freshly ground black pepper,** to taste

INGREDIENTS

Cauliflower, 1 medium head

Olive oil, 3 tablespoons plus ⅔ cup

Toasted bread crumbs, 1 cup

Garlic, 2 cloves, minced

Crushed red pepper flakes, 1 ½ teaspoons

Anchovies, 1 can (2 ounces)

Ground black pepper, ½ teaspoon

Gemelli, 1 pound

Pecorino Romano cheese, ½ cup grated

Spicy Gemelli with Cauliflower

Gemelli arrabbiati con Cavolfiore

DIRECTIONS:

Remove the leaves and core of the cauliflower and cut the head into small uniform florets. Set aside.

In a small frying pan, with 3 tablespoons olive oil, heat bread crumbs; stirring until golden brown. Remove the bread crumbs and set aside. In a large frying pan, heat the remaining 2/3 cup olive oil. Add the garlic and sauté until the garlic is soft. Stir in the pepper flakes and cook for 1 minute. Stir in the anchovy fillets and oil (the anchovies will disintegrate and break up with fork), and black pepper. Cook for 1 minute longer. Keep the sauce warm over very low heat.

Meanwhile, in a large pot of salted boiling water, cook the cauliflower and the pasta Gemelli until the cauliflower is crisp-tender and the pasta is al dente (about 7–8 minutes). Drain, reserving ½ cup of the cooking water.

Lightly grease a extra-large serving platter with olive oil. Transfer the Gemelli and cauliflower to the platter and toss to coat with the oil. Add the reserved cooking water to the sauce and stir to blend (if needed). Pour the sauce over the Gemelli and cauliflower and toss well. Sprinkle with the cheese, black pepper to taste, and the bread crumbs. Serve immediately.

PASTA & RICE

Sausage with Potato Lasagna

Saliccia con Lasagna di Patate

DIRECTIONS:

In a large skillet, cook the sausage and mushrooms; stirring until the sausage is brown. Drain fat.

In a large covered saucepan, cook the sliced potatoes in boiling water for 5 minutes (the potatoes won't be thoroughly cooked). Drain and set aside.

To make the filling, stir together the egg, Ricotta and Parmesan or Romano cheese. Stir in the spinach.

To make the Béchamel sauce, use a medium saucepan. Cook the onion and garlic in hot butter until the onion is tender but not brown. Stir in the flour and nutmeg. Add milk all at once. Cook and stir until thickened and bubbly.

Layer half of the potatoes in a greased 2-quart rectangular baking dish. Top with half of the spinach filling. Top with half of the sausage/mushroom mixture, half of the sauce and half of the Mozzarella cheese. Repeat layers; but, reserve the remaining cheese. Cover dish with foil.

Bake at 350 degrees for 35 minutes or until the potatoes are tender. Uncover and sprinkle remaining cheese atop. Bake for another 5–8 minutes or until cheese is melted. Let stand for 10 minutes. It will make the lasagna easier to cut and serve.

INGREDIENTS

- **Italian sausage or ground turkey sausage,** ½ pound (remove casings)
- **Fresh mushrooms,** 2 cups, sliced
- **Potatoes,** 4 cups, peeled and thinly sliced
- **Egg,** 1 beaten
- **Ricotta cheese,** 1 ½ cups, drained
- **Parmesan or Romano cheese,** ½ cup grated
- **Frozen chopped spinach,** 1 package (10 ounces) thawed and well drained
- **Onion,** 1 medium, chopped
- **Garlic,** 2 cloves, minced
- **Butter,** 2 tablespoons
- **All-purpose flour,** 2 tablespoons
- **Ground nutmeg,** a pinch
- **Milk,** 1 ½ cups
- **Mozzarella,** 1 cup shredded cheese

INGREDIENTS

Olive oil, ½ cup

Onion, 1 cup, chopped

Garlic, 2 cloves, chopped

Black olives, 15, pitted

Capers, 3 tablespoons

Anchovies, 10 fillets, chopped

Basil, 4 leaves, chopped

San Marzano tomatoes, 1 can (28 ounces) crushed

Water, 1 cup

Tomato paste, 3 tablespoons

Butter, 3 tablespoons

Red wine, 4 ounces

Spaghetti, 1 pound, cooked and drained

Romano cheese, ½ cup grated

Parsley, 2 tablespoons chopped

Salt and pepper, to taste

Spaghetti with Anchovies and Tomato Sauce

Spaghetti con Acciughe e salsa di Pomodoro

This is a Sicilian recipe

DIRECTIONS:

Heat the oil in a frying pan. Cook the onion and garlic until golden. Add the olives, capers, anchovy fillets, basil, San Marzano tomatoes, 1 cup water, tomato paste, butter, red wine and salt and pepper to taste. Simmer for 15–20 minutes.

In a large pot, boil the spaghetti according to the package directions. Place the spaghetti on a serving platter, pour the sauce on top and lightly toss with two forks. Sprinkle with Romano cheese and parsley. Quick and easy!

Serves 6–8.

TIP: *Reserve 1 cup of boiled pasta water to thin the sauce if it is sticking together.*

PASTA & RICE

Spaghetti with Asparagus

Spaghetti con Asparagi

INGREDIENTS

Butter, ½ stick

Olive oil, 1 ½ tablespoon

Onion, 1 (thinly sliced)

Parma prosciutto or ham, about ⅓ pound sliced (thinly sliced)

Asparagus, ½ pound cut into slivers

Water, ½ cup

Chicken bouillon, 1 cube

Half and half, ½ cup

Spaghetti or spaghettini, 1 pound

Parmigiano-Reggiano cheese, ½ cup grated

Fresh ground pepper, to taste

Salt, to taste

DIRECTIONS:

Heat butter and oil in a large fry pan. Add onion and sauté lightly. Add ham and sauté for 5 minutes. Add asparagus, water, bouillon and simmer on low heat for about 5–8 minutes. Set aside.

Cook spaghetti in salted water (al dente), and drain.

Add asparagus mixture, half & half, and stir together on very low heat so flavors absorb. Top with Parmesan, pepper and salt to taste.

Serves 4–6.

TIP: *Reserve 1 cup of boiled pasta water to thin the sauce if it is sticking together.*

TIP: *It is important to remove the tough ends of the asparagus before cooking.*

TIP: *Add extra cheese on top of pasta when you serve.*

PASTA & RICE

SALADS

Avocado Shrimp Salad   142

Beans and Tuna Salad   143

Beef Tongue Salad   144

Broccoli Rabe Salad with Vinaigrette   146

Broccoli Salad   147

Broccoli with Garlic and Anchovy Sauce   148

Cauliflower Salad   149

Cod Salad   150

Fennel Salad   153

Green Salad with Oranges   154

Honey Mustard Pecan Salad   155

Italian Potato Salad   157

Italian Tomato Salad   158

Mena's Italian Salad Dressing   156

Mena's Seafood Salad   166

Orange Salad Sicilian Style   159

Orecchiette with Broccoli, Onion, and Sausage   160

Pasta Orzo   161

Pasta Salad with Grilled Chicken, Apples, and Cheddar   162

Roasted Potato, Garlic and Red Pepper Salad   163

Summer Fresh Deli Sandwich   152

Tuna Nicoise Salad   164

MARINADE INGREDIENTS
COMBINE & HAND WHIP

Balsamic vinegar, ½ cup

Water, ⅓ cup

Lemon juice, ½ cup

Olive oil, 1 cup

Parsley, ¼ cup chopped

Garlic, 2 cloves, minced

Salt, 1 tablespoon

Paprika, ¼ cup

Black pepper, ¼ teaspoon

Sugar, 1 tablespoon

Dry mustard, 1 teaspoon (or 1 tablespoon prepared mustard)

Thyme, 1 teaspoon, crushed

Oregano, ½ teaspoon, crushed

Red onions, 3 small or 1 large, sliced

Sweet red pepper, ⅓ cup, chopped

SALAD INGREDIENTS

Frozen shrimp, 2 pounds (raw, peeled, deveined)

Avocados, 2, sliced

Bibb lettuce, 1 head (or iceberg lettuce)

Avocado Shrimp Salad

Insalata di gamberi e avocado

This is a wonderful summer salad.
You can make a meal out of it!

DIRECTIONS:

Combine all marinade ingredients and hand whip.

Boil the raw shrimp according to package directions (approximately 2 minutes); let cool. Place the shrimp in a large bowl and mix with marinade; stir together and place plastic wrap over top of bowl. Marinate in refrigerator for 8 hours or overnight.

Put marinated shrimp mixture in lettuce leaves and garnish with avocado slices. Drizzle with remaining marinade.

Beans and Tuna Salad

Fagioli E Tonno

DIRECTIONS:

If using canned white kidney beans: drain them and discard the liquid. In a large salad bowl, add tuna, chopped parsley, beans, grape tomatoes, onion, celery, cucumber and red pepper.

In small bowl, add the olive oil, salt, pepper, vinegar, and whisk together. Pour this salad dressing mixture into the large salad bowl mixture. Toss together. Add salt to taste, drizzle with 2 tablespoon of olive oil on top. Let it rest for 1 hour before serving.

TIP: *Serve with Italian bread.*

TIP: *Keep the canned tuna in the juice and oil and add to salad.*

SALAD INGREDIENTS

Cannellini beans (white kidney), 2 cans (20 oz.)

Italian tuna fish, 2 cans (7 oz.), do not drain (packed in olive oil)

Italian parsley, 2 tablespoons, chopped

Grape tomatoes, 1 ½ cup, cut in halves

Red onion, 1 medium, thinly sliced

Celery, 2 stalks, thinly sliced

English cucumber, 1 small, thinly sliced

Sweet red pepper, ½, thinly sliced

DRESSING INGREDIENTS

Olive oil, ½ cup + 2 tablespoons

Freshly ground Pepper, to taste

Wine vinegar, 2 tablespoons

SALADS

INGREDIENTS – BRINE

Water, 3 quarts
Salt, ½ cup
Bay leaves

INGREDIENTS – BOIL

Beef tongue, 3 – 3 ½ pounds
Water, enough to cover the tongue
Onion, 1, quartered
Bay, 2 leaves
Celery, 1 stalk

Beef Tongue Salad

Insalata di Lingua di Bue alla Calabrese

This is a true Calabrese dish that is well worth the time!

DIRECTIONS:

Mix brine in a large bowl. Submerge the tongue in the brine and refrigerate for 4–6 hours or overnight.

Remove tongue from brine. Place in a large pot and cover tongue with water; add 1 onion (quartered), 2 bay leaves, and 1 celery stalk. Let boil for 5 minutes then simmer for 2–2 ½ hours until fork tender.

Remove tongue from pot and let rest for 10–15 minutes until cool enough to handle. Starting at the root end peel the outer skin (it will peel quite easily). Trim away any fat on the root end.

Slice tongue into ½-inch sections and cut in quarters; cut the larger end into 6 pieces.

In a large bowl mix together the tongue, vegetables, and dressing; toss well. Marinate for ½ an hour.

(recipe continues)

SALAD INGREDIENTS

Beef tongue, 1

Celery, 3 stalks, cut into ¼ inch sections (diagonally)

Red onion, ½ cup, cut in half and sliced

Green olives, ½ cup sliced

Pickled Giardiniera, ½ cup, coarsely chopped

Red cabbage, ½ cup, thinly sliced

Italian parsley, 3 tablespoons, coarsely chopped

Sweet red peppers, ½, cubed (½-inch)

Sweet yellow peppers, ½, cubed (½-inch)

DRESSING INGREDIENTS

Garlic, 1 clove, crushed

Black pepper, ½ teaspoon

Oregano, 1 teaspoon

Celery salt, 1 teaspoon

Lemon, 1, juiced

Olive oil, 1 cup

Wine vinegar, ⅓ cup

Salt, 1 teaspoon or to taste

TIP: *If water reduces while cooking the tongue, add a little more water. Can eat as an appetizer or a salad.*

SALADS

Broccoli Rabe Salad with Vinaigrette

Insalata di Broccoli Rape con Vinaigrette

When I first came to America in the 60s, "Rapini", as it's called in Italy, were not available. My family and I use to go to Canada to get some. Today, they are made this way and are now called "Broccoli Rabe" (Rah-beh).

INGREDIENTS

Broccoli rabe, 1 bunch (about 1 pound); washed & chopped into 2 inch pieces

Extra virgin olive oil, ⅓ cup

Red wine vinegar, ¼ cup

Garlic, 1 clove, finely chopped

Salt, ½ teaspoon

Black pepper, ¼ teaspoon

Short Pasta, ½ pound cooked according to package directions (drain and cool)

DIRECTIONS:

Bring a large pot of water to a boil. Add the broccoli rabe and boil for 3 to 4 minutes, until crisp-tender. Drain. Place in a bowl with ice water. Set aside to cool to room temperature. Drain well. Add pasta, then add the olive oil, vinegar, garlic, black pepper and salt to the broccoli rabe. Toss salad lightly and mix well. Serve and enjoy.

TIP: *Broccoli Rabe is naturally bitter. But, if it is blanched, much of the bitterness is reduced. Do not overcook it.*

TIP: *This is an excellent recipe when you are looking for a healthy alternative.*

SALADS

Broccoli Salad

Insalata di Broccoli

MARINADE INGREDIENTS

Paprika, ½ teaspoon

Celery salt, ½ teaspoon

Salt, ¼ teaspoon

Light olive oil, ¼ cup

Wine vinegar, 2 tablespoons

VEGETABLE INGREDIENTS

Fresh mushrooms, 2 cups, sliced

Fresh broccoli florets, 2 cups, with stalk peeled

Green onions, 3, sliced

Raisins, ½ cup

Salt and pepper, to taste

DIRECTIONS:

Combine and whip marinade sauce ingredients until foamy and thick. Pour over the vegetables and marinate in the refrigerator overnight.

TIP: *The longer you marinate in the refrigerator, the better it taste. Serve and enjoy!*

SALADS

INGREDIENTS

Olive oil, ½ cup

Garlic, 2 cloves, chopped or minced

Anchovies, 3 fillets

Broccoli florets, 1 head and tops, cut up

Salt, 1 teaspoon

Black pepper, ¼ teaspoon

Cold water, 1 cup

Short pasta, 1 pound (shells, penne, or tubetti), cooked according to package directions

Broccoli with Garlic and Anchovy Sauce

Broccoli con aglio e salsa di acciughe

DIRECTIONS:

In a large frying pan, heat the olive oil and garlic. Sauté for 1 minute until garlic is light golden brown. Add fillets of anchovy and cook smashing anchovy with a fork, about 1–2 minutes. Toss the cut up broccoli in this sauce to coat well; add salt and pepper. Add the water. Place lid on large pan and steam over low-heat for 7–8 minutes until tender. Remove lid; turn heat on high and stir until half the water evaporates. Toss with pasta.

TIP: *Reserve ½ cup of boiled pasta water and add a tablespoon or two at a time to thin the sauce if needed.*

TIP: *Cut and discard the tough end of the broccoli stems (3-inch bottom end); stalk should be peeled. If you desire you can sprinkle pasta with Parmigiano, Reggiano or Romano cheese.*

SALADS

Cauliflower Salad

Insalata di Cavolfiore — Sicilian style

I had this in Messina. It was delicious!

DIRECTIONS:

Have a pot of salted boiling water ready on the stove. Break the cauliflower into small uniform-size florets. Add the florets to the boiling water and cook for 2 minutes. Drain well and cool. Transfer the florets to a salad bowl. Add the remaining ingredients to the salad bowl, stir to combine and toss with the dressing. Add salt and pepper to taste.

Serves 6–8.

SALAD INGREDIENTS

- **Cauliflower,** 1 medium head, outer stems and core removed
- **Green or black kalamata (non-pitted) olives,** ½ cup diced
- **Sweet red pepper,** ½ cup, cut into large chunks
- **Italian parsley,** ¼ cup chopped
- **Capers,** 2 tablespoons in brine, drained and minced
- **Cherry tomatoes,** 1 cup, cut in half or ¼ cup diced sun-dried tomatoes in olive oil
- **Chickpeas,** 1 cup canned, drained and well rinsed
- **Salt and pepper,** to taste

DRESSING INGREDIENTS

WHISK INGREDIENTS UNTIL BLENDED TOGETHER WELL

- **Extra virgin olive oil,** ½ cup
- **Garlic,** 1 clove, peeled and minced (fine)
- **Red wine vinegar,** 4 tablespoons
- **Salt,** ½ teaspoon

INGREDIENTS

Dried salted cod, 2 pounds

Onions, 3 medium or 2 large, thinly sliced

Potatoes (Yukon gold), 2 pounds, cook with peel on until tender then peel and cut into small chunks and set aside

Milk, 2 ½ cups

Eggs, 4 hardboiled, sliced

Kalamata or Italian green olives, ½ cup pitted and cut in half

Italian parsley, 2 tablespoons chopped

Olive oil, 1 ¼ cups

Salt and ground pepper, to taste

Cod Salad

Insalata de Baccalá

This Cod Salad can be served either hot or cold. It is delicious either way. Traditionally we eat this as a dinner.

DIRECTIONS:

Rinse the salted cod in cold water. Place in a large container (1–2 gallons). Cut the cod into 2x4-inch pieces. Store in refrigerator to soak and de-salt for 2–3 days, changing the water at least 2 times per day. Cod will taste salty if the water is not changed.

Remove the fish from water, place in a medium size saucepan. Cover with cold milk. Bring to a boil then reduce the heat to low and cook uncovered, until it becomes opaque (about 10 minutes). Turn the heat off and let the cod rest in milk about 15 minutes. Using a slotted spoon, remove the cod and discard the milk. Flake the fish with your hands into small-medium chunks.

Place the whole potatoes in a large saucepan. Cover with cold water, add a pinch of salt. Bring to a boil, turn down, and simmer until tender. Drain, cool down, then peel and cut about ½ inch thick and set aside.

Place 1 cup of olive oil in a large skillet and cook onion over low heat (set aside leaving the oil inside the fry pan). Stir occasionally until they are tender, sweet, and golden brown, about 10–12 minutes.

(recipe continues)

In a large bowl mix the cod, onion, potatoes, parsley, and pepper to taste.

Spread the mixture above in an 9x13 dish with ¼ cup olive oil. Drizzle oil in pan so it will not stick. Bake in oven until bubbly, about 15–20 minutes. Remove dish from the oven. Spread the eggs (sliced) and olives over the top. Cover with lid or foil paper, bake 6–10 minutes. Serve hot.

TIP: *If you do not bake, add all ingredients, toss and serve at room temperature with parsley for flavor.*

SALADS

INGREDIENTS

Sub buns, 4–6 fresh

Salami, ½ pound thinly sliced

Spicy capicola, ½ pound thinly sliced

Mortadella, ½ pound thinly sliced

Provolone, ½ pound thinly sliced

Iceberg lettuce, 2 cups shredded

Red onion, ¼ cup thinly sliced

Fresh basil, 8 leaves, chopped (medium-chunks)

Extra-virgin olive oil, 3–4 tablespoons

Salt, ¼ teaspoon

Black pepper, ¼ teaspoon

Summer Fresh Deli Sandwich

Panino Calabrese

In Calabria we make these beautiful sandwiches; it's the fresh basil that makes it special. What a fresh taste of summer.

DIRECTIONS:

Shred the lettuce in a bowl; add the red onion and basil. Drizzle with olive oil and add salt and black pepper. Toss until lightly coated. Set aside. Layer the meats and cheeses on the bread, then top with the lettuce and basil mix and press down. Bite into it. Delicious! Welcome to summer.

Fennel Salad

Insalata di Finocchio

DIRECTIONS:

In a large bowl, combine the thinly sliced fennel, sliced red onions, parsley, sliced green onions, and toasted almonds; toss together.

DRESSING:

In another small bowl, add vinegar, lemon, olive oil, black pepper and salt. Whisk together well. Add mixture to the fennel salad. Toss very well. Set aside for about ½ hour to allow flavor to absorb. Taste and season as necessary.

SALAD INGREDIENTS

Fennel, 2 bulbs (medium or large, very thinly sliced)

Red onion, ½ cup, sliced

Italian parsley, 3 tablespoons finely chopped

Green onions, 2 (cut on a diagonal into slices)

Toasted almonds, ½ cup

DRESSING INGREDIENTS

White balsamic vinegar, 2 tablespoons

Lemon juice, 1 tablespoon

Olive oil, ½ cup

Black pepper, ¼ teaspoon

Salt, 1 teaspoon (season to taste)

INGREDIENTS

Iceberg lettuce, 1 medium head

Black olives, 1 can sliced (drained), or non-pitted Kalamata

Oranges, 2 peeled and sectioned

Olive oil, ¼ cup

Orange juice, ¼ cup

Orange zest, ½ teaspoon

White balsamic vinegar, 2 teaspoons

Salt, ¾ teaspoon

Black pepper, ¼ teaspoon

Paprika, ¼ teaspoon

Green Salad with Oranges
Insalata Siciliana alle Arance

DIRECTIONS:

Wash lettuce and pat dry with paper towel; tear into small pieces. Mix lettuce, olives, and oranges.

In a bowl, whisk together the oil, orange juice, zest, vinegar, salt, black pepper, and paprika for dressing.

Pour dressing over salad, mix and serve.

SALADS

Honey Mustard Pecan Salad

Insalata di Noci Pecan al Miele e Mostarda

DIRECTIONS:

In a screw-top jar, combine vinegar, sugar, honey mustard, salt and pepper; shake to combine. Add olive oil and shake well. Chill till serving time (can be up to one week ahead of time). Just before serving, in a large salad bowl, combine apple slices, greens, and pecans. Shake dressing; pour some over greens and toss. Add enough remaining dressing to coat greens. Toss again. Serve immediately.

TIP: *Place leftovers in a glass bottle in the refrigerator.*

INGREDIENTS

Red wine vinegar, ¼ cup

Sugar, 4 teaspoons

Honey mustard, 1 teaspoon (or other mustard)

Salt, ¼ teaspoon

Freshly ground pepper, ¼ teaspoon

Olive oil, ⅓ cup

Apples, 1 cup, sliced thinly (toss with mixed greens)

Mixed greens, 8 cups torn (such as: butter head lettuce, red-tipped leaf lettuce, Romaine, radicchio, arugula and watercress)

Toasted pecans, ½ cup chopped

SALADS

INGREDIENTS

Light olive oil, 1 ⅓ cup

Red wine vinegar, ½ cup

Parmigiano-Reggiano cheese, ¼ cup freshly grated

Sugar, 1 teaspoon

Salt, 2 teaspoons

Celery salt, 1 teaspoon

White pepper, ½ teaspoon

Dry mustard, ½ teaspoon

Paprika, ½ teaspoon

Garlic, 1 clove, minced

Mena's Italian Salad Dressing

Condimento per Insalata

DIRECTIONS:

In a screw-top jar, blend all ingredients together; chill for 2 hour. Shake well before serving. I like this best on a Romaine salad, Arugula salad, or a blend of greens.

Italian Potato Salad

Insalata di patate alla Contadina

I love this. We could eat this with fresh crusty Italian or Calabrese bread. We love to dip the bread in the salad juice ("Scarpetta").

DIRECTIONS:

Cook the beans in salted boiling water until just tender. Drain in a colander and let cool. Cook potatoes in jackets until done. Set aside to cool.

In a large bowl, cut tomatoes into cubes. Slice onion, peel potatoes once cooled, and cut into cubes. Toss the vegetables together with oil, vinegar, oregano, salt and pepper. Mix together gently with long spoon. Let it sit at least 10 minutes before serving.

Serves 6–8.

TIP: **Scarpetta:** *This is the act of mopping up the remaining juices on your plate with a piece of crunchy Italian bread. Scarpetta literally means "to do the little shoe" in Italian; this is because some say the little piece of bread looks like a small shoe when we dip and drag it along our plates in the remaining sauce. Delicious!*

INGREDIENTS

Green beans, 1 pound (cut in half)

Potatoes (Yukon Gold), 1 ½ pound

Fresh tomatoes, 3 medium-size

Red Italian onion, ½, sliced

Olive oil, ½–¾ cup

Wine vinegar, ¼ cup (scant)

Oregano, ½ teaspoon

Fresh basil, 1 teaspoon, chopped

Fresh Italian parsley, 1 teaspoon

Salt and pepper, to taste

SALADS

Italian Tomato Salad

Insalata di Pomodori

INGREDIENTS

Red onion, ½ medium, thinly sliced (soak in water with a pinch of salt for ½ hour then drain well)

Tomatoes, 3 medium-large sized cut into wedges

Green olives, ½ cup sliced

Olive oil, 4–5 tablespoons

Wine vinegar, 1 teaspoon

Oregano, ½ teaspoon

Black pepper, ¼ teaspoon

Basil, 3–4 leaves, chopped

Garlic, 1 small clove, chopped (for flavor)

Salt, ½ teaspoon

Optional:

Bell pepper, ½, sliced (for color and added flavor)

English cucumber, ½, halved and sliced

DIRECTIONS:

In a large salad bowl, mix ingredients; toss together well and serve.

Orange Salad Sicilian Style

Insalata di Aranci

INGREDIENTS

Oranges, 6 seedless

Olive oil, 6 tablespoons

Salt, ½ teaspoon, or to taste

Black olives, 24 (Sicilian or Greek)

Lemon Juice, ½ lemon

Salt, to taste

Black pepper, a pinch

DIRECTIONS:

Marinate the olives in the lemon juice for 10–15 minutes.

Peel the oranges, taking off as much of the white inner peel as possible. Slice in thin rounds and spread out on a large serving plate. Sprinkle with olive oil, a pinch of black pepper and salt to taste.

Distribute the olives over the orange slices. Tilt the plate. With a large spoon, scoop up the olive oil and juices and baste the oranges. Press down gently on some of the slices so that more juice mingles with the oil. Baste a bit more and serve.

SALADS

INGREDIENTS

Extra-virgin olive oil, ½ cup

Italian sausage, 1 pound uncooked (remove casings)

Onion, 1 cup, chopped

Garlic, 1 clove, sliced

Crushed red pepper, ¼ teaspoon

Chicken or vegetable stock (or both), 2 cups

Broccoli, 1 large-size head broken into florets

Orecchiette pasta, 1 pound

Unseasoned dry bread crumbs, ½ cup (toasted)

Pecorino Romano cheese, ½ cup freshly grated

Fresh Italian parsley, ½ cup chopped

Orecchiette with Broccoli, Onion, and Sausage

Orecchiette con Broccoli, Cipolle e Salsiccia

DIRECTIONS:

In a large saucepan, heat oil over medium-heat. Add sausage, onion, garlic, and crushed red pepper. Stir with a wooden spoon and cook until sausage is browned and the onion is tender. Add stock and broccoli; bring to a boil. Reduce heat to simmer and cook about 10 minutes (until desired tenderness).

Meanwhile, cook pasta according to package directions; drain well and return to pot. Add sausage-broccoli mixture; toss to coat. Combine bread crumbs, grated Pecorino Romano cheese, and parsley; toss with pasta mixture.

Serves 6–8.

TIP: *Reserve 1 cup of boiled pasta water to thin the sauce if it is sticking together.*

TIP: *Substitute medium-sized pasta shells for orecchiette pasta if desired*

SALADS

Pasta Orzo

Pasta Orzo

Orzo is the Italian word for "barley". In Italy, the word can of course refer to the grain itself, but might also describe a beverage made from roasted barley or a wheat-based pasta that looks like barley. The term is also always used for pasta in other parts of the world, though pasta is also called risoni in some places. Its small shape makes it a popular addition to soups and stews, and it can also be prepared as a pilaf in much the same way that rice could be.

DIRECTIONS:

Preheat a 6 quart pot with a tight fitting cover over moderate heat. Add oil, butter, onion, and garlic and sauté for 2–3 minutes. Add broth to the pan and bring to a boil. Stir in orzo and return broth to a boil. Cover pot and reduce heat to simmer. Cook 15 minutes, stirring occasionally, or until liquid is absorbed and pasta tender. Remove lid and stir in cheese and parsley. Season with salt and pepper to taste. Add your favorite fresh herbs (I especially like basil!). Stir 1 chopped tomato into the orzo to add flavor and more color!

INGREDIENTS

Orzo pasta, 2 cups

Extra-virgin olive oil, 2 tablespoons

Butter, 3 tablespoons

Onion, ½ medium sized, chopped

Garlic, 1 clove (chopped)

Chicken or vegetable broth, 2 cans (14 oz.) or homemade stock

Parmigiano-Reggiano cheese, ½ cup grated (or Romano cheese)

Fresh Italian parsley, 1 tablespoon, chopped

Tomato, 1 chopped

Salt and freshly ground black pepper, to taste

SALADS

Pasta Salad with Grilled Chicken, Apples, and Cheddar

Insalate di pollo con Mele e Formaggio

A great Michigan recipe from a customer. Wonderful to enjoy in the fall.

SALAD INGREDIENTS

Pennette, 8 ounces, cooked and cooled

Grilled chicken breast, 6 ounces thinly sliced

Apple, 1 peeled, cored and coarsely chopped

Dried cherries, ½ cup

Celery, ½ cup

Fresh tarragon, 1 teaspoon chopped

Salt, ½ teaspoon

Pistachios, ½ cup chopped

Sharp Cheddar or Fontina cheese, ½ cup shredded

DRESSING INGREDIENTS

Light olive oil, ⅓ cup

Balsamic vinegar, 2 tablespoon

Mayonnaise, ¼ cup

Dijon mustard, ¼ teaspoon

Honey, 1 tablespoon

Salt, ½ teaspoon

Black pepper, ¼ teaspoon

DIRECTIONS:

Mix together dressing ingredients. Refrigerate until ready to use.

In a large bowl, combine Pennette, chicken, apple, dried cherries, celery, tarragon and salt. Stir in dressing; mixing to combine. Season with pepper. Refrigerate 1–2 hours to combine flavors. To serve, top with chopped pistachios and cheddar cheese.

Serves 6.

TIP: *If you do not have Pennette pasta, any style of pasta will go well with this recipe!*

Roasted Potato, Garlic and Red Pepper Salad

Insalata di Patate con Aglio e Peperoni Rossi

INGREDIENTS

Potatoes, 3 pounds small (white, red, or fingerling)

Red bell peppers, 2

Extra-virgin olive oil, 6 tablespoons

Salt and pepper, to taste

Garlic, 6 cloves, unpeeled

White balsamic vinegar, 3 tablespoons

Fresh chopped basil, 2 tablespoons

DIRECTIONS:

Preheat oven to 450°F.

Cut the potatoes in half and cut bell pepper into 1-inch pieces. In a large bowl, toss potatoes, bell peppers, and 3 tablespoons olive oil with salt and pepper to taste. Wrap garlic cloves together in foil.

Arrange potatoes and bell peppers in one layer in 2 large shallow baking pans. Roast in the middle and lower thirds of an oven (roast wrapped garlic on either rack), stirring occasionally and switching position of pans halfway through roasting time; roast until potatoes are tender and golden brown (about 35 minutes).

In a bowl, immediately toss potatoes and bell peppers with 2 tablespoons vinegar and cool. Remove garlic from foil and squeeze pulp in a small bowl. With a fork, mash garlic with remaining 3 tablespoons oil and 1 tablespoon vinegar. Toss garlic together with the potatoes, bell peppers, salt and pepper to taste. Just before serving, add basil. Serve potato salad at room temperature.

Serves 6.

TIP: *Suggested additions: any type of olives, pine nuts, goat cheese, grilled chicken, tuna, or prosciutto.*

SALADS

SALAD INGREDIENTS

- **Red potatoes,** ½ pound scrubbed and cut lengthwise into ¼-inch thick slices
- **Green beans (small thin),** ¼ pound with ends trimmed
- **Fresh tuna steaks,** 2 pounds (½ pound per person)
- **Salt,** 1 teaspoon
- **Ground black pepper,** 1 teaspoon
- **Olive oil,** 2 tablespoons
- **Fresh thyme,** 1 teaspoon
- **Romaine or Bibb lettuce,** 1 large head, rinsed and patted dry
- **Fresh Italian parsley,** 2 teaspoons, chopped
- **Roma plum tomatoes,** 4, cut into 1-inch cubes
- **Kalamata olives,** ⅓ cup pitted halved
- **Green pitted cerignola olives ⅓ cup,** halved and seeded
- **Red onion,** ½ cup, thinly sliced
- **Eggs,** 4 hardboiled

Tuna Nicoise Salad

Insalata di Tonno Nizzarada

This is a delicious, healthy dish to enjoy!

DIRECTIONS:

Bring 2 medium pots of salted water to a boil. Add the potatoes and cook until tender; about 5–6 minutes. Drain in a colander, pat dry, and set aside. Add the green beans to the other pot and blanch until tender, for 4–5 minutes. Drain in a colander, pat dry and set aside.

Arrange tuna into 4 equal portions. Season each of the tuna steaks with ¼ teaspoon salt and ¼ teaspoon pepper. Heat the oil in a large skillet, over medium-high heat. When the oil is hot but not smoking, add the thyme, tuna steaks and sear for about 30 seconds on each side until medium-rare. Remove from the pan and dice the tuna into 1 inch pieces.

(recipe continues)

Tear the lettuce into bite-size pieces and combine with chopped fresh parsley and tarragon. Toss with enough of the Anchovy Dressing just to coat. Adjust seasonings with salt and pepper as needed. Toss the potatoes and green beans in ¼ cup of the Anchovy Dressing. Arrange the lettuce along the side of 4 large plates. Spoon the vegetables along the other side of the plate. Arrange the diced tuna over the lettuce. Arrange the tomatoes, olives, sliced red onions, and eggs on the other side of the plates. Garnish with additional herbs if desired and serve immediately.

Serves 4.

ANCHOVY DRESSING INGREDIENTS
COMBINE WITH FOOD PROCESSOR

Anchovy, 2 fillet, drained (finely chopped)

Salt, ¼ teaspoon

Freshly ground black pepper, ¼ teaspoon

Paprika, ½ teaspoon

Garlic, 1 teaspoon, crushed

Egg, 1 yolk

Fresh lemon juice, 5 teaspoons

Dijon mustard, 1 teaspoon

Olive oil, 7 tablespoons

Salt and Pepper, to taste.

SALADS

INGREDIENTS – SET 1

MIX IN A LARGE BOWL

Raw shrimp, 1 ½ pounds medium-sized, frozen or fresh (de-veined, shells & tails removed)

Frozen calamari with tentacles, 1 ½ pound (Clean and wash calamari bodies and tentacles. Refer to the package directions on how to clean and wash if needed.) Cut calamari bodies into ½-inch rings

Scallops, 1 pound medium-sized, frozen (ready to cook); refer to package for cleaning directions

Crab meat, 1 cup in a can or frozen but already cooked (real or artificial), cut into chunks

Mena's Seafood Salad

Insalata di Pesce alla Siciliana

In my house growing up, we loved seafood salad as an appetizer; especially on Christmas Eve.

DIRECTIONS:

In a large pot, bring 3 quarts water to a boil. Add the shrimp, calamari (bodies & tentacles), and scallops and boil for 2–3 minutes until shrimp is tender and pink in color (do not overcook or will be tough). Remove from pot and drain in colander until cool.

Mix all of the fish in a large bowl: calamari, shrimp, scallops, and crab; then add the celery, green olives, red cabbage, and Italian parsley into the sea food mixture – blend together well, tossing with a spoon or your hands.

(recipe continues)

SALADS

In another small bowl, mix the marinade dressing: garlic, lemon juice, wine vinegar, sea salt, black pepper, celery salt, oregano, paprika, olive oil, and whisk together well. Pour marinade into large bowl of fish mixture, toss well and taste combined salad mixture.

Marinate in the Refrigerator for 1 hour; Taste and check for salt; continue to taste until it is to your flavor. Add round wedges of lemon if desired.

TIP: *Before you serve, you can refrigerate the salad to allow the flavor to develop; but not for too long. Taste the salad and serve at room temperature.*

INGREDIENTS – SET 2

Celery, 3 stalks, cut into quarters at an angle

Manzanilla green olives (jumbo with pimento), ¾ cup large cut in half

Radicchio or red cabbage, 1 cup cut into medium slices (like in Cole slaw)

Fresh Italian parsley, ¼ cup chopped

Garlic, 1–2 medium cloves, very finely chopped or crushed

INGREDIENTS – SET 3

MIX IN SMALL BOWL

Fresh lemon juice, 2 tablespoons

White wine vinegar, ¼ cup

Sea salt, 1 teaspoon

Black pepper, ¾ teaspoon

Celery salt, ½ teaspoon

Oregano, ½ teaspoon

Spanish paprika, ½ teaspoon

Olive oil, 1 cup

SALADS

SAUCES

Béchamel Sauce   170

Creamy Herb Sauce   171

Garlic and Anchovies, Sauce or Dip   172

Garlic Sauce for Fish or Meat   173

Lemon Butter Sauce   174

Lemon Oil Dressing   174

Mamma's Spare Rib Sauce with Meatballs (Sunday Dinner)   176

Marinara Sauce   178

Parmigiano-Reggiano Cheese Sauce   184

Pesto Sauce   182

Pesto Sauce with Fresh Basil   183

Quick, 20 Minute Marinara Sauce   180

Sweet and Sour Italian Salsa   175

Tomato Meat Sauce   181

Vodka Sauce   185

INGREDIENTS

Butter, 4 tablespoons
Flour, 4 tablespoons
Milk, 2 cups
Salt, ¼ teaspoon
Nutmeg, a pinch (optional)

Béchamel Sauce

Besciamella

You can use this white cream sauce with Lasagna, cannelloni, or other pastas of your choice. This is delicious with anything!

DIRECTIONS:

Melt butter and flour, whisk together. Cook well. Pour in milk; stirring constantly until it comes to a full boil and is thickened. Add ¼ teaspoon salt and a pinch of nutmeg (if preferred); taste.

Yields 2 ⅓ cups of sauce.

TIP: *If you need more sauce, double the recipe.*

SAUCES

Creamy Herb Sauce

Crema di Erbe

Used as a condiment over beef, pork or veal.

DIRECTIONS:

Cook the first five ingredients in the butter for five minutes. Stir in flour for 1 minute. Add half and half and chicken broth, continue stirring. Cook and stir over medium heat until thick and bubbly. Add parsley, cognac or brandy, and lemon juice. Cook for 1 minute to heat through. Serve over beef, pork or veal. Makes 1 ⅓ cups.

INGREDIENTS

Butter, 2 tablespoon
Fresh mushrooms, 1 cup sliced
Shallots, 1 tablespoon finely chopped
Garlic, 2 cloves, minced
Fresh thyme, 1 tablespoon, snipped
Fresh tarragon, 1 tablespoon, snipped
Flour, 1 tablespoon
Half and half, ¾ cup
Chicken broth, ¼ cup
Fresh parsley, 2 tablespoons, snipped
Cognac or brandy, 1 tablespoon
Lemon juice, 1 ½ teaspoon

SAUCES

INGREDIENTS

Butter, 1 cup

Olive oil, 4 tablespoons

Garlic, 4 cloves, finely chopped

Anchovy, 6 fillets, chopped

Salt, to taste

Garlic and Anchovies, Sauce or Dip

Salsa di Aglio e Acciughe

DIRECTIONS:

In a frying pan, heat butter and oil together, sauté garlic until it is soft (golden brown). Take pan off the heat and add the anchovies, stir with a wooden spoon. Return pan to low heat and continue cooking, stirring until the anchovies dissolve into a paste. Season with a pinch of salt. Serve hot with fresh vegetables or a crusty loaf of bread. May also be tossed with 1 or 2 tablespoons of Spaghetti or Fettuccine of choice.

SAUCES

Garlic Sauce for Fish or Meat

Salsa all aglio

INGREDIENTS

French or Italian bread, ½ loaf, crust removed

Garlic, 1–2 cloves

Egg, 1 yolk

Lemon juice, 1 lemon or 2 tablespoons vinegar

Olive oil, ½ cup

Salt, ½ teaspoon

Pepper, ½ teaspoon

Fresh Italian parsley, ½ teaspoon (or dried dill)

DIRECTIONS:

Cut crust off the bread, moisten with water and squeeze out the excess water. In a food processor or blender with the blade running through the entire process, add the garlic and mix until fine. Add the bread and egg yolk. Mix lemon juice with oil and pour with a slow stream into the mixture. Next, add salt, pepper and parsley; mix until the mixture is thick and smooth. Can be served cold with boiled or baked meat or fish.

INGREDIENTS

Butter, ¼ cup
Lemon juice, 1 tablespoon

INGREDIENTS

Olive oil, ½ cup
Garlic, 1 clove, minced
Oregano, ½ teaspoon
Fresh lemon juice, 1 lemon
Salt, ½ teaspoon
Pepper, ½ teaspoon
Water, 2 tablespoons
Worcestershire sauce, 1 teaspoon

Lemon Butter Sauce

Salsa di Limone e Burro

Lemon butter sauce is delicious service on top of chicken, fish, or vegetables.

DIRECTIONS:

In a saucepan, melt the butter over low heat. Continue heating until butter turns light brown. Add lemon juice.

Lemon Oil Dressing

Salmoriglio alla Siciliana

This sauce is great on steak, fish or chicken. Sicilian style

DIRECTIONS:

Whisk all ingredients well in a large bowl. Let it sit for 1 hour before serving. Serve at room temperature.

After meat is grilled, dip in the sauce and serve. Place leftover sauce in a bowl and use as desired.

SAUCES

Sweet and Sour Italian Salsa

Macedonia agrodolce per Pesce o Pollo

This is a wonderful salsa to serve with fish or chicken. It has a fresh citrus taste that is so refreshing.

DIRECTIONS:

Toss all ingredients together in a large bowl. Let stand on counter for ½ hour (best served at room temperature). Put ½ cup of the mixture on each piece of fish or chicken.

We use fish, salmon, or chicken—pan-fried (with a little olive oil or butter for flavor), or on the grill.

INGREDIENTS

Peach or mango, 1 cup peeled and cubed (small)

Papaya, ½ cup, peeled and cubed (small)

Red pepper, ½ cup, chopped

Red onion, ¼ cup, chopped

Orange, ½ cup, peeled, sectioned, and cubed (small)

Fresh Italian parsley, 2 tablespoons, chopped

Lemon juice, 1 large lemon

Salt, ¼–¾ teaspoon (taste)

Sugar, ½ teaspoon

Black pepper, ¼ teaspoon

Olive oil, 2 tablespoons

TIP: *If you prefer spicy, add ½ teaspoon fresh chopped hot pepper to the Italian salsa.*

SAUCES

INGREDIENTS (SPARE RIB SAUCE)

Olive oil, ¼ cup

Pork baby back ribs, 1 ½ pounds, cut between ribs

Oregano, 1 teaspoon

Salt, 2 teaspoons

Onion, 1 medium, chopped

Garlic, 2 cloves, sliced

San Marzano tomatoes, 1 can (28 ounces), crushed

Tomato puree, 1 can (28 ounces)

Salt and Black pepper, to taste

Water, ¾ cup

Basil, 6 leaves (fresh)

Mamma's Spare Rib Sauce with Meatballs (Sunday Dinner)

Salsa della Mamma con Polpette e Carne

Mama would make this every Sunday. She started it about 7:30 in the morning and by the time we got home from church it was ready. You could smell it before you walked in the door. You couldn't resist taking a chunk of bread and dipping it in the sauce. Makes me hungry just thinking about it!

DIRECTIONS FOR SPARE RIB SAUCE:

Heat the oil in a large sauce pan. Add the meat; sprinkle with oregano and salt, brown lightly. Add the chopped onion and garlic, and sauté until translucent. Add the tomatoes, tomato puree, pepper, and water. Cook for 1 ½ hours on slow heat, stirring occasionally. Add fresh basil approximately 10 minutes before serving.

DIRECTIONS FOR MEATBALLS:

Mix the ground chuck and pork in a large bowl; add salt, pepper, garlic, cheese, parsley, and eggs. Mix well with hands. Wet the slices of Italian bread, squeeze out water, and combine into meat mixture; add dried bread crumbs and spare rib sauce. Mix well with hands; folding in all ingredients. Don't over mix. Shape mixture into 2-inch balls; fry in oil. Cook in batches until lightly browned (3–5 minutes); drain on paper towels. When the spare rib sauce is almost cooked, add the meatballs and cook 20–25 minutes longer.

(recipe continues)

SAUCES

Sunday Dinner with Penne Pasta.

INGREDIENTS (MEATBALLS)

Ground chuck, 1 ½ pound

Ground pork, ½ pound

Salt, 1 teaspoon

Black pepper, to taste

Garlic, 1–2 teaspoons, crushed

Romano cheese, ⅓ cup

Fresh Italian parsley, 3 tablespoons, chopped

Eggs, 2 large

Day-old Italian bread, 6 slices

Water, ½ cup

Unseasoned bread crumbs, 1 cup

Spare rib sauce, ½ cup

Vegetable oil, 1 cup, for frying

TIP: *Use your choice of pasta cut.*

SAUCES

INGREDIENTS

Extra-virgin olive oil, ¾ cup

Garlic, 6 large cloves, peeled and sliced (or chopped)

Fresh ripe plum tomatoes, 4–5 pounds, peeled, seeded and coarsely chopped

Tomato paste, 3 tablespoons with fresh tomatoes only (do not mix with canned tomatoes)

Salt, 2 teaspoon

Sugar, ½ teaspoon (optional)

Fresh basil, ¼ cup, about 10 leaves, torn by hand into pieces

Crushed red pepper flakes, a pinch (optional)

Black pepper, to taste

Pasta, 1 pound of choice: spaghetti, spaghettini, penne, rigatoni (you can serve this sauce with anything you like!)

Parmigiano-Reggiano cheese, freshly grated (or Romano)

Marinara Sauce

La salsa di Pomodoro

A basic, yet delicious, tomato sauce for pasta.

DIRECTIONS:

Put ¼ cup of olive oil and garlic in a large skillet over medium-heat and cook for 1–2 minutes until the garlic begins to sizzle.

(recipe continues)

SAUCES

Add the fresh tomatoes and tomato paste. If using fresh tomatoes, you will notice that they will give off a fair amount of liquid. When the liquid begins to reduce, season with salt and sugar Add ¼ cup basil leaves. Reduce heat and let simmer for 1–1 ½ hours. Stirring occasionally with wooden spoon.

Add the torn basil leaves and cook for last 3 minutes.

Continue cooking over medium heat until tomatoes have reduced and separated from the oil. At this point, you have the option to add the red pepper flakes if desired.

Cook pasta of choice to al dente. Drain pasta and toss with the sauce in a skillet. Drizzle remaining ¼ cup of olive oil on top of pasta. Serve individual portions of pasta with sauce. Top with grated Parmigiano-Reggiano or Romano cheese and remaining basil.

Mena making Tomato Puree every September.

TIP: *If you do not have fresh tomatoes you can use 2 cans (28 oz.) Italian plum tomatoes (San Marzano), crushed. If you use canned tomatoes you do not need tomato paste.*

TIP: *If you are using canned tomatoes, let simmer for 30 minutes (everything else is the same).*

TIP: *It is important to drizzle olive oil over top of the pasta after it is cooked. This brings back some of the raw olive oil flavor that was reduced when cooking the pasta.*

TIP: *Freshly grated Parmigiano-Reggiano cheese (or Romano) can be used to top any kind of pasta!*

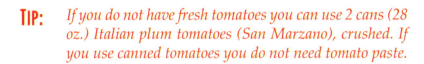

SAUCES

INGREDIENTS

Extra-virgin olive oil, ½ cup

Onion, 1 small, finely chopped (or ½ of a large onion)

Garlic, 3 cloves, finely chopped

Salt, ½ teaspoon plus 1 tablespoon

San Marzano plum tomatoes, 1 can (28 oz.), crushed

Tomato puree, 1 can (15 oz.)

Water, ½ cup

Sugar, ½ teaspoon (optional)

Fresh parsley, 2 tablespoons, finely chopped

Fresh basil, 4 to 6 leaves, coarsely chopped

Pasta, 1 pound (spaghetti, vermicelli, or linguine)

Romano cheese, freshly grated

Quick, 20 Minute Marinara Sauce

La salsa di Pomodoro

This quick version of my marinara sauce may be substituted for the original, traditional marinara in almost any recipe!

DIRECTIONS:

Warm the olive oil in a medium saucepan over medium heat. Add the onion, garlic and ½ teaspoon of the salt. Cook, stirring, for 2–3 minutes until the onion has softened. Add the tomato puree, San Marzano, sugar, water, parsley and basil. Cover partially and cook at a low boil, stirring occasionally, for 20–25 minutes. If the tomatoes condense too much, add a little water.

Meanwhile, combine 4 ½ to 5 quarts of water with 1 tablespoon of salt in a large pot and bring to a boil. Add the pasta and cook until al dente. Drain thoroughly.

Place the pasta in a serving dish and toss with the sauce. Top with cheese and serve immediately. This sauce is ready in 20–30 minutes; it is easy and delicious!

Serves 4–6.

SAUCES

Tomato Meat Sauce

Salsa di carne per Lasagna e Spaghetti

This is a basic meat sauce used for Lasagna or Spaghetti. Easy and delicious!

INGREDIENTS

Olive oil, ¼ cup

Garlic, 1 clove, minced or crushed

Onion, 1 medium, chopped (about 1 cup)

Ground chuck, 1 pound

Italian Sausage, 1 link with casing removed (or ½ pound ground pork)

San Marzano plum tomatoes, 1 can (28 oz.), crushed

Tomato puree, 1 can (28 oz.)

Salt, 2 teaspoon

Oregano, ½ teaspoon

Fresh basil, 1 tablespoon, chopped

Water, 1 ½ cups

Salt and pepper, to taste

DIRECTIONS:

Heat olive oil in a saucepan and add garlic and onion. Sauté until translucent. Add both meats to pan. Crumble with a wooden spoon and cook thoroughly.

Once meat is browned, add tomatoes, tomato puree, salt, oregano, basil, and 1 ½ cups water. Simmer over low heat for 1 to 1½ hours, stirring occasionally. Taste. Add additional salt and pepper to taste, if desired.

TIP: *In order to achieve desired consistency, a little more water may be required.*

SAUCES

Pesto Sauce

Salsa di Pesto

At Roma, we serve this as a cold pasta salad. You can also enjoy it as a hot pasta!

INGREDIENTS

Basil, 1 cup leaves, lightly packed

Parsley, ½ cup leaves

Garlic, 2 cloves, peeled

Onion, 2 tablespoons

Pine nuts, ¼ cup

Salt, 1 teaspoon

Pepper, ½ teaspoon

Romano or Parmesan cheese, 4 tablespoons, grated

Extra virgin olive oil, ½ cup

Bow tie pasta, 1 pound

DIRECTIONS:

In a food processor, combine basil, parsley, garlic, onion, pine nuts, slat, pepper, and cheese. Blend for a few minutes. With the motor running, add the extra-virgin olive oil in a thin stream and blend to make a smooth paste.

For pasta with pesto: Bring 4 quarts of water with 1 tablespoon salt to boil in a large pot. Add the bow tie pasta and cook until al dente. Drain, put on a platter, and cool pasta completely. Place pasta in a bowl and add pesto sauce, sprinkle with cheese and serve.

TIP: *This pesto can be used in a variety of ways! It is delicious in hot or cold pastas, pizza, or Minestrone soup; or you can freeze it and use it later.*

SAUCES

Pesto Sauce with Fresh Basil

Pesto con Basilico fresco

This sauce can be put in a jar covered with olive oil. It can be stored in the refrigerator for 1 to 2 days or pesto may be put in the freezer. Pesto sauce can be used with any type of pasta, sandwich, fish, or pizza.

DIRECTIONS:

Combine the garlic and pine nuts in a food processor and pulse for a few minutes. Add parsley, basil, salt, black pepper and pulse for a few more minutes. Slowly add the oil in a constant stream while the food processor is running. Stop to scrape down the sides of the food processor with a rubber spatula. Add the grated cheese and pulse for a few more minutes until blended.

TIP: *You can freeze the pesto sauce in a glass jar or plastic container. Make sure to add a little oil on top of pesto when freezing.*

INGREDIENTS

Garlic, 2–3 cloves, medium sized

Pine nuts, ½ cup

Italian parsley, ½ cup tightly packed

Fresh basil, 2 cups loosely packed

Salt, 1 teaspoon

Black pepper, ¼ teaspoon

Extra-virgin olive oil, 1 cup (do not substitute with other oils)

Parmesan or Romano cheese, ½ cup fresh grated

SAUCES

Parmigiano-Reggiano Cheese Sauce

Salsa di formaggio al Parmigiano Reggiano

This can be used as a pasta sauce, or dip for red or yellow pepper, broccoli, cauliflower, or toasted baguette.

INGREDIENTS

- **Parmigiano,** ½ pound (not too dry)
- **Asiago cheese,** ½ pound (not too dry)
- **Garlic,** 2 teaspoons, minced
- **Dried oregano,** 1 teaspoon
- **Red pepper flakes,** 1 teaspoon
- **Green onion,** 2 tablespoons, chopped
- **Extra-virgin olive oil,** 1 ½ cup
- **Freshly ground black pepper,** 1 teaspoon

DIRECTIONS:

Remove any rind from the cheeses and chop the cheeses into roughly 1-inch chunks. Place the cheese in a food processor with the garlic, oregano, and red pepper flakes and pulse until reduced to the size of rice. Stir in the green onion, olive oil and black pepper. Pulse again. Cover and let stand at room temperature for at least 2 hours before using.

TIP: *This can be used as a sauce or dip.*

SAUCES

Vodka Sauce

Salsa alla Vodka

This recipe is from my friend Dr. Gino Corrado, from Rome. My family loves this sauce. It's smooth, creamy and delicious. I hope you enjoy it!

INGREDIENTS

Olive oil, ¼ cup
Butter, 2 tablespoon
Onion, 1 cup finely diced
Vodka, ½ cup
Tomato puree, 1 can (28 oz.)
Water, ½ cup
Salt, ½ teaspoon
Black pepper, ¼ teaspoon
Heavy cream, 1 cup
Penne pasta, 1 pound
Parmigiano-Reggiano cheese, ½ cup

DIRECTIONS:

In a large skillet on medium heat, warm the olive oil and butter until melted. Add the onion, cook and stir for 2–3 minutes until translucent. Add the vodka and cook for about 1 minute, so that the alcohol will evaporate. Add tomato puree, ½ cup water, salt and pepper. Simmer on medium heat for 15–20 minutes until it thickens. Lower the heat, add heavy cream and stir for about 1 minute. Set aside.

Bring 4 quarts of water in a large pot to a boil and add 1 tablespoon of salt. Add the penne and cook until al dente. Drain. Pour pasta into sauce and stir. Sprinkle Parmigiano-Reggiano on top.

SAUCES

DOUGHS & BREADS

Bread Sticks   188

Calabreze Doughnuts   190

Italian Sweet Egg Bread   192

Mena's Pizza Dough   196

Pizza Dough   197

Seasoned Italian Bread Crumbs   189

Toasted Italian Bread with Tomato, Basil, and Olive Oil   195

Bread Sticks

Grissini

INGREDIENTS

Dry yeast, 1 package (or 1 yeast cake)

Warm water, ⅔ cup

Salt, 1 teaspoon

Sugar, 1 tablespoon

Olive oil, ½ cup or shortening

All-purpose flour, 2 cups sifted, plus additional flour to dust surface

Egg, 1 yolk, whisked

Sesame seeds, (optional)

DIRECTIONS:

In a large bowl, add yeast and dissolve in ⅔ cups warm water (100–110°F). Add salt, sugar, and olive oil (or shortening) and beat until smooth. Mix in 2 cups of flour. Dust a clean counter top with flour. Knead dough on floured surface until smooth and elastic. Place in a greased bowl and cover with plastic wrap. Let rise in a warm place for about 1 hour or until it has doubled in bulk.

Preheat oven to 400°F. Divide dough in half, cut each half into 12 equal parts. Roll each piece into a strip (about 6–8 inches long), place on greased cookie sheet or a cookie sheet lined with parchment paper, making sure the pieces are 1 inch apart. Brush tops with egg, sprinkle with seeds (if preferred). Bake 20–25 minutes or until golden brown.

Makes 2 dozen.

TIP: *Use a 12x18-inch cookie sheet or any size you have.*

TIP: *Sprinkle a little bit of garlic powder or sesame seeds on top of breadsticks for flavor or eat plain.*

DOUGH & BREADS

Seasoned Italian Bread Crumbs

Mollica di Pane con Sapore

DIRECTIONS:

Mix all the ingredients together. Keep refrigerated or in the freezer.

TIP: To make coarse homemade bread crumbs; use 2–3 day old dried white Italian or French bread.

TIP: If you have fresh bread, place in a 150°F oven for 2 hours until dry and golden but not toasted. Tear dried bread into smaller pieces and place in your food processor. Process until desired coarseness. If you need finer crumbs, just regrind the amount needed.

INGREDIENTS

Bread crumbs, 1 cup

Romano cheese, ⅓ cup

Garlic, 1 teaspoon fresh, finely chopped (or ¼ teaspoon garlic powder)

Salt, ¼ teaspoon

Black pepper, ¼ teaspoon

Fresh Italian parsley, 1 tablespoon, finely chopped

DOUGH & BREADS

Calabrese Doughnuts

Cuddurieddi-Ciambella

INGREDIENTS

Russet potatoes, 2 ½–3 pounds, washed, peeled, cut into chunks, and boiled (about 4 cups mashed down)

Warm water, 2 cups (you can use the potato water)

All-purpose flour, 9 cups

Salt, 1 ½ tablespoon

Yeast, 2 packages (dissolved in water)

Vegetable oil, 1 quart for frying

DIRECTIONS:

Place chunks of potatoes in a large pot and cover with cold water. Bring to a boil and cook until potatoes are tender. Drain potatoes and reserve any remaining water. After potatoes are boiled and drained, take chunks of potatoes, 1 cup at a time, and mash them down, flattening and leveling off the tops, until you have four cups.

Use a standing mixer (with bowl and paddle attached), set on medium-speed, to mash the 4 cups of potatoes until smooth, about 4–5 minutes. Remove the paddle attachment and replace with a dough hook.

Add flour and salt into the mixer. Add yeast (which has been dissolved in warm water, 100–110°F) into flour mixture.

Before adding yeast mixture to potatoes, check that potatoes aren't too hot (they should be about 100–110°F as well). Pour yeast mixture into potatoes and knead on high speed until dough is smooth, soft, and shiny (about 10 minutes).

Place dough into a very large, oiled, bowl. Cover tightly with plastic wrap and top with a cloth, let rise until dough has doubled in size, about 1–2 hours (make sure

(recipe continues)

DOUGH & BREADS

bowl is extra-large—you want to leave room for dough to rise and not stick to plastic wrap).

In a large, deep frying pan, add sufficient vegetable oil to deep fry. Heat the oil to 375°F.

Punch the dough down with oiled hands, take ½ cup of dough and round into the size of a small ball. Make a hole in the center and create a doughnut shape (make sure the hole is big enough to avoid closing up during frying).

Drop the doughnuts in hot oil and fry until golden brown on both sides. Remove from oil (with tongs) and place on paper towels to drain. Enjoy hot or cold!

TIP: *Can be enjoyed sweet (by dusting with granulated sugar) or savory (served as is).*

DOUGH & BREADS

INGREDIENTS

Stage 1:

Lukewarm water, 1 cup (100–110°F)

Yeast, 2 packages

Sugar, 1 tablespoon

Flour, 1 cup

Stage 2:

Milk, 2 cups

Sugar, 1¼ cup

Salt, 1 teaspoon

Eggs, 6 large (1 for brushing on top)

All-purpose flour, 4 ½ pounds

Butter, 1 stick, softened

Parchment paper

Italian Sweet Egg Bread

Pan Dolce (di Pasqua)

This bread is very good for Easter or any other time of the year. Traditionally, we make this in a ring shape and add eggs in the shells, pressed into the dough after braiding, let rise, brush top with egg wash and bake.

DIRECTIONS STAGE 1 (DOUGH SPONGE):

Add water, yeast, sugar, and flour into the very large bowl of a stand mixer fitted with a dough hook attachment. Mix well, for 3–4 minutes. Cover the mixture bowl with a kitchen cloth. After 15 minutes uncover and check to see if it is foamy. If it is not foamy, let sit for another 5–6 minutes until foam and/or bubbles begin to form. *(Note: while waiting for mixture to foam, begin stage 2.)*

DIRECTIONS STAGE 2:

Preheat oven 350–375°F

In a small saucepan, add 2 cups milk, 1¼ cup sugar, and 1 teaspoon salt, mix well, and warm over low heat until mixture is lukewarm (100–110°F; if the mixture is any hotter, you will scramble the eggs in the following step). Remove from heat. In a small mixing bowl, mix 5 large eggs. While continuously whisking the mixture, pour the eggs into the saucepan and set aside.

In a separate bowl, add 4 ½ pounds all-purpose flour.

Add 1 stick of butter (softened to room temperature) to the foamy stage 1 mixture, in the bowl of the stand mixer. Keep the dough hook attached.

Add all of the stage 2 mixture (from the saucepan) into the stage 1 mixture. Add about half of the flour

(recipe continues)

DOUGH & BREADS

This is a lamb shaped for Easter with sweet almond paste inside.

mixture (if you add it all at once, you will be covered in flour). Start mixing on low speed for 2 minutes. When the first half of the flour is mostly incorporated, slowly add the rest while mixing on low. Allow to incorporate, then increase speed to medium for about 10 minutes. Finally, mix on high speed for another 3–5 minutes, until the dough smooth and shiny. Dough should be pulling away from the bottom of the bowl and look sticky.

Remove dough from mixing bowl, scraping down sides of the bowl. Place the ball of dough on a clean, well-floured surface. Punch the dough down. Knead for about 2–3 minutes, dough should feel silky and smooth.

Lightly oil the mixing bowl, then return the dough and cover with plastic wrap first, then with a kitchen cloth. Set aside and let rise for about 1 hour to 75 minutes. Check to see if dough has risen; if it has not, wait a little bit longer. Depending on the room temperature and humidity, you may need more time. Dough should be left to rise until it has doubled (which should mean that it puffs up to the brim of the mixing bowl).

(recipe continues)

DOUGH & BREADS

Dust kitchen counter or a board with a little bit of flour (leave a small pile of flour on the side for you to use while manipulating dough). Knead for 5 minutes. Divide the dough into 4 equal pieces with a dough scraper (cut the ball of dough in half, then turn and half again to make 4 pieces). Roll each piece of dough into a round ball and set aside.

DIRECTIONS FOR BRAIDING:

Layer two 12x18 baking sheets with parchment paper.

Cut each ball of dough into 3 equal pieces. Roll each piece into a long rope (about 12 inches long).

Make an "X" shape with two pieces and place the third piece on top, through the center of the "X". Braid the three dough ropes in a traditional braid. Repeat the process with each ball of dough.

Place two loaves of bread on each baking sheet. Set aside. Cover with a kitchen towel and let rise for 45 minutes (checking occasionally, adjusting time as needed). Whisk the remaining 1 egg in a small bowl with 1 teaspoon water. Using a pastry brush, brush the egg wash over top of each loaf.

Bake at 350–375°F for 30–35 minutes (depending on the oven), or until golden. Remove and let sit for 10–15 minutes. Place on a rack and let cool for 1 hour before serving. This bread also stores very well!

TIP: *This bread is also delicious with raisins or dried cranberries added right into the dough. To make this fruity variation simply add ½ cups dried fruit to the dough after initial kneading. Add the dried fruit and knead dough for another minute or so, until fruit is distributed and dough is smooth. From there, proceed with the recipe as written above.*

DOUGH & BREADS

Toasted Italian Bread with Tomato, Basil, and Olive Oil

Friselle con Ponodoro alla Calabrese

INGREDIENTS

Friselle bread from Roma Bakery, 2 sliced in half, lightly toasted in oven

Garlic, 1 large clove, peeled

Tomatoes, 2 medium-sized (or 1 ½ cup chopped cherry tomatoes)

Fresh basil, 8 leaves, chopped (chevron style)

Oregano, ¼ teaspoon

Olive oil, 3 tablespoons

Salt, ½ teaspoon

DIRECTIONS:

Take the toasted Friselle bread and rub garlic over the bread (in a circular fashion). Drip water lightly over the bread (3–4 seconds) and let set on platter; should be softened but some areas still crunchy. Combine tomato, basil, oregano, olive oil and salt in a bowl. Let stand for 5 minutes. Spread the tomato mixture over each half of Frisella bread (covering the bread completely); gently press on the tomatoes to allow the bread to absorb some juice. Cut into quarters and this is ready to serve!

TIP: *Variation (Mena's favorite): Drizzle 2 tablespoons of olive oil, 1 tablespoon wine vinegar, ¼ teaspoon oregano, salt and pepper on Friselle and enjoy!*

DOUGH & BREADS

Mena's Pizza Dough

La Pasta della Pizza di Mena

INGREDIENTS

Water, ¼ cup plus 2 tablespoons, lukewarm (110°F)

Bread flour, 1 cup (King Arthur)

Active dry yeast, 2 teaspoons (or 1 package)

Sugar, ½ teaspoon

Semolina flour, ¼ cup

White whole wheat flour, ½ cup (King Arthur)

All-purpose flour, ¼ cup

Salt, ½ teaspoon

Water, ½ cup, lukewarm (110°F)

Olive oil, 2 tablespoons

DIRECTIONS:

Combine ¼ cup plus 2 tablespoons lukewarm water (110°F), ¼ cup bread flour, yeast, and ½ teaspoon sugar in a small bowl; lightly mix. Let stand for 30 minutes until it bubbles up.

After proofing the yeast (when it bubbles up), mix in the remaining ¾ cup bread flour, ¼ cup semolina flour, ½ cup whole wheat flour, ¼ cup all-purpose flour, ½ teaspoon salt, ½ cup of lukewarm water, and 2 tablespoons olive oil. Mix dough thoroughly. (If it seems too sticky, add a little bread flour, if it seems too dry, add a little water).

If using a food processor, pulse the dry ingredients with dough blade to mix. Then add all other ingredients and pulse until it balls up.

Turn out onto a floured surface and knead until smooth, elastic, but still a little tacky to the touch (3–5 minutes).

Place in an oiled bowl and turn to coat with oil. Cover with plastic wrap and let rise in a warm place (75°F), until it doubles in size (1–1 ½ hours).

Alternatively, you can let the dough rise in refrigerator overnight. The next day, bring dough to room temperature and proceed.

Bake at 475–500°F for 20–25 minutes (more or less, depending on how crispy you prefer your pizza).

Makes 18–20 ounces of dough or 1 thick 14-inch pizza or 2 thinner 12-inch pizzas.

DOUGH & BREADS

Pizza Dough

La Pasta della Pizza

This recipe was given to me by one of my longtime customers. Thank you so much for sharing this recipe with me. It is one of my favorites.

DIRECTIONS:

Mix the yeast, sugar and water together in a bowl. When the top has formed a foam, add the flour and salt. Knead for five minutes until dough is smooth and does not stick to hands. Form the dough into a ball and let rise for two hours or until dough doubles in size. The dough can be made and refrigerated for several days after rising. Just punch it down and place in a zip lock bag or plastic container and refrigerate. Makes 3 pounds of dough, enough for two large, thick-crust pizzas. Pull or roll into shape.

Add the pizza toppings of your choice. Drizzle the top of the pizza with olive oil for flavor! Bake at 475–500°F. Remove from the oven after 20–25 minutes depending on how crispy you prefer your pizza.

INGREDIENTS

Fast acting yeast, 1 package

Sugar, 1 tablespoon

Lukewarm water, 2 cups (100–110°F)

Semolina flour, 2 cups

Bread flour, 3 ½ cups

Salt, ¼ teaspoon

Olive oil, 2 tablespoons

DOUGH & BREADS

DESSERTS & COOKIES

Almond Clusters   200
Almond Crescent Cookies   201
Almond Half Moon Cookies   202
Almond Pudding   238
Amaretti Cookies   208
Anise Cookies   204
Baked Stuffed Peaches   228
Butter Cookies   206
Calabrese Doughnuts   190
Carmela's Finger Cookies   212
Christmas Honey Cookies   216
Cookies with a Kiss   209
Fresh Fruit Dessert   229
Galatobouriko   224
Honey Sliced Cookies   218
Italian Fig Cookies   210
Ladyfingers   214
Macaroons   219

Mamma's Finger Cookies   215
Mamma's Italian Pastry Cream   235
Mamma's Torte   236
Mamma's Vodka Cherries   233
Panna Cotta   234
Peaches in Red Wine   230
Pear Caramel Cake   231
Pears Poached in Red Wine   232
Ricotta Pudding   239
Roma's Pastiera Ricotta Filling   240
Roma's Sweet Pastry Dough   242
Sesame Seed Cookies   220
Shaved Coffee Ice — Granita with Cream   226
Shaved Lemon Ice — Granita   227
Sliced Biscotti with Cashew Nuts   203
Thumbprint Cookies   221
Zeppole   222

Almond Clusters

Croccantini di Mandorla

This recipe was given to me by friend Juliana from Windsor, Canada. Mille grazie!

DIRECTIONS:

Preheat oven to 375–400°F. In a large mixing bowl add egg whites and whip on medium speed for 1 minute. Slowly incorporate sugar into the egg whites while mixing continuously; add almond extract; whip on medium-high speed for another minute until mixture is soft and peaks. Remove bowl from mixer. Add the almond slices; gently mix with a spatula.

Layer a 12x18-inch baking pan with parchment paper; drop 1 tablespoon of the mixture on the pan at a time, leaving ½-inch of space between each cluster. Bake for 8–10 minutes until golden brown.

Remove from oven and let cool.

DIRECTIONS (CHOCOLATE DRIZZLE):

In a microwaveable bowl, combine 1 cup of semi-sweet morsels. Heat in microwave until melted; make sure to check it every 30 seconds to avoid scorching. Use a form to drizzle melted chocolate over each cookie. Let dry for 30 minutes.

TIP: *This is a Gluten free recipe!*

TIP: *You can eat these plain or if desired, with a drizzle of chocolate on top.*

INGREDIENTS

Almond slices, 1 ⅛ pound, (lightly toasted for 5–6 minutes)

Eggs, 4 egg whites

Sugar, ½ cup

Almond extract, 1 teaspoon

DESSERTS & COOKIES

Almond Crescent Cookies

Mezzelune di Mandorla

DIRECTIONS:

You can buy sliced almonds in any grocery store. I prefer whole crushed almonds because they have more almond flavor.

Place one cup of almonds in a food processor and pulse quickly just to crush, probably about 6 pulses. Put in a plate.

Cream almond paste and sugar until light in texture, about 3 minutes, using an electric mixer. Add 1 egg white, almond extract, and salt, mix for 1 minute.

Cover a cookie sheet with a piece of parchment paper. Lightly oil your hands, divide dough into 16 equal-sized balls. Roll dough between your hands to make cylinders about 2 inches long.

Roll each cylinder in sprinkles (if you choose), almond slices, or crushed almonds, and bend into a crescent shape as you place them on the cookie sheet. Refrigerate for 30 minutes.

Preheat oven to 350–375°F.

Place cookies in pre-heated oven for 12–15 minutes, until they are a light golden brown. Let cool slightly for 4–5 minutes, then remove to a cooling rack to cool completely. It's always the cook's prerogative to eat a few right out of the oven.

TIP: *If you like, you can dip half of each crescent into chocolate and dry on a rack before serving.*

INGREDIENTS

Almonds, 1 cup, sliced

Almond paste, 1 tube (7 oz.) (not marzipan)

Sugar, ⅓ cup

Egg white, 1 unbeaten

Almond extract, 1 teaspoon

Salt, a pinch

Canola oil, 1 teaspoon or other light oil (use on hands to form cookies)

Variations:

Use crushed macadamia nuts in place of almonds

Use vanilla extract and mix a pinch of grated nutmeg in the dough.

DESSERTS & COOKIES

Almond Half Moon Cookies

Biscotti—Mezzelune di Mandorla

INGREDIENTS

Toasted almonds, 1 cup slivered

All-purpose flour, ¾ cup

Salt, ¼ teaspoon

Powdered sugar, ¾ cup, separated

Unsalted butter, ½ cup (1 stick), room temperature

Vanilla extract, 1 ½ teaspoons

Almond extract, ¼ teaspoon

DIRECTIONS:

Finely grind the almonds, flour and salt in a food processor. Set aside. Using an electric mixer, beat ½ cup of the powdered sugar, butter, vanilla, and almond extract in a large bowl until fluffy. Add almond mixture and beat just until blended. Cover; chill until firm, for about 1 hour.

Preheat oven to 350°F. Line two 12x18-inch baking sheets with parchment paper. For each cookie, roll 1 rounded tablespoonful of dough into a cylinder; pinch ends to taper. Place in half moon shape on baking sheet. Bake until bottoms of cookies are just golden, for about 15 minutes. Let cool for a few minutes then transfer to cooling racks. When cookies are completely cooled, sift ¼ cup powdered sugar on top.

Makes about 18–20 cookies.

TIP: Can be made 3 days ahead. Store airtight at room temperature.

Sliced Biscotti with Cashew Nuts

Biscotti con noci di anacardio

INGREDIENTS

Crisco, 1 pound

Sugar, 2 cups

Eggs, 7 large

Whole milk, 2 cups

Orange or Lemon zest, 1 orange or lemon

Vanilla extract, 2 teaspoons

Flour, 10 cups

Baking powder, 9 teaspoon

Salt, ½ teaspoon

Lightly toasted cashew nuts, 2 cups chopped (or substitute almonds or hazelnuts)

DIRECTIONS:

Preheat oven at 375°F. Set aside two 12x18-inch baking sheets lined with parchment paper.

Mix flour, baking powder, and salt together in a bowl and set aside.

In a standing mixer with a large bowl, add in the Crisco and sugar; mix well for 3–4 minutes until fluffy. Add one egg at a time while mixing. Pause; then add milk, orange zest, vanilla and flour mixture. Reduce to low speed and mix well. Add the cashew nuts; mix for a few seconds. Remove dough mixture and place into a bowl. Cover with clear plastic wrap and place in the refrigerator for 30 minutes.

Dust counter with flour. Take 2 cups of dough and round into a baseball shape. Roll each piece into a log 2x10 inches long. Place 3 logs on a cookie sheet lined with parchment paper. Beat 1 egg and brush over top of each log. Place into a 375°F oven for 10–12 minutes until light brown. Let cool on a wire rack.

CUTTING:

Place the biscotti on a cutting board; using a serrated knife, cut on a diagonal into ¾-inch thick slices. Arrange the biscotti cut side down on the baking sheet. Bake until they are toasted or lightly golden for 8–10 minutes. Put biscotti on the rack and let it cool.

TIP: *If you store biscotti in an air tight container, they will be good for about 2 weeks. If you store them in the freezer, they are good for 2–3 months. This was my friend's recipe. You may have more than 6 logs. Enjoy!*

DESSERTS & COOKIES

INGREDIENTS

Flour, 3 ¾ cups

Baking powder, 2 teaspoons

Salt, ¼ teaspoon

Unsalted butter, 2 sticks

Sugar, 1 ½ cup

Eggs, 6 large

Vanilla extract, 1 teaspoon

Anise extract, 2 tablespoons (or ⅛ teaspoon of anise oil)

Egg, 1, beaten, whisk with sea salt (brush over top)

Anise Cookies

Biscotti All Anice

You can enjoy the biscotti two different ways: You can cut and eat them right away while they maintain a soft texture or, if you prefer them toasted, bake the biscotti in the oven until firm.

DIRECTIONS:

Preheat oven at 375°F. Set aside two 12x18-inch baking sheets lined with parchment paper.

In a medium bowl, combine flour, baking powder, salt, and set aside.

Using a standing electric mixer with a paddle, add butter and sugar; mix well on medium-high for 5 minutes. Add 2 eggs at a time until eggs are incorporated (about 1 minute). Add vanilla and anise extract; mix. Reduce speed, add flour mixture, and blend well together for 1–2 minutes.

Remove bowl from mixer. Dust clean kitchen counter with ½ cup flour. With your hands separate dough into two halves (each half will make into logs). Form the dough into two long, domed logs (dust with flour if necessary for rolling the dough into logs). Logs should be about 12–13 inches long and 2—2 ½ inches wide. Place the dough onto a baking sheet layered with parchment paper. Beat 1 egg and brush over top of each log. Bake at 375°F. Bake for 20–25 minutes, until light golden brown. Cool on a wire rack.

(recipe continues)

DESSERTS & COOKIES

CUTTING:

Place the biscotti on a cutting board; using a serrated knife, cut on a diagonal into ¾-inch thick slices. Arrange the biscotti cut side down on the baking sheet. Bake until they are toasted or lightly golden for 10 minutes. Put Biscotti on the rack again.

TIP: *If you have biscotti stored in an air tight container, they will be good for about 2 weeks. If you store them in the freezer they are good for 2–3 months.*

DESSERTS & COOKIES

INGREDIENTS

Flour, 8 cups (approximately)

Baking powder, 4 teaspoons

Baking soda, ¼ teaspoon

Salt, ⅛ teaspoon

Unsalted butter, 1 pound

Sugar, 2 ½ cups

Eggs, 6 large

Orange juice, 1 orange

Orange zest, 1 orange

INGREDIENTS FOR TOPPING

Egg, 1 yolk

Milk, 2 tablespoons (or water)

Sesame or poppy seeds, ¼ cup (or finely chopped almonds)

Butter Cookies

Biscotti dolci al burro

DIRECTIONS:

Preheat oven to 350°F. Line a baking sheet (12x18-inch, or any size) with parchment paper and set aside.

In a medium bowl, blend flour, baking powder, baking soda, and salt; set aside.

In a large standing mixer, add butter and sugar; beat until smooth and creamy (about 5–6 minutes), on medium-speed.

In a separate small bowl, beat the eggs. Add one or two eggs at a time into the butter/sugar mixture and fully incorporate.

Add the orange juice, and zest (if using). Mix for another minute or so.

Gradually add dry ingredients (step 1) to the butter/sugar mixture, about 2 cups at a time. Fully incorporate before adding more. If the batter becomes too stiff for the electric mixer, incorporate remaining flour by hand.

Dump dough onto a floured surface and knead gently, just to be sure that flour is fully incorporated. Shape the dough into a ball shape.

Return the dough to the bowl. To shape the cookies, pinch off a rounded tablespoon of dough and roll into

(recipe continues)

DESSERTS & COOKIES

a walnut-sized ball. From there, you may shape the ball into a football shape or continue rolling into a log, and form an "S" shape.

Arrange formed cookies about a half-inch apart on baking sheets.

Whisk together the egg yolk with the milk or water, and lightly brush the cookies with the mixture. Sprinkle with seeds or nuts and place in the preheated oven. Bake at 350°F for 15–20 minutes.

Remove cookies from oven and place on a wire rack to cool for about 10 minutes. Place cooled cookies on a platter and enjoy!

TIP: *For an optional topping, you can dust the cookies with confectioner's sugar.*

TIP: *If cookies are stored in an air-tight container, they may be kept for 1–2 weeks.*

Amaretti Cookies

Biscotti di Amaretto

This recipe was from my cousin (Ida Baldino) in Cosenza.

These cookies have a crisp texture. Light and airy.

INGREDIENTS

Unblanched whole almonds, 1 pound

Confectioner's sugar, 2 ¼ cup

Baking powder, 1 teaspoon

Egg, 4 large egg whites, at room temperature

Parchment paper

DIRECTIONS:

Preheat oven to 375°F.

Line four 12x18-inch cookie sheets with parchment paper.

In a food processor, finely chop the almonds, place them in a large bowl, and set aside.

In a medium bowl, mix the confectioner's sugar and baking powder together. Add to the almonds and mix well.

In a separate bowl, beat the egg whites with an electric mixer until stiff peaks form. With a rubber spatula, gently fold the egg whites into the almond mixture a little at a time until the mixture is well blended.

Using two soup spoons, shape the batter into balls about 2 inches in diameter and place them about 1 inch apart on the cookie sheets. They will spread while baking.

Bake for 10–12 minutes or until firm to touch and golden brown. Let the cookies cool completely on the parchment paper before removing; otherwise, they will break. Store the cookies in an airtight container.

Cookies with a Kiss

Biscotti al bacio di cioccolato

DIRECTIONS:

Preheat oven to 350°F. Set aside two 12×18-inch baking sheets lined with parchment paper.

Cream butter and sugar with a hand held or standing mixer until light and fluffy. Beat in egg yolks, flour, and ground hazelnuts. Mix well. Take a teaspoon of each dough and shape into a ball. Place them well apart on the baking sheets. Press one whole hazelnut into the center of each cookie. Place into the oven and bake for 10–12 minutes or until lightly brown. Cool on baking sheet; then transfer to a wire rack and let cool completely. Makes 5 dozen.

CHOCOLATE DIP:

In a microwave proof bowl, combine the 12 ounces dark chocolate. Microwave until it melts; checking every 30 seconds to avoid scorching. Dip a portion of each cookie into the chocolate. And let it dry for about 30 minutes. Make sure the chocolate is completely dry on the cookie.

TIP: *If you don't want any chocolate you can just dust the cookies with confectioners' sugar. If you don't have hazelnut you can also use almonds.*

INGREDIENTS

Unsalted butter, 2 sticks, softened

Confectioners' sugar, 1 ½ cups

All-purpose flour, 2 cups

Hazelnut, ½ cup, ground

Egg, 2 large egg yolks

Hazelnut, 60 whole (placed on top of each cookie)

Dark chocolate, 12 oz. melted and dipped

INGREDIENTS

Shortening, 2 cups

Sugar, 3 cups

Eggs, 6 large

Whole milk, 2 cups

Vanilla extract, 2 tablespoons

All-purpose flour, 10–12 cups (reserve 2 cups to flour the counter top and to adjust the consistency)

Baking powder, 7 teaspoons

Salt, a pinch

FILLING INGREDIENTS

Dry figs, 3 pounds

Brandy, 1 ½ cups

Water, ¾ cup

Dates, 1 pound

Golden raisins, 1 pound

Sugar, ½ cup

Cinnamon, 2 teaspoons

Nutmeg, ½ teaspoon

Orange juice, ¼ cup

Orange peel, 1, finely chopped

Apple, 1, peeled and cut into chunks (remove core)

Pecans, 2 cups chopped

Italian Fig Cookies

Pasticciotti di Fichi Secchi

Fig cookies are a favorite because Italians love figs. We use figs in so many ways, but fig cookies are a favorite.

DOUGH DIRECTIONS:

Using a standing mixer, with a paddle, cream the shortening and sugar, until light and creamy (4–5 minutes). Add the eggs, mix for 1 minute. Add milk and vanilla, mix slowly. Add 10 cups of flour, baking powder, and salt; mix on low speed until smooth. Place on floured counter and knead about 3 times. Put in a medium bowl, cover with plastic wrap and put in the fridge for 4 hours or overnight (until firm).

FILLING DIRECTIONS:

Cut up the figs, put in a bowl and add the brandy. Let it sit (covered), on the counter overnight. Put the figs in a food processor, add half of the water, and mix again until it becomes a paste. Place in a large bowl and set aside. In a food processor, mix together the dates, raisins, sugar, cinnamon, nutmeg, orange juice, orange peel, apple, and the other half of the water. Make into a smooth paste. Add chopped nuts to the processor and pulse only 4–5 times so it stays slightly chunky. Add this mixture to the bowl of fig paste. Take a wooden spoon (or hands) and mix well. Cover and refrigerate for 4 hours.

(recipe continues)

GLAZE INGREDIENTS

Confectioner's sugar, 1 pound

Lemon juice, 5–6 tablespoons (or as needed)

Colored sprinkles, optional

BAKING DIRECTIONS:

Preheat oven to 375°F. Line 12x18-inch cookie sheets with parchment paper.

Flour your counter and rolling pin (flour again between pieces of dough). Take a ball of dough about the size of a large orange and roll it into a rectangle, about 4 inches by 14 inches, and ¼ inch thick. Cut the rectangle in half so you have 2 long strips. Roll out the filling so you have a ¾ (quarter sized) rope of filling and lay it in the middle of the dough. Roll over the edges of the dough then roll the log over so the seam is on the bottom. Cut the logs into 1 ½ inch pieces using a wet knife. Cut a slit in the cookie. Transfer cookies to the cookie sheets (easier to do with a spatula).

Cookies should be about 1 inch apart. Bake for 15–20 minutes in preheated oven until very light golden color. Transfer cookies to a wire rack to cool.

Mix confectioner's sugar and lemon juice with a whisk until the glaze reaches the consistency of pancake batter. Dip the top of cookies in the glaze, add sprinkles, and then lay them down on a wire rack to dry.

DESSERTS & COOKIES

INGREDIENTS

Canola oil, 2 quarts, for frying
Eggs, 4 large
Sugar, 1 cup
Vegetable oil, ¼ cup
Sour cream, 1 cup
Anisette liquor, 1 tablespoon
Vanilla extract, 1 teaspoon
All-purpose flour, 4 cups
Baking powder, 4 teaspoons
Salt, 1 teaspoon

GLAZE INGREDIENTS

Confectioner's sugar, 1 pound for glaze
Cold water, ¼ cup (or as needed)

Carmela's Finger Cookies

Biscotti di Carmela

This recipe was given to me by my friend Carmela Porco.

DIRECTIONS:

Set aside a deep fryer or 4-quart deep sauce pan, with 2 quarts of oil.

In a standing mixer with a paddle, add eggs, sugar, vegetable oil, sour cream, anisette and vanilla. Mix on low speed for about 1–2 minutes. Add flour, baking powder, and salt. Mix gently until consistency looks like cookie dough. Don't over mix (over mixing makes dough tough).

Dust your kitchen counter with ¼ cup flour. Use a plastic spatula to scrape the dough out of the bowl. Rub a little flour on your hands and pat down the dough. With floured hands, roll a little bit of dough into the size of a small walnut, then further roll into the size of a finger. Place each finger cookie on a cookie sheet until the dough is used up.

Heat oil in a deep fryer or 4-quart deep saucepan to 350°F (use a thermometer to measure the heat if using the pot). Fill in a strainer spoon with dough and drop into the oil (do not overcrowd the pan). Fry for 4–5 minutes or until they are golden brown. Fry all the dough. Make sure the oil is hot (350°F) before frying a new batch. Remove with slotted spoon and drain them on paper towels. Let cool.

(recipe continues)

DESSERTS & COOKIES

To make the glaze, put confectioner's sugar in a medium bowl. Slowly incorporate 2–3 tablespoons cold water, mix well. Continue to add water by the tablespoon until the glaze reaches the consistency of pancake batter. When finger cookies are completely cooled, glaze them. Place cookies on a wire rack to dry.

TIP: *If you need more oil to fry, add more as needed.*

DESSERTS & COOKIES

Ladyfingers

ITALIAN NAME??

Ladyfingers are used in Tiramisu or are also eaten plain with an afternoon espresso. This is our recipe from Roma Bakery.

DIRECTIONS:

Preheat oven to 425°F. Line two 12x18-inch baking sheets with parchment paper.

You will need a large pastry bag with a plain ½-inch round tube tip.

Place egg whites in a large bowl; beat on high using a standing electric mixer until foamy with soft peaks. Slowly incorporate sugar 2 tablespoons at a time, while beating continuously, until 1 cup is incorporated completely into the mixture. Continue beating; add egg yolk and vanilla mixture. Keep machine beating for 45–50 seconds until very pale in color. Mixture should look stiff and glossy. Remove bowl from mixer. Add 1 cup flour. Using a plastic spatula, softly fold the flour into the mixture until absorbed.

Transfer batter into large pastry bag. Holding the bag at a 45° angle above the baking sheet, pipe out 3-inch long ladyfingers on prepared baking sheet (ladyfingers look like little soldiers in a row).

Bake for 6–7 minutes with oven door remaining closed entire time. Remove baking sheet from oven. Slide parchment paper from baking sheet onto a wire rack. Allow ladyfingers to cool for a few minutes and release them from the parchment paper using a flat spatula. Finish cooling the ladyfingers on a wire rack. Store ladyfingers in an airtight container or freeze if you are not using them right away.

INGREDIENTS

Eggs, 6 large, whites and yolks separated

Sugar, 1 cup

All-purpose flour, 1 cup, sifted

Vanilla extract, 1 teaspoon (added to egg yolks)

DESSERTS & COOKIES

Mamma's Finger Cookies

Biscotti di Sposalizi

Finger cookies are a traditional Italian wedding dessert.

DIRECTIONS:

Mix the sugar and Crisco in a standing mixer with a paddle for about 5–6 minutes until creamy. Add in the Anisette liquor, and the eggs (two at a time). Mix on medium speed until incorporated. In the same bowl, add in 8 ¾ cups of flour first and then the baking powder. Incorporate a little at a time until the dough is soft. You may need the extra flour for your hands to handle dough. Be sure not to over mix or the dough will get tough.

Dust your kitchen counter with ½ cup flour. Use a plastic spatula to scrape the dough out of the bowl. Rub a little flour on your hands and pat down the dough. With floured hands, roll a little bit of dough into the size of a small walnut, then further roll into the size of a finger. Place each finger cookie on a cookie sheet until the dough is all rolled out.

Heat oil in a deep fryer or 4–6 quart, deep pot to 350°F (use a thermometer to measure the heat if using the pot). Fill a strainer spoon with dough and drop into the oil, but do not crowd the pan. Fry for 4–5 minutes or until they are golden brown. With your first batch, you may have to open one up to see if it is cooked in the center. Fry all the cookies. Make sure the oil is hot (350°F) before frying a new batch. Remove with a slotted spoon and drain them on paper towels. Let cool.

To make the glaze, put the confectioner's sugar in a bowl and slowly add water, mixing until glaze reaches the consistency of pancake batter. When the finger cookies are cooled, glaze them. Set cookies on a wire rack to dry.

INGREDIENTS

Sugar, 2 cups

Crisco, 1 cup

Anisette liquor, 2 tablespoons

Eggs, 12 large

Flour, 8 ¾ cups, save extra ½ cup

Baking powder, 6 teaspoons

Vegetable or Canola oil, 2 quarts, for frying

GLAZE INGREDIENTS

Confectioner's sugar, 1 pound (or as needed)

Water, ¼ cup (or as needed)

Christmas Honey Cookies

Turdilli con Miele

This recipe was given to me by Maria Dionise. She was such a nice person and wonderful lady. She was also the mother of my son-in-law Mark.

LIQUID INGREDIENTS

Canola oil, 10 ounces

Eggs, 2 large

White wine or Moscato, 10 ounces

Sugar, 4 ounces

Anisette liquor, 2 tablespoons

Orange zest, 1 tablespoon grated

DRY INGREDIENTS

Cake flour, 10 cups

Baking powder, 2 teaspoons

Salt, a pinch

Cinnamon, ½ teaspoon

DIRECTIONS:

In a medium bowl, mix together the liquid ingredients. Whisk by hand for 1–2 minutes until well blended. Set aside.

In a large bowl, sift together dry ingredients. Pour the liquid ingredients into the dry ingredients and blend together well with hands until dough looks smooth like pasta dough (this takes 10 minutes).

Transfer to a clean work surface (sprinkle with a little bit of flour first) and knead 1–2 minutes; form dough into a ball; flatten the dough and cut into 6–8 square sections (first cut the dough into two chunks horizontally, then vertically into smaller sections).

Roll the sections into long ropes (1-inch in diameter). Cut each roll into 1 ¼-inch pieces; roll the dough on a gnocchi board, butter paddle, or fork to make a ridged pattern design (press with two fingers on the inside of the dough to create these deep ridges on the outside of each pieces) These ridges make the dough look nice and hold the honey you coat the cookies in; make sure the ridges are deep or else they will disappear when you fry the dough.

(recipe continues)

Heat 1 quart of Canola oil (or more depending on the size of your pan) in a deep fryer or saucepan (heat to 375°F). Fry the cookies in about 4 batches until puffed and mid-light brown. If you are using a deep pan make sure to stir the cookies a few times (fry for about 10–12 minutes). It is easier to pile cookies in a sieve or fry basket and them dip them into the hot oil. Each batch should include enough cookies to cover the surface of the oil. Any fewer and the oil gets took hot and browns the cookies before they are cooked through. Stir the cookies while they fry to avoid them sticking together. The number of cookies you add to the oil and the amount of oil will change the timing. The cookies first turn light brown, then a medium brown and finally golden brown in color. Remove when they get to this golden brown color. Drain on paper towels. Be sure oil is hot before frying the next set of cookies.

HONEY GLAZE:

Mix ½ cup grape jelly and 1 tablespoon sugar—stir this mixture until smooth, and then add 4 cups of honey. Warm over medium heat until glaze liquefies and becomes hot. Add a few Turdilli at a time until coated. Drain and put on a platter.

HONEY GLAZE INGREDIENTS

Grape jelly, ½ cup
Sugar, 1 tablespoon
Honey, 4 cups

This crivello was given to me by Nonna.

TIP: *A crivello or crivo is an Italian basket used to make Turdilli in Calabria but is often hard to find. In different regions they call this "Turdiddi". Either way it is a delicious and beautiful cookie!*

DESSERTS & COOKIES

Honey Sliced Cookies

Mostazolli

This recipe was given to me by my friend Anna.

DIRECTIONS:

Preheat oven to 350°F. Set aside two 12x18-inch baking sheets lined with parchment paper.

In a standing mixer, with a paddle, combine honey, oil, eggs, orange zest, anisette, flour, cocoa, baking powder, clove, cinnamon, and salt. Mix well on low speed; add walnuts and mix for 30 seconds (it is normal for the dough to be very sticky). Remove dough mixture and place into a bowl. Cover with saran wrap and place in the refrigerator for 30 minutes.

Dust counter with flour. Dust hands with flour and roll dough into a ball (rub hands with flour as needed to work with sticky dough). Cut dough into 8 pieces. Roll each piece into 2 x 8 inch long pieces. Place 4 logs on a cookie sheet. Beat one egg and brush over the surface of each log. Bake for 20 minutes in preheated oven. Let cool.

CUTTING:

Place desired amount of biscotti logs on a cutting board. Using a serrated knife, cut on a diagonal into ½ –inch thick slices.

TIP: *It is a very chewy dough but delicious. I hope you enjoy it. This is a Calabrese favorite. You can save the remaining logs (whole) in a plastic storage bag or container. These can stay in the refrigerator for up to 1 month.*

INGREDIENTS

Honey, 4 cups

Vegetable oil, 5 tablespoons

Egg, 1 large (whisked)

Orange zest, 2 tablespoons grated

Anisette, 2 teaspoons

All-purpose flour, 7 ½ cups (set aside 1 cup)

Cocoa, 2 teaspoons

Baking powder, 3 teaspoons

Clove, ¼ teaspoon

Cinnamon, ½ teaspoon

Salt, a pinch

Chopped walnuts, 1 cup (optional)

DESSERTS & COOKIES

Macaroons

"Dessert" alle Mandorle

One of our bestselling cookies at Roma Bakery are the Amaretti Macaroon cookies. The delicate almond flavor is delightful with a cup of tea or espresso.

DIRECTIONS:

Preheat oven to 375°F. Place rack in center of oven. Line a 12x18-inch baking sheet with parchment paper.

Cut almond paste into pieces and place into an electric mixer. Add sugar, pastry flour, and pinch of salt; mix well for 2–3 minutes. Add in almond extract and vanilla; add egg whites one at a time, blend well. Stop and check consistency of batter; it should be soft like cookie dough but not runny (add another egg if needed). Stop and scrape down sides of bowl; place almond batter onto a plate to work with.

Drop the batter by teaspoon onto baking sheets; leaving approximately 1-inch between cookies. Sprinkle sugar over top of cookies. Bake for 10 minutes or until light in color. Cool completely on parchment paper; store in air tight container; layering cookies between waxed paper.

TIP: *Use a piping bag with a star-shaped tip to make cookies. You can make cookies into other shapes (white or colored) like crescents with almonds or a round-shape with pine nuts or chocolate.*

INGREDIENTS

YIELDS 5 DOZEN

Almond paste, 16-ounces (not marzipan)

Granulated sugar, 1 cup

Pastry flour, 6 ounces

Salt, a pinch

Vanilla extract, 1 teaspoon

Almond extract, 2 teaspoons

Eggs, 3 egg whites at room temperature (start with 3 egg whites, add 1 if needed)

Sugar, 4 tablespoons, for sprinkling on top

INGREDIENTS

Flour, 4 cups sifted
Sugar, 1 cup
Baking powder, 1 tablespoon
Salt, ¼ teaspoon
Nutmeg, ⅛ teaspoon
Shortening, ¾ cup (butter Crisco flavor)
Unsalted butter, ½ cup
Eggs, 2 large, slightly beaten
Milk, ¼ cup
Vanilla extract, 2 teaspoon
Lemon zest, 2 tablespoon
Sesame seeds, 1 cup

Sesame Seed Cookies

Biscotti ai Semi di Sesamo

DIRECTIONS:

Preheat oven to 375°F. Set aside two 12x18-inch baking sheets lined with parchment paper.

In a food processor add the flour, sugar, baking powder, salt and nutmeg; pulse for ½ a minute (two pulses). Add in the shortening and butter; pulse again until pieces look like small peas. Stir in the eggs, milk, vanilla, and lemon zest; pulse together until dough comes together. Remove dough from bowl. Wrap the dough in plastic wrap; refrigerate for 1 hour.

Break off small pieces of dough (size of large walnut) and roll into 1½ inch logs, with hands. Roll dough in sesame seeds (may need more seeds) and place on baking sheet.

Bake at 375°F for 15–20 minutes, or until lightly browned. Makes about 5–6 dozen cookies, depending on the size.

TIP: *Store cookies in sealed, air-tight container. Good for 2–3 weeks.*

DESSERTS & COOKIES

Thumbprint Cookies

Biscotti con l'imprinta del police

Kids love helping with the "thumbprint!"

DIRECTIONS:

Preheat oven to 400°F. Line an 12x18-inch baking sheet with parchment paper and set aside.

Combine all-purpose flour, pastry flour, baking powder, and the salt in a bowl and set aside.

Using a standing electric mixer beat shortening, butter, and sugar until fluffy. Add the egg and mix well for about 2 minutes. Add the orange zest and vanilla, and mix.

Next add the flour mixture on low speed, until combined. Then add the walnuts and mix on a slow speed to incorporate the nuts, but being careful not break them. Add the sour cream and blend for 30 seconds.

Take one tablespoon of dough and roll into a ball, and place on the cookie sheet. Or you can use a small ice cream scoop with a cup that measures 1¼ in. Make sure there is a ¾ in space between balls. Once you have all the cookies on the sheets take your thumb and press into each cookie, enough for about ¼ of a teaspoon of the jam. Bake for between 8–9 minutes. Cool until you can pick them up with a spatula and move them to cooling racks.

TIP: *If you have a larger thumb or you push down more you will need more jam. You may also dust cookies with confectioner's sugar.*

INGREDIENTS

Shortening, ¾ cup

Butter, ¾ cup (unsalted)

Sugar, 1 ¼ cup

Egg, 1 large

Orange zest, 1 tablespoon

Vanilla extract, 1 teaspoon

Flour, 1 ½ cup

Pastry flour, ½ cup

Salt, a pinch

Baking powder, a pinch

Walnuts, 2 cups chopped small

Sour cream, ¼ cup

Jam, 10–12 ounce jar of your choice, for topping

DESSERTS & COOKIES

Zeppole

Zeppole

This is a traditional dessert for Saint Joseph's Day in Italy.

INGREDIENTS

Water, 1 cup
Salt, a pinch
Sugar, 1 tablespoon
Butter, ½ cup
Lemon zest, 1 teaspoon
Pastry flour, 1 cup (or all-purpose flour)
Eggs, 4 large
Vegetable or canola oil, 5–6 cups (or more if needed), for frying

INGREDIENTS (RICOTTA FILLING)

Ricotta, 1 ½ pounds
Sugar, ½ cup and 2 tablespoons
Almond extract, 1 teaspoon (or vanilla if preferred)
Chocolate "petites" or mini chips, 3 tablespoons
Orange zest, 1 teaspoon

DIRECTIONS:

In a medium saucepan, combine water, salt, sugar, and butter. Bring to a boil over medium heat, stirring with a wooden spoon to melt butter. Add the lemon zest and stir.

Stirring constantly, slowly add flour, continue to stir constantly with the wooden spoon until the flour is incorporated and the dough begins to pull away from the sides of the pan.

Remove the dough from the stove. Place the dough into a food processor. In a small bowl, add 4 eggs. Gently pour the eggs one at a time into the food processor, mixing vigorously to be sure each egg is incorporated before adding the next (1 minute). Continue to mix until dough is completely smooth (additional 2 minutes).

Heat oil to 350–375°F in a deep fryer or heavy, deep pot. Drop dough into the oil by the heaping tablespoon (use a silverware tablespoon not a measuring tablespoon), being sure not to crowd the dollops (which will expand as they cook). Fry the dough until light golden brown, turning them on all sides—about 5 minutes. Drain on a paper towel. Continue to fry remaining dough in batches.

(recipe continues)

While the zeppole are cooling, you may prepare the filling. First drain the ricotta. Use a food processor to whip the ricotta, almond extract, orange zest, and sugar; mix continuously for 2 minutes until smooth. Fold in the mini chocolate chips and mix with a plastic spatula (until blended). Chill the filling in the refrigerator for at least a half an hour before using.

When the zeppole have completely cooled, make a slit in the side of each one. Using a pastry bag (or a spoon), pipe the filling into the bottom half of the zeppole (about 1–2 tablespoons). Dust with confectioner's sugar and serve! Makes about 2 dozen.

DESSERTS & COOKIES

GALATOBOURIKO SYRUP INGREDIENTS

Sugar, 4 cups

Water, 3 cups

Fresh lemon juice, 2–3 tablespoons

Cinnamon, 1 stick

INGREDIENTS FOR DOUGH

Filo (strudel dough), 2 pounds; 1 pound for bottom and 1 pound for the top

Clarified butter, 1 ½ pound

GALATOBOURIKO MIXTURE INGREDIENTS

Eggs, 16 large

Sugar, 1 ½ cups

Vanilla extract, 1 teaspoon extract

Whole milk, 10 cups

Farina, 1 ⅓ cups

Butter, ¼ cup, melted

Galatobouriko

Galatobouriko (Greek Recipe)

This recipe was given to me by my best friend Elaine Kritselis. This is a dessert similar to baklava with a cream filling. Lovely with a cup of coffee.

DIRECTIONS FOR SYRUP*:

* Make syrup first.

Combine all ingredients in a large saucepan. Bring to a boil, being careful it does not over boil. Reduce heat so liquid is barely simmering. Simmer for 25 minutes. Remove from heat and allow to cool.

DIRECTIONS FOR DOUGH:

First, to clarify butter, melt 1 pound butter; allow it to reach a boil so impurities will separate from butter. You should see white foam. Pour butter into a ceramic bowl and refrigerate for 1–2 hours in order to solidify (or put in freezer for half an hour or so). This can be done the day before but don't leave in freezer too long. When butter is solidified; run a knife along the edge of the bowl to release butter from the sides; a chunk of butter will slip out leaving the impurities on the bottom. Scrape off impurities from top and bottom of butter chunk (if necessary). Re-melt when ready to use filo.

Second, prepare the Galatobouriko mixture; beat together the eggs (I use two mixers because 16 eggs are too much for one mixer). Whip 10–15 minutes until frothy. Gradually add sugar and vanilla. Beat well. Transfer eggs to large saucepan (6 or 8 quart).

(recipe continues)

DESSERTS & COOKIES

Heat milk until barely warm. Remove from heat. Slowly pour milk into eggs while whisking so the eggs don't curdle (use all the milk).

Place mixture on stove on low heat. Gradually incorporate farina. Stir constantly, gradually increasing the heat. Cook until thickened (about when it starts bubbling). Tip: I sometimes increase heat to medium-high to get it to bubble. Do not leave the mixture or it will stick to the bottom and burn. May take 1 hour to thicken. When thickened, add ¼ cup melted butter and mix. Remove from heat and let it cool.

Preheat oven to 350°F. Layer half the filo dough, buttering each layer with the melted butter. Use 12 x 18-inch pan. Add all the above mixture. Top with remaining filo, buttering each layer and turning ends down inside the pan to seal. Pour remaining butter on top.

Bake for one hour in pre-heated 350°F oven.

Remove from oven. Pour cooled syrup over hot Galatobouriko. Allow it to thoroughly cool. Cut into whatever size serving pieces you desire. Don't worry about leftovers; it freezes nicely.

TIP: *When preparing galatobouriko or baklava, one secret is having the syrup cool and pouring it over the hot item. That's why I advise making the syrup first*

TIP: *Recipe may be halved also (9 x 13).*

Shaved Coffee Ice — Granita with Cream

Granita di Caffe

This recipe comes from Sicily. Granita di caffe is a dessert that Sicilians love in the heat of summer months. They sometimes have it for breakfast with sweet bread (Brioce).

INGREDIENTS

- **Sugar,** 1 ¼ cup
- **Cold water,** 2 cups
- **Espresso,** 3 cups, cooled and set aside
- **Heavy cream,** 1 cup
- **Sugar,** 1 tablespoon (whip cream and sugar together)

DIRECTIONS:

Put sugar and water in a saucepan. Lower the heat and simmer, stirring until the sugar is dissolved (about 2 minutes). Add the espresso and stir. Remove the pan and let it cool for about 20 minutes. Transfer the mixture to a 9x13 tray and place in the freezer for between 2 and 3 hours.

Using a fork, scrape the semi-frozen mixture, allowing crystals to form. Check the mixture in 30 minute intervals, each time using the fork to fluff the mixture. Freeze for an additional 30 minutes until a slushy consistency is achieved. To serve, place a scoop in a fluted glass and top with the whipped cream. Serve immediately. Serves 4–6.

TIP: *This dish can also be served plain, without the whip cream.*

TIP: *You can add the frozen mix to a food processor to make it shaved.*

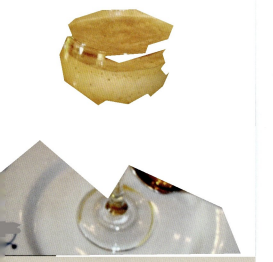

DESSERTS & COOKIES

Shaved Lemon Ice — Granita

Granita di Limone

Sicilian style shaved ice is perfect at the end of a long, hot summer day.

INGREDIENTS

Sugar, 1 ¼ cup
Cold water, 2 cups
Fresh lemon juice, ½ to ¾ cups
Lemon zest, 1 teaspoon

DIRECTIONS:

In a saucepan, melt the sugar in cold water; bring to a boil. Lower the heat and let simmer for 2 minutes until sugar is dissolved. Remove pan and let sit for about 20 minutes. Add remaining ingredients (lemon juice and zest). Pour the mixture into a 9x13 tray; put into freezer for about 2–3 hours until mixture begins to crystallize; check after 2 hours to see how much the top has crystallized (scrape with a fork and mix around); check every 30–45 minutes thereafter; mixing around until granita looks slushy.

To serve, place granita in a fluted glass. Serve immediately.

TIP: *The amount of lemon juice is subjective to one's palate. More lemon juice will result in a tart flavor. Adjust to fit your desired taste.*

TIP: *You can add the frozen mix to a food processor to make it shaved.*

DESSERTS & COOKIES

INGREDIENTS

Peaches, 6 firm ripe

Sugar, ½ cup

Blanched almonds, ½ cup sliced

Amaretti almond macaroons, 6 large, broken

Egg, 1 egg yolk

Amaretto, ⅓ cup (or liquor of choice)

Baked Stuffed Peaches

Pesche Ripiene

A delicious dessert any time of the year. The almond macaroons give a delightful flavor to the peaches. Using fresh summer peaches you cannot go wrong.

DIRECTIONS:

Preheat oven to 350°F. Butter a large shallow baking dish. Wash and dry peaches and cut into halves. Remove pits and scoop out no more than 1 tablespoon pulp from each half.

In a blender or food processor fitted with a metal blade, combine peach pulp, sugar, almonds, almond macaroons, egg yolk and liquor. Blend to a fine paste.

Divide mixture between peach halves. Arrange the peaches in a single layer, in buttered baking dish. Bake 25 minutes. Serve warm or at room temperature.

TIP: *If using small amaretti cookies, use 12.*

DESSERTS & COOKIES

Fresh Fruit Dessert

Macedonia di Frutta

We love fresh fruit salad for dessert. Especially in my home in Italy. My favorite seasonal fruit is fresh figs.

INGREDIENTS

SERVES 6

Apples, 2
Pears, 2
Peaches, 2
Bananas, 2
Strawberries, 12 hulled
Seedless grapes, 18 (if large cut in half)
Tangerine, 6 sections
Confectioner's sugar, ½ cup
Limoncello, ½ cup
Fresh lemon juice, 1 tablespoon
Vanilla ice cream, 1 pint
Heavy cream, 1 cup, whipped

DIRECTIONS:

Peel and core the apples, pears and peaches and cut into cubes. Peel and slice the bananas. Add hulled strawberries, grapes and tangerine slices, cut into pieces. Combine fruit in a large bowl. Add confectioner's sugar and Limoncello, and lemon juice. Mix well and chill. Place the fruit mixture in the bottom of individual serving cups. Top with ice cream and then with whipped cream.

TIP: *Limoncello is a lemon flavored liquor. This can be made without Limencello for an alcohol-free option by adding some lemon zest.*

DESSERTS & COOKIES

Peaches in Red Wine

Pesche al Vino

A favorite of Papá

DIRECTIONS:

In a bowl, combine peach slices, and sugar; toss gently until sugar dissolves completely. Add wine and stir gently to combine. Cover and chill for about ½ hour.

TO SERVE:

Spoon mixture into serving goblet. Garnish with additional fresh mint leaves.

INGREDIENTS

SERVES 2-4

Fresh peaches, 4 peeled, pitted, and sliced

Sugar, 4 tablespoons

Dry red wine, 1 cup

Fresh mint leaves, for garnish

TIP: *Substitute nectarines for peaches in this recipe as well*

DESSERTS & COOKIES

Pear Caramel Cake

Torta di Pere caramellate

DIRECTIONS:

Butter a 9-inch cake pan. Do not use one with a removable bottom as the liquid may seep out. Line the bottom with parchment paper and butter it as well. Arrange the pear slices in a circle to cover the bottom of the cake pan.

Cream the butter and brown sugar until light and fluffy. Then add the eggs one at a time. Mix until well blended. Mix all the dry ingredients in a bowl. Then mix the milk and vanilla in another small bowl. Add the dry ingredients and milk mixture alternately in layers to the brown sugar mixture, ending with the last of the dry ingredients. Set aside while you make the caramel.

To make the caramel, put the white sugar, lemon juice, lemon zest and water in a heavy saucepan. Keep a glass filled with water and a pastry brush at hand. Swirl the sugar mixture by holding the pan handle. Do not use a spoon to mix. Bring the mixture to a boil and boil until the caramel is light brown. If sugar crystals form around the edge of the pan, use the pastry brush dipped in the water to brush them back into the sugar mixture. When the caramel is light brown, remove from the heat and add the salted butter a little at a time. Stir until the mixture is smooth and creamy. Pour it over the pears in the cake pan, spreading evenly over the whole surface. Pour the cake batter over the pears and caramel. Bake in the oven at 350°F for 30–35 minutes. Let it cool for 10 minutes before inverting onto a serving plate. Serve the cake alone or with a dollop of cream or ice cream.

CAKE INGREDIENTS

SERVES 8

Flour, 1 ½ cups
Baking powder, 1 ¾ teaspoon
Ginger, ½ teaspoon
Cinnamon, ½ teaspoon
Salt, ¼ teaspoon
Whole milk, ½ cup
Vanilla extract, 2 teaspoons
Butter, 8 tablespoons (1 stick), softened
Brown sugar, 1 cup
Eggs, 2 large

TOPPING INGREDIENTS

Pears, 2 Anjou or Barlett, peeled, cored, and cut into ¼-inch slices
Salted butter, 4 tablespoons
Basic caramel recipe (see below)

CARAMEL INGREDIENTS

Sugar, 1 cup
Lemon juice, ¼ teaspoon
Water, ¼ cup
Lemon zest, ½ teaspoon

INGREDIENTS

Pears, 8 Bosc or Anjou (preferably), firm ripe

Good dry red wine, 4 cups

Marsala or sherry, 1 cup

Sugar, 1 cup

Lemon zest, 1 lemon, grated

Lemon juice, 1 lemon

Pears Poached in Red Wine

Pere al Vino Rosso

We Italians like wine and fruit in desserts. "Papá loved this!"

DIRECTIONS:

Peel pears leaving stems attached. Flatten the pear bottoms by cutting off a thin slice from bottom of each pear. Stand pears close together in a large saucepan. Add red wine, Marsala or sherry, ¾ cup sugar and lemon zest. Bring to a boil. Reduce heat to medium and cover pan. Cook pears for 25 to 30 minutes or until tender. Use a basting spoon to taste several times during cooking.

Place pears in a glass bowl or platter. Let it stand at room temperature until ready to serve. Add ¼ cup sugar and lemon juice to the liquid in the saucepan. Boil for 10–15 minutes until it has the consistency of syrup. Spoon hot sauce over pears and serve.

TIP: *Serve with Ricotta pudding on the side.*

DESSERTS & COOKIES

Mamma's Vodka Cherries

Ciliege sotto spirit della Mamma

An after dinner treat!

INGREDIENTS

Bing sweet cherries, 1 ½ pounds

Sugar, ½ cup

Cinnamon, 1 three-inch stick

Vodka, 2 cups (100 proof) or enough to cover the cherries

DIRECTIONS:

Make sure that the cherries you buy for this kind of preserving are not extremely ripe. Choose very firm, red Bing cherries that are fresh with bright green stems, well attached to the fruit. Wash the cherries and spread them out on a clean paper towel to dry. When they are dry, cut off the top of each stem, leaving just ¼ inch. Do not use cherries without stems because they tend to fall apart in the jar.

Put the sugar in the bottom of a 1-quart sterilized jar with a tight seal. Add cinnamon, and cherries. Give the jar a shake or two to settle the fruit, and pour on enough vodka to cover the cherries completely. Seal tightly and let stand at least 4 weeks before serving.

INGREDIENTS

Unflavored gelatin, 1 ½ teaspoons

Water, 2 tablespoons

Milk, 1 cup

Sugar, ½ cup

Vanilla bean, ½, split lengthwise

Heavy cream, 2 cups

Fresh berries, raspberries, blueberries, or strawberries

Panna Cotta

Panna Cotta

Panna cotta is Northern Italian cookie cream custard. It is eaten either plain or with berries, caramel, chocolate sauce, hazelnuts or fruit puree. A beautiful light dessert.

DIRECTIONS:

In a small bowl, sprinkle gelatin over the water; let it stand for 5 minutes. In a medium saucepan, combine milk, sugar, and split vanilla bean; bring just to a boil. Remove pan from heat. Stir gelatin mixture into milk mixture; continue stirring until gelatin is dissolved. Remove vanilla bean; with a small knife, scrape seeds from bean into milk mixture. Strain mixture through a fine-mesh sieve into a large bowl. Cool to room temperature.

In a medium bowl, beat heavy cream with electric mixer until it holds stiff peaks. Stir a small amount of the whipped cream into the cooled milk mixture. Fold in remaining whipped cream. Spoon mixture into 8 (6-ounce) ramekins of custard cups. Cover and chill until set, at least 2 hours. Garnish with raspberries, blueberries, or strawberries (any of your choice). Makes 8 servings.

Mamma's Italian Pastry Cream

Crema Pasticcera

This cream is used in Italian tortes, cream puffs, or just eat it the way it is. Enjoy!

INGREDIENTS

Whole milk, 4 cups
Sugar, 1 cup
Flour, ¾ cup
Cornstarch, 1 tablespoon
Eggs, 5 egg yolks
Lemon zest, 1 teaspoon
Vanilla extract, 1 teaspoon

DIRECTIONS:

Place 3 ¼ cups of milk in saucepan (reserve ¾ cup of milk to mix into the following ingredients). In a mixing bowl, slowly mix together the sugar, flour, and cornstarch; add the ¾ cup cold milk until it forms a paste; then add the egg yolks, lemon zest, and vanilla. Whisk until the mixture is smooth; add this mixture to the 3 ¼ cups of milk in the sauce pan over medium heat and cook while stirring. Keep stirring for 2–3 minutes until it thickens and becomes smooth. Remove the pan from the stove, pour the mixture into a bowl, cover with a plastic wrap and refrigerate. This will make about 5 cups of cream.

INGREDIENTS

Eggs, 7 large

Sugar, 1 cup

Flour, 2 cups

Baking powder, 2 teaspoons

Vanilla extract, 1 teaspoon

Lemon zest, 1 teaspoon

Salt, a pinch

Italian Pastry Cream, ½ recipe

Mamma's Torte

Pan di Spagna

This is a sponge cake you can eat plain or fill with Italian pastry cream and flavored liquor. Mamma would make this light and delicious dessert for company.

DIRECTIONS:

Preheat oven to 350°F.

Grease a 9x13-inch pan with flour or non-stick cooking spray.

Place eggs and sugar in an electric mixer bowl, mix for 15–20 minutes on high speed until eggs and sugar become stiff and smooth. Set aside. Mix the flour and baking powder in separate bowl; take half of the flour mixture and add it to the egg mixture. Mix in electric mixer on low speed; add the other half of the flour mixture; then vanilla & lemon zest. Place the batter in the baking pan.

Bake at 350°F for 45 minutes. Poke a toothpick into the center. If it comes out clean, the torte is done. Let it cool for 10 minutes. Remove the torte from the pan and place onto a wire rack to cool. Let it cool completely for 15–20 minutes.

TIP: *This can be served plain or with powdered sugar dust; or fill the torte with a Limoncello and cream mixture.*

(recipe continues)

DESSERTS & COOKIES

SYRUP INGREDIENTS

Water, 1 cup

Sugar, 1 tablespoon

Limoncello Liquor, 1 cup (or liquor of your choice)

WHIPPED CREAM (OPTION 1)

Cream, 1 cup (8 oz)

Confectioner's Sugar, 2 tablespoons

Vanilla extract, ¼ teaspoon

GLAZE (OPTION 2)

Confectioner's Sugar, 1 pound

Milk, 4–5 tablespoons (more if needed)

Mix together until consistency is like pancake batter.

SYRUP MIXTURE RECIPE:

Mix ingredients together then separate batter in half. Slice the torte horizontally into two pieces (top and bottom); remove the top half; drizzle ½ of the syrup mixture on the bottom half; then add Italian pastry cream (2 ½–3 cups).

Place the top half of the torte back on the bottom of the torte; gently pressing it down with your fingers. Drizzle the other half of the syrup mixture on top of the torte; put fluffy whipped cream or glaze on top and refrigerate for 2 hours. This is delicious!

TIP: *Use any liquor of your choice for this recipe; Mama's favorite liquor was Anisette.*

TIP: *Mom would mix confectioner's sugar and a little bit of milk to form a glaze to pour over top of the torte (instead of whipped cream).*

TIP: *If topping with whipped cream, then the top layer must be placed with the inside (cut surface) facing up. If using the glaze, then position the top layer with the outside facing up.*

INGREDIENTS

Whole milk, 5 cups

Cornstarch, ¾ cup

Sugar, 1 cup

Almond extract, 2 ½ teaspoons

Ground cinnamon, for garnish

Finely chopped pistachios or toasted almonds, for garnish

Almond Pudding

Crema di Mandorle Siciliana

Thank you to my cousin Maria, from Sicily, for this wonderful almond crema.

DIRECTIONS:

Pour together the cold milk, cornstarch, sugar, and almond extract in a medium saucepan and whisk well. Cook over medium heat, whisking constantly to prevent sticking, until thickened and creamy (the custard should have the consistency of pudding). Remove from the heat and divide the custard among compote glasses. Garnish with a dusting of cinnamon, sprinkling of pistachios or chopped almonds (put plastic film over top of each compote glass). Place in the refrigerator until it's cold. Serves 6–8.

TIP: *It is also used for cannoli filling. Make sure you fluff the filling after it is cold in a standing mixer or with a spoon. Put mini chocolate chips or finely grated chocolate at the ends of the cannoli dipped in chopped pistachios.*

DESSERTS & COOKIES

Ricotta Pudding

Budino di Ricotta

DIRECTIONS:

Using a hand held mixer, add the ricotta, vanilla, and orange juice in a medium-bowl; whip until smooth. Stir in the cherries and orange zest with a plastic spatula. Set aside.

In a separate bowl, whip the cream and sugar until the cream is stiff (adding the sugar a little at a time). Pour into the ricotta mixture and blend together gently. Divide and spoon the mixture into goblets and garnish each with some of the toasted slivered almonds and whole cherries. Refrigerate until ready to serve.

TIP: *Delicious with poached pears added on the side!*

INGREDIENTS

- **Whole milk ricotta cheese,** 1 ½ cup
- **Vanilla,** ½ teaspoon
- **Orange juice,** ¼ cup fresh squeezed
- **Dried cherries,** ½ cup, plus a few whole to garnish
- **Orange zest,** 1 medium-size orange
- **Heavy cream,** 1 cup
- **Sugar,** ⅓ cup
- **Toasted almonds,** ⅓ cup, silvered

DESSERTS & COOKIES

BOILED BARLEY INGREDIENTS

Barley, ½ cup
Water, 7 cups
Salt, ¼ teaspoon

RICOTTA FILLING INGREDIENTS

Ricotta, 2 cups
Boiled barley, 2 cups
Sugar, 2 cups
Mascarpone, 8 ounces
Eggs, 8 large, reserve one for caking topping
Vanilla extract, 1 teaspoon
Salt, ½ teaspoon
Orange zest, 1 tablespoons
Orange blossom water, 1 tablespoon (Sold at Roma Bakery or any Middle Eastern market)

Sweet Pastry Dough (Pasta Frolla), 1 recipe

Roma's Pastiera Ricotta Filling

Torta di Pasqua con Ricotta

Pastiera is our traditional Easter dessert. No Italian home is without this meaningful dish on Easter!

DIRECTIONS:

Bring ½ cups barley, 7 cups water, and ¼ teaspoon salt to a boil. Cook on medium low for 2–3 hours until it is very tender. Stir once in a while. If the water is absorbed and the barley is not tender, add a little more water. Cool in the refrigerator. I often make the day before.

Make Sweet Pastry Dough (Pasta Frolla).

To make the ricotta filling use a standing mixer with the whisk attachment or hand mixer on medium speed, to blend the ricotta, about 2 minutes. Next add the sugar and mix for 1–2 minutes. Now add the Mascarpone and mix for 1 minute. Add 2 eggs at a time, mixing well in between (on medium-speed), until 7 eggs are incorporated. Add vanilla, salt, orange zest, and orange blossom water. Mix well for about 1 minute.

Preheat oven to 350°F.

After pasta frolla dough is removed from the refrigerator, divide into ¾ for bottom crust and set aside the ¼–⅛ dough for top crust. Roll out the ¾ portion of dough on a floured surface. Make into a 12-inch circle, ¼–⅛ inch thick. Use a pastry scraper to lift the dough. Line a 9-inch cake pan with the dough. Cut around the top edge with a paring knife, saving scraps for the top crust.

(recipe continues)

DESSERTS & COOKIES

Pour 6 cups of the ricotta filling into the crust, leaving room for the pastry strips-topping.

Roll the remaining ¼ dough and cut scraps on floured surface. Roll to 10 inches and ¼–⅛ inch thick. Cut into ½–¾-inch wide strips with knife or flute pastry wheel. Lay the extra strips across the top. Trim excess at edges. Using a pastry brush, lightly coat top with one whisked egg.

Place the pan on a cookie sheet to catch any overflow. Bake for 15–20 minutes until edges are set. Lower heat to 325° and cook another 50–60 minutes. The center should be puffed up and if pierced with a toothpick, it should come out clean.

TIP: *In Italy traditional Pastiera is made with wheat berries. When we came here we couldn't find it so we made it with Arborio (Italian rice). Prepare dry rice per package directions to make 2 cups cooked rice. It's delicious no matter which filling you use.*

TIP: *You may also roll the dough out on parchment paper, place pan upside down, then flip over onto pan. Mend any cracks by pressing lightly with your fingers. This method is easier if the dough is separating when you try to lift to put in pan.*

TIP: *You can use leftover filling to pour into a muffin tin, small ramekin or other baking dish for mini pies. Extra dough can be used to make cookies. Or, all extra ingredients can be made into an additional 6 inch pie.*

DESSERTS & COOKIES

Roma's Sweet Pastry Dough

Pasta Frolla

INGREDIENTS

Butter, ½ cup (1 stick), softened

Shortening, ¼ cup, softened

Sugar, ½ cup

Egg, 1 large

Orange zest, 1 tablespoon

Vanilla extract, 1 teaspoon

Italian flour or pastry flour, 1 ½ cup "00 tipo"

All-purpose flour, 1 cups

Baking powder, 1 teaspoon

Salt, ⅛ teaspoon

DIRECTIONS:

In a food processor, place butter, shortening, and sugar. Pulse in processor a few times until well blended. Add 1 egg, orange zest, and vanilla. Pulse the processor 3–4 times until well absorbed into the mixture and is creamy.

In a separate bowl, mix the flours, baking powder and salt. Add the flour mixture into the cream mixture. Pulse a few times, then change to continuous mixing until ball of dough is formed. Shape into smooth, round ball with hands. Place into plastic wrap. Refrigerate for 2 hours or overnight. After 2 hours, dough should be ready to work with. If refrigerated overnight, set out for about 1–2 hours until a bit cooler than room temperature and soft enough to work with. Place the dough between two pieces of parchment paper and roll it out on a flat surface (it is easier to roll the dough when it is place between parchment paper). The dough should be ¼–⅛ inch thick.

TIP: *This dough is good for Pastiera, Crostata, cookies, or anything that needs a sweet crust. Extra dough can be made into cookies.*

DESSERTS & COOKIES

PHOTOGRAPHIC HISTORY

ROMA BAKERY

Started by Sostine and Mena way back in 1969, Roma has provided the Lansing, Michigan area authentic Italian delicacies and products. We were embraced by Lansing and would like to thank everyone for their support over the years.

Sostine and Mena at Roma Bakery with a wedding cake.

Sostine stirring the tomatoes for canning.

One of my cooking classes at Roma. Most recipes I taught were Calabrian.

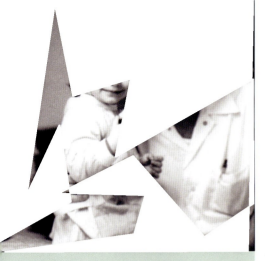

Sostine with our oldest daughter, AnneMarie (2), at Roma Bakery.

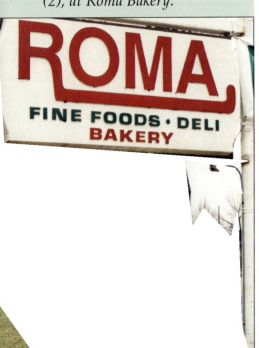

The Lansing State Journal took this photo to go with an article they wrote about the 25th Anniversary celebrations we had for the bakery.

Sostine and I outside Roma Bakery for a party in honor of our customers on our 25th anniversary of opening. The Coliseum Rum Cake was gone by the end of the party.

Sostine making our Puff Pastry.

PHOTOGRAPHIC HISTORY

MENA

Papá and I in my hometown of Caricchio, Calabria. I was ten months old.

My first Communion in Italy when I was seven.

This is where I lived until I was twelve, with my parents and my four siblings, in the small town of Caricchio.

This was my school while I was in Italy.

This is a picture from my school in Italy. That's me on the far right.

Papá and I in Italy.

Gino and I outside our home in Italy. We reminisce about it all the time.

I went back to Italy for my Nonna Annunziata's ninetieth birthday. I used to go back to Italy every two to three years to visit family and stayed with my Zia Emilia and Nonna, in Cosenza.

Friends and family were my constant companions growing up in Italy. Back row from L to R Silvana, Alba (cousin), Rose (cousin), Mena and Pierino (friend). Front row from L to R: Marianna, Pietro (friend), Gino, and Lilliana (friend and Pierino's sister).

PHOTOGRAPHIC HISTORY

MENA'S FAMILY

Nonno Luigi Gallo and Nonna Annunziata Bonofiglio-Gallo, my maternal grandparents.

AnneMarie and I went to visit the area where my Papá was born in the mountain village of Serra Soprano. From L to R: Me, Baby AnneMarie, Cousin Teresa, Cousin Giovanni, and Cousin Elio.

This is my Nonna (Grandmother) Filomena with my Papá Mario on the right and on the far left is Zia (Aunt) Assunta and Zia Giovannina (Ginnina) next to Nonna.

PHOTOGRAPHIC HISTORY

This is Papá and his friend at the flour mill where they worked, in Cosenza which is the big city near Caricchio.

My cousin, Eugenio, used to come and visit all the time in Italy.

Our family with Zia Maria, Cousin Gina, and Julie, our first American baby.

Front sitting L to R: Silvana, baby Julie, and Mamma. Middle L to R: Lori, Papá, and Marianna. Standing L to R: Gino, Me, and Nonno Baldino.

PHOTOGRAPHIC HISTORY

Every summer we would go to Fuscaldo Beach in my uncle Santo's car. L to R: Mamma Rita, baby Silvana, Gino, myself, and Zia Ginnina.

We were so excited for our first family Christmas in America.

1959 — This is my Zia Giovannina, Nonno Luigi Baldino, and Zia Assunta. Nonno owned a grocery store called Northtown Grocery.

PHOTOGRAPHIC HISTORY

My Zia Ginnina (Giovannina) came back from America to get married in Caricchio. She stayed at our house and took this picture our balcony. My cousin Teresa, and my brother, Gino, are also in the picture.

At my cousin Virginia Baldino's wedding, in Cosenza, Italy. I am the little flower girl in the white dress. Most of the people in this picture are my aunts and cousins.

Standing L to R: Zia Rosina Baldino-Bozz, —, Pietro Baldino, Salvatore Gallo, Mario DeMarco, Gaetano (Guy) Perna, Angela Perna-DeMarco, Amedio DeMarco, Giovanni Baldino, Zia Julia DeLuca-Baldino, Mamma Rita Gallo-Baldino, Papá Mario Baldino holding Luigi (Gino) Baldino, Zia Raffella Baldino.

Sitting L to R: Pasquale Bozzo, Zia Ginnina Baldino-Pecara, —, Dave Maglicco, Zia Virginia Baldino-Litrenta, Natale Litrenta, Zia Maria Baldino Perna.

On the floor L to R: Erma Perna-VanZwoll, Filomena "Mena" Baldino (Castriciano), Ida Perna, Conni Perna-Khun.

Mamma, Me and Papá at their 50th Wedding Anniversary.

Mamma and Papá on their wedding day in September 1946.

Mamma, Papá, Me and Sostine at our 25th Wedding Anniversary

PHOTOGRAPHIC HISTORY

Papá and I making pork cutlets for dinner.

In Cosenza for a visit with my cousins. Back row L to R: Cousin Teresa, Me, Zia Emilia, Nella, Cousin Peppino, Silvana, Patrizia. Middle row L to R: Cousin Enzo and Antonio. Front row L to R: Mario and Cousin Immacolata.

My sisters and brothers. From L to R: Robert, Silvana, Mena, Lori, Gino, Marianna, and Julie.

Mamma and I are very close; she taught me how to cook and I always helped her. This picture is one of our lunches. We used to have lunch every Monday, but now she lives too far away for me to drive. She is now ninety-two and I love her very much. May God keep her safe.

PHOTOGRAPHIC HISTORY

My brother Gino and I at Roma.

My brother Gino and sister Silvana helping out at the bakery making turdilli.

My cousin Gaetano and I at a Lamb picnic.

Christmas at Mamma and Papá's home on Grand River in Lansing.

My brother Gino making Liver Sausage and Italian Sausage.

PHOTOGRAPHIC HISTORY

Mamma and Papá at Thanksgiving.

Mamma, Zia Ginonina, and Mena making Christmas Pasta Alici.

Zia Emilia, Mamma, and Zia Ida came to Lansing.

Mamma with her sisters Zia Emilia and Zia Ida.

PHOTOGRAPHIC HISTORY

SOSTINE

Sostine and his parents, Papá Giuseppe and Mamma Maria. They came to America for a year and stayed with us. This was their going away party.

Sostine's cousin, Franco Galletta, owned a bakery in Hamilton, Ontario, called Frank's Sicilia (Sicilian) Bakery. My husband's friend, Nicola, on the left his cousin Franco in the middle, and Sostine on the right all working on a rum torte.

My husband, Sostine, at his cousin's bakery in Hamilton, Ontario, where he was working when I first met him.

PHOTOGRAPHIC HISTORY

MENA & SOSTINE

Sostine and Mena on their way to their honeymoon on Mackinac Island.

Sostine and I have been blessed with our three beautiful daughters, AnneMarie, Elisabeth, and Filomena.

Sostine and I were married on October 26, 1968 at Lansing's St. Therese Catholic Parish.

PHOTOGRAPHIC HISTORY

Sostine and I on our 25th wedding anniversary in 1993.

Mena and Sostine, catering at Roma's Bakery.

ITALY

This is the fountain from the mountain where I used to go and get water every day, twice a day. We did not have running water in our home. From L to R: Zia Emilia, me, and Little Mena.

Zia Emilia cooked our dinner outside for our picnic on a farm in Sila. They are known for the tastes and color of their potatoes in Sila. They are delicious with a little olive oil, salt, and pepper!

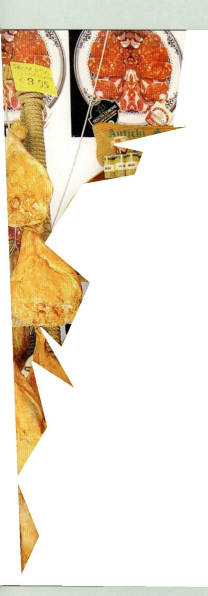

While in Italy with Elisabeth we traveled to Camigliatello and we found homemade proscutto... yummy!

PHOTOGRAPHIC HISTORY

The city of Sila is known for having fresh water from the mountains. A few cousins, Little Mena, and I went to get some.

My daughters in Cosenza.

My daughter Elisabeth in Rome to see a friend and get a pork sandwich "Porchetta."

PHOTOGRAPHIC HISTORY

In the summer in Sila, they have a lot of markets like this. Little Mena and I enjoyed some homemade Calabrian food.

While staying with Sostine's brother in Messina, Sicily, we went shopping for fresh seafood.

In January 2004 Elisabeth and I traveled to visit my cousin Franco and stay with him. We traveled to Sila where he has a house. This is a market in Camigliatello where everything is homemade and is fresh daily.

PHOTOGRAPHIC HISTORY

Cosenza, where Mena is from.

Sicily, where Sostine is from.

Serra Soprano, the farm in the hills.

PHOTOGRAPHIC HISTORY

MY FAITH

This is our church in Caricchio; it could only fit about 35 people.

Sostine and I welcomed Our Lady of Fatima in our home for a visit. We had about thirty people to our house to say the rosary in honor of her. She has worked many miracles for me.

In August, Silvana, Irene and I went to St. Ippolito in Calabria "Banker Hill."

PHOTOGRAPHIC HISTORY

This is St. Joseph, Father of Jesus. His feast day is March 19, which is also Father's Day in Italy. My Papá would take me to Cosenza; he knew how much I loved it. We would get mustazzoli from the stalls and zeppole from the bakeries. I dream about it all the time. Roma Bakery is the only place around that I have found zeppole.

This is the blessed mother that guards the port of Messina. Sostine is from Messina, Sicily.

Every July, the blessed mother has a feast and festival on July 16, but she is known as Our Lady of Mount Carmel. On the nearest Saturday, you say your rosaries and go out to walk among the stalls with different vendors with all kinds of sweets. On Sunday the day starts with a morning mass and taking the blessed mother to a wooden platform. The men carry her through the streets in a processional. Then we bring her back to the church and the party starts.

PHOTOGRAPHIC HISTORY

INDEX

A

Almond Clusters   200
Almond Crescent Cookies   201
Almond Half Moon Cookies   202
Almond Pudding   238
Amaretti Cookies   208
Anise Cookies   204
Antipasti, Soups & Dips
   Artichoke and Cheese Casserole   2
   Artichokes with Stuffing   6
   Artichoke Tapenade   4
   Asparagus Patties, Small   10
   Chicken Broth with Pasta and Eggs   8
   Chicken Soup with Little Meatballs   9
   Creamy Tomato Bisque   11
   Crispy Eggplant Flat Meatballs ("Meatless")   12
   Eggplant Appetizer   14
   Eggplant Rolls   16
   Eggplant (Spread)   18
   Flaming Cheese   22
   Fried Artichoke Hearts   5
   Fried Stuffed Zucchini Blossoms   19
   Fried Zucchini   20
   Italian Fish Soup   21
   Lentil Soup with Sausage & Pancetta   23
   Marinated Artichokes   24
   Mushrooms Stuffed with Ricotta   25
   Mushrooms Stuffed with Sausage   26
   Panini (Grilled)   27
   Pickled Zucchini, Sweet & Sour   28
   Potato Garlic Soup   29
   Ricotta Dumpling Soup   30
   Roasted Red Pepper and Sun-Dried Tomato Tapenade   31
   Sausage Soup with Minestrone   32
   Spinach and Olive Tapenade   33
   Spinach Pie   34
   Taramasalata Dip   37
   Tomato and Mozzarella Fondue   36
Artichoke and Cheese Casserole   2
Artichokes with Stuffing   6
Artichoke Tapenade   4
Asparagus Patties, Small   10
Avocado Shrimp Salad   142

B

Baked Chicken and Potato with Rosemary   90
Baked Halibut   48
Baked Lasagna with Meat Sauce   114
Baked Pasta with Eggplant   115
Baked Stuffed Peaches   228
Baked Swordfish Steaks   49
Beans and Tuna Salad   143
Béchamel Sauce   170
Beef Pizzaiola   67
Beef Tongue Salad   144
Biscotti with Cashew Nuts   203
Braciole — Rolled Sirloin Tip   66
Bread Crumbs   189
Bread Sticks   188
Broccoli Rabe Salad with Vinaigrette   146
Broccoli Rabe with Sausage   80
Broccoli Salad   147
Broccoli with Garlic and Anchovy Sauce   148
Butter Cookies   206

C

Calabrese Doughnuts   190
Cannelloni Filling   116
Carmela's Finger Cookies   212
Cauliflower Salad   149
Cheese Sauce   184
Chicken and Potato with Rosemary   90
Chicken Breasts   99
Chicken Breast Saltimbocca   92
Chicken Broth with Pasta and Eggs   8
Chicken Cacciatore   93
Chicken or Veal Cutlets   94
Chicken Piccata   95
Chicken Soup with Little Meatballs   9
Chicken Tetrazzini   96
Christmas Honey Cookies   216
Codfish Salad (Sicilian Style)   51
Codfish Stew (Baccalá)   52
Codfish Stew (Fresh)   54

Cod Salad   150
Cod Sautéed with Shrimp Sauce   50
Cookies with a Kiss   209
Creamy Herb Sauce   171
Creamy Tomato Bisque   11
Crêpes   118
Crispy Eggplant Flat Meatballs ("Meatless")   12

D

Deep-Fried Squid   55
Deli Sandwich   152
Desserts & Cookies
    Almond Clusters   200
    Almond Crescent Cookies   201
    Almond Half Moon Cookies   202
    Almond Pudding   238
    Amaretti Cookies   208
    Anise Cookies   204
    Baked Stuffed Peaches   228
    Butter Cookies   206
    Carmela's Finger Cookies   212
    Christmas Honey Cookies   216
    Cookies with a Kiss   209
    Fresh Fruit Dessert   229
    Galatobouriko   224
    Honey Sliced Cookies   218
    Italian Fig Cookies   210
    Ladyfingers   214
    Macaroons   219
    Mamma's Finger Cookies   215
    Mamma's Italian Pastry Cream   235
    Mamma's Torte   236
    Mamma's Vodka Cherries   233
    Panna Cotta   234
    Peaches in Red Wine   230
    Pear Caramel Cake   231
    Pears Poached in Red Wine   232
    Ricotta Pudding   239
    Roma's Pastiera Ricotta Filling   240
    Roma's Sweet Pastry Dough   242
    Sesame Seed Cookies   220
    Shaved Coffee Ice — Granita with Cream   226
    Shaved Lemon Ice — Granita   227
    Sliced Biscotti with Cashew Nuts   203
    Thumbprint Cookies   221
    Zeppole   222
Doughnuts   190
Doughs & Breads
    Bread Sticks   188
    Calabrese Doughnuts   190
    Italian Sweet Egg Bread   192
    Mena's Pizza Dough   196
    Pizza Dough   197
    Seasoned Italian Bread Crumbs   189
    Toasted Italian Bread with Tomato, Basil, and Olive Oil   195

E

Egg Dishes
    Eggs Poached in Tomato Sauce   40
    Eggs with Tomatoes   41
    Frittata (Easter Omelet)   42
    Frittata – Ham and Cheese   45
    Frittata (Mamma's Spaghetti)   44
    Frittata with Artichokes   45
Egg Pasta   122
Eggplant Appetizer   14
Eggplant Flat Meatballs   12
Eggplant Parmesan   104
Eggplant Rolls   16
Eggplant (Spread)   18
Eggs Poached in Tomato Sauce   40
Eggs with Tomatoes   41

F

Fennel Salad   153
Fettuccine Alfredo   120
Fettuccine with Artichokes   121
Fig Cookies   210
Finger Cookies   212, 215
Fish
    Baked Halibut   48
    Baked Swordfish Steaks   49
    Codfish Salad (Sicilian Style)   51
    Codfish Stew (Baccalá)   52
    Codfish Stew (Fresh)   54
    Cod Sautéed with Shrimp Sauce   50
    Deep-Fried Squid   55
    Halibut and Onions   48
    Mixed Fried Fish   56
    Mussels Marinara   57
    Salmon with White Bean Salad   58
    Scallop Kabobs   61
    Scallops and Mushrooms   60
    Shrimp Scampi with Artichokes   62
    Spicy Shrimp   63
    Tiella (Casserole)   59
Flaming Cheese   22
Fresh Fruit Dessert   229
Fried Artichoke Hearts   5
Fried Rice Balls   130
Fried Stuffed Zucchini Blossoms   19

Fried Zucchini   20
Frittata (Easter Omelet)   42
Frittata – Ham and Cheese   45
Frittata (Mamma's Spaghetti)   44
Frittata with Artichokes   45
Fruit Dessert   229

G

Galatobouriko   224
Garlic and Anchovies, Sauce or Dip   172
Garlic Sauce for Fish or Meat   173
Gemelli with Cauliflower   136
Gnocchi   128
Grandma's Beef Pizzaiola   67
Granita   227
Granita with Cream   226
Green Beans with Mint   106
Green Beans with Tomatoes   107
Green Salad with Oranges   154

H

Halibut and Onions   48
Halibut, Baked   48
Homemade Egg Pasta   122
Honey Cookies   216
Honey Mustard Pecan Salad   155
Honey Sliced Cookies   218

I

Italian Bread   195
Italian Bread Crumbs   189
Italian Fig Cookies   210
Italian Fish Soup   21
Italian Pastry Cream   235
Italian Potato Salad   157
Italian Salad Dressing   156
Italian Salsa   175
Italian Sweet Egg Bread   192
Italian Tomato Salad   158

J

Jumbo Stuffed Shells   124

L

Ladyfingers   214
Lamb Shanks in Tomato Sauce with Orecchiette   68
Lasagna, Sausage with Potato   137
Lasagna with Meat Sauce   114
Leg of Lamb   70
Lemon Butter Sauce   174
Lemon Oil Dressing   174
Lentil Soup with Sausage & Pancetta   23
Linetta's Chicken   98
Linguine Carbonara   125

M

Macaroons   219
Mamma's Finger Cookies   215
Mamma's Italian Pastry Cream   235
Mamma's Pasta & Anchovy Sauce   126
Mamma's Potato Cassarole   110
Mamma's Spare Rib Sauce with Meatballs (Sunday Dinner)   176
Mamma's Torte   236
Mamma's Vegetable Zucchini Stew   105
Mamma's Vodka Cherries   233
Manicotti Crêpes   118
Marinara Sauce   178, 180
Marinated Artichokes   24
Meat
    Braciole — Rolled Sirloin Tip   66
    Broccoli Rabe with Sausage   80
    Grandma's Beef Pizzaiola   67
    Lamb Shanks in Tomato Sauce with Orecchiette   68
    Leg of Lamb   70
    Meatballs   73
    Oxtail Style Sauce   74
    Pan-Roasted Rabbit with Marsala   75
    Papá's Pork Rolls in Tomato Sauce   76
    Sausage with Sweet Red Pepper   79
    Stuffed Beef Roll   82
    Stuffed Eggplant   84
    Tripe with Sauce   72
    Veal Scaloppine with Marsala Wine Sauce   69
    Veal Stuffed Jumbo Shells with Mushroom Béchamel   86
Meatballs   73
Meat Sauce   181
Mediterranean Pasta   127
Mena's Gnocchi   128
Mena's Italian Salad Dressing   156
Mena's Manicotti Crêpes   118
Mena's Pizza Dough   196
Mena's Seafood Salad   166
Mixed Fried Fish   56
Mushrooms Stuffed with Ricotta   25

Mushrooms Stuffed with Sausage   26
Mussels Marinara   57

O

Orange Salad Sicilian Style   159
Orecchiette with Broccoli, Onion, and Sausage   160
Orzo Pasta or Rice Pilaf   133
Oxtail Style Sauce   74

P

Panini (Grilled)   27
Panna Cotta   234
Pan-Roasted Rabbit with Marsala   75
Papá's Pork Rolls in Tomato Sauce   76
Parmigiano-Reggiano Cheese Sauce   184
Pasta & Anchovy Sauce   126
Pasta Frolla   242
Pasta Orzo   161
Pasta & Rice
    Baked Lasagna with Meat Sauce   114
    Baked Pasta with Eggplant   115
    Cannelloni Filling   116
    Fettuccine Alfredo   120
    Fettuccine with Artichokes   121
    Fried Rice Balls   130
    Homemade Egg Pasta   122
    Jumbo Stuffed Shells   124
    Linguine Carbonara   125
    Mamma's Pasta & Anchovy Sauce   126
    Mediterranean Pasta   127
    Mena's Gnocchi   128
    Mena's Manicotti Crêpes   118
    Orzo Pasta or Rice Pilaf   133
    Rice Croquettes   132
    Rice with Tuna   134
    Risotto — Basic   135
    Sausage with Potato Lasagna   137
    Spaghetti with Anchovies and Tomato Sauce   138
    Spaghetti with Asparagus   139
    Spicy Gemelli with Cauliflower   136
Pasta Salad with Grilled Chicken, Apples, and Cheddar   162
Pasta with Eggplant   115
Pasta with Peas and Onions   108
Pastiera Ricotta Filling   240
Pastry Cream   235
Pastry Dough   242
Peaches, Baked Stuffed   228
Peaches in Red Wine   230

Pear Caramel Cake   231
Pears Poached in Red Wine   232
Peppers & Eggplant   109
Pesto Sauce   182
Pesto Sauce with Fresh Basil   183
Pickled Zucchini, Sweet & Sour   28
Pizza Dough   197
Pork Rolls in Tomato Sauce   76
Potato Garlic Soup   29
Potato Gratin   111
Poultry
    Baked Chicken and Potato with Rosemary   90
    Chicken Breast Saltimbocca   92
    Chicken Cacciatore   93
    Chicken or Veal Cutlets   94
    Chicken Piccata   95
    Chicken Tetrazzini   96
    Linetta's Chicken   98
    Skillet Chicken Breasts   99
    Turkey Breast with Lemon Sauce   100
    Turkey Cutlets with Spinach, Crab, and Asiago Cheese Sauce   101

Q

Quick, 20 Minute Marinara Sauce   180

R

Rabbit with Marsala   75
Rice Croquettes   132
Rice with Tuna   134
Ricotta Dumpling Soup   30
Ricotta Filling   240
Ricotta Pudding   239
Risotto — Basic   135
Roasted Potato, Garlic and Red Pepper Salad   163
Roasted Red Pepper and Sun-Dried Tomato Tapenade   31
Roma's Pastiera Ricotta Filling   240
Roma's Sweet Pastry Dough   242
Rosemary Potato Gratin   111

S

Salad Dressing   156
Salads
    Avocado Shrimp Salad   142
    Beans and Tuna Salad   143
    Beef Tongue Salad   144
    Broccoli Rabe Salad with Vinaigrette   146

    Broccoli Salad   147
    Broccoli with Garlic and Anchovy Sauce   148
    Cauliflower Salad   149
    Cod Salad   150
    Fennel Salad   153
    Green Salad with Oranges   154
    Honey Mustard Pecan Salad   155
    Italian Potato Salad   157
    Italian Tomato Salad   158
    Mena's Italian Salad Dressing   156
    Mena's Seafood Salad   166
    Orange Salad Sicilian Style   159
    Orecchiette with Broccoli, Onion, and Sausage   160
    Pasta Orzo   161
    Pasta Salad with Grilled Chicken, Apples, and Cheddar   162
    Roasted Potato, Garlic and Red Pepper Salad   163
    Summer Fresh Deli Sandwich   152
    Tuna Nicoise Salad   164
Salmon with White Bean Salad   58
Sauces
    Béchamel Sauce   170
    Creamy Herb Sauce   171
    Garlic and Anchovies, Sauce or Dip   172
    Garlic Sauce for Fish or Meat   173
    Lemon Butter Sauce   174
    Lemon Oil Dressing   174
    Mamma's Spare Rib Sauce with Meatballs (Sunday Dinner)   176
    Marinara Sauce   178
    Parmigiano-Reggiano Cheese Sauce   184
    Pesto Sauce   182
    Pesto Sauce with Fresh Basil   183
    Quick, 20 Minute Marinara Sauce   180
    Sweet and Sour Italian Salsa   175
    Tomato Meat Sauce   181
    Vodka Sauce   185
Sausage Soup with Minestrone   32
Sausage with Potato Lasagna   137
Sausage with Sweet Red Pepper   79
Scallop Kabobs   61
Scallops and Mushrooms   60
Seafood Salad   166
Seasoned Italian Bread Crumbs   189
Sesame Seed Cookies   220
Shaved Coffee Ice — Granita with Cream   226
Shaved Lemon Ice — Granita   227
Shrimp Scampi with Artichokes   62
Skillet Chicken Breasts   99
Sliced Biscotti with Cashew Nuts   203
Spaghetti with Anchovies and Tomato Sauce   138
Spaghetti with Asparagus   139
Spare Rib Sauce with Meatballs   176
Spicy Gemelli with Cauliflower   136
Spicy Shrimp   63
Spinach and Olive Tapenade   33
Spinach Pie   34
Stuffed Beef Roll   82
Stuffed Eggplant   84
Summer Fresh Deli Sandwich   152
Sweet and Sour Italian Salsa   175
Sweet Egg Bread   192
Sweet Pastry Dough   242
Swordfish Steaks   49

T

Taramasalata Dip   37
Thumbprint Cookies   221
Tiella (Casserole)   59
Toasted Italian Bread with Tomato, Basil, and Olive Oil   195
Tomato and Mozzarella Fondue   36
Tomato Meat Sauce   181
Torte   236
Tripe with Sauce   72
Tuna Nicoise Salad   164
Turkey Breast with Lemon Sauce   100
Turkey Cutlets with Spinach, Crab, and Asiago Cheese Sauce   101

V

Veal Cutlets   94
Veal Scaloppine with Marsala Wine Sauce   69
Veal Stuffed Jumbo Shells with Mushroom Béchamel   86
Vegetables
    Eggplant Parmesan   104
    Green Beans with Mint   106
    Green Beans with Tomatoes   107
    Mamma's Potato Cassarole   110
    Mamma's Vegetable Zucchini Stew   105
    Pasta with Peas and Onions   108
    Peppers & Eggplant   109
    Rosemary Potato Gratin   111
Vodka Cherries   233
Vodka Sauce   185

Z

Zeppole   222

Index of Italian Names

A
Agnello con Orecchiette in Salsa di Pomodoro   68
Arancine Sicilian Style   130

B
Besciamella   170
Biscotti ai Semi di Sesamo   220
Biscotti al bacio di cioccolato   209
Biscotti All Anice   204
Biscotti con l'imprinta del police   221
Biscotti con noci di anacardio   203
Biscotti di Amaretto   208
Biscotti di Carmela   212
Biscotti di Sposalizi   215
Biscotti dolci al burro   206
Biscotti—Mezzelune di Mandorla   202
Braciole   66
Broccoli con aglio e salsa di acciughe   148
Broccoli Rabe con Salsiccia   80
Budino di Ricotta   239

C
Calamari Fritti   55
Caponata Siciliano   14
Cappa Santa con Funghi   60
Cappa Santa Kabob   61
Carciofi Marinati   24
Carciofi Ripieni   6
Ciliege sotto spirit della Mamma   233
Coda di Bue   74
Conchiglioni Ripieni   124
Conchiglioni Ripieni di Vitello con Besciamella di Funghi   86
Condimento per Insalata   156
Coniglio Arrosto al Marsala   75
Cosciotto di Agnello   70
Cotoletta   94
Cotolette di Tacchino con salsa di spinaci, granchio e formaggio Asiago   101
Cozze alla Marinara   57
Crema di Erbe   171
Crema di Mandorle Siciliana   238
Crema Pasticcera   235
Croccantini di Mandorla   200
Crocchetti di Riso   132
Cuddurieddi-Ciambella   190
Cuori di Carciofi Fritti   5

D
Dessert alle Mandorle   219
di Melanzane   18

F
Fagioli E Tonno   143
Fagiolini all Menta   106
Fagiolini con Pomodoro   107
Falsomagro o Braciolone Calabrese   82
Fettuccine Alfredo   120
Fettuccine con Carciofi   121
Fiori di Zucchini Fritti Ripieni   19
Friselle con Ponodoro alla Calabrese   195
Fritelli di Asparagi   10
Frittata   42
Frittata Contadina   45
Frittata di Carciofi   45
Frittata di spaghetti della Mamma   44
Frittelle con Zucchine   20
Frittelle di Polpette di Melanzane—"Senza Carne"   12
Fritto Misto di Pesce   56
Funghi Ripiene con Ricotta   25
Funghi ripieni con Salsiccia   26

G
Galatobouriko (Greek Recipe)   224
Gamberi Arrabbiati   63
Gamberi con Carciofi   62
Gemelli arrabbiati con Cavolfiore   136
Gnocchi di Mena   128
Granita di Caffe   226
Granita di Limone   227
Grissini   188

I
Impasto di Peperoni Rossi arrostiti e Pomodori essicata al sole   31
Impasto di Spinaci e Olive   33
Insalata de Baccalá   150
Insalata di Aranci   159
Insalata di Broccoli   147
Insalata di Broccoli Rape con Vinaigrette   146
Insalata di Cavolfiore—Sicilian style   149
Insalata di Finocchio   153
Insalata di gamberi e avocado   142
Insalata di Lingua di Bue alla Calabrese   144
Insalata di Merluzzo-Baccalá   51
Insalata di Noci Pecan al Miele e Mostarda   155
Insalata di patate alla Contadina   157
Insalata di Patate con Aglio e Peperoni Rossi   163
Insalata di Pesce alla Siciliana   166
Insalata di Pomodori   158
Insalata di Tonno Nizzarada   164
Insalata Siciliana alle Arance   154
Insalate di pollo con Mele e Formaggio   162
Ippoglosso al forno   48
Ippoglosso e Cipolle   48

L
La Pasta della Pizza   197
La Pasta della Pizza di Mena   196
Lasagna con Salsa di Carne   114
La salsa di Pomodoro   178, 180
Linguine Carbonara   125

M
Macedonia agrodolce per Pesce o Pollo   175
Macedonia di Frutta   229
Manicotti di Mena con Crêpes   118
Manzo Pizzaiola della Nonna   67
Melanzane alla Parmigiana   104
Melanzane Ripiene   84
Merluzzo salato in padella con salsa di gamberi   50
Mezzelune di Mandorla   201
Minestrone con Salsiccia   32
Mollica di Pane con Sapore   189
Mostazolli   218

O
Orecchiette con Broccoli, Cipolle e Salsiccia   160
Orzo o Riso Pilaf   133

P
Pan di Spagna   236
Pan Dolce (di Pasqua)   192
Panini   27
Panino Calabrese   152
Panna Cotta   234
Papá's Pork Rolls in Tomato Sauce   76
Parmiggiana di Carciofi   2
Pasta al Forno con Melanzane   115
Pasta Alici   126
Pasta all Uovo Fatta in Casa   122
Pasta Frolla   242
Pasta Mediterraneo   127
Pasta Orzo   161
Pasticciotti di Fichi Secchi   210
Pastina in brood con le uova   8
Peperonata di Zia Rosina Baldino   109
Pere al Vino Rosso   232
Pesce Spada al Forno   49
Pesche al Vino   230
Pesche Ripiene   228
Pesto con Basilico fresco   183
Petti di Pollo con Aglio e Olio   99
Petti di Pollo Saltimbocca   92
Petto di Tacchino al Limone   100
Piselli e Cipolle Pasta   108
Pollo al forno con patate e Rosmarino   90
Pollo alla Cacciatora di Papá Cacciatore   93
Pollo alla Mena   96
Pollo di Linetta   98
Pollo Piccata   95
Pollpetti di Ricotta in Brodo   30
Polpette di Carne   73
Pomadore e Mozzarella Fonduta   36

R
Ricette per Salsicce   78
Ripieno per Cannelloni   116
Risotto   135
Risotto con Tonno   134
Rollatini di Melanzane   16

S
Saganaki (Greek Recipe)   22
Saliccia con Lasagna di Patate   137
Salmone con Insalata di Cannellini   58
Salmoriglio alla Siciliana   174
Salsa all aglio   173
Salsa alla Vodka   185
Salsa della Mamma con Polpette e Carne   176
Salsa di Aglio e Acciughe   172
Salsa di carne per Lasagna e Spaghetti   181
Salsa di formaggio al Parmigiano Reggiano   184
Salsa di Limone e Burro   174
Salsa di Pesto   182
Salsiccie con Peperoni Rossi   79
Scaloppine alla Marsala   69
Spaghetti con Acciughe e salsa di Pomodoro   138
Spaghetti con Asparagi   139
Spanakopita (Greek Recipe)   34
Spauma di Patate   110
Spezzatini di Trippa alla Calabrese   72
Stufato di Merluzzo alla Calabrese   52
Stufato di Merluzzo—Baccala all Siciliana   54
Stufato di verdure di Mamma   105

T
Tapenade di carciofi   4
Taramasalata (Greek Recipe)   37
Tiella or Tiedda Calabrese   59
Torta di Pasqua con Ricotta   240
Torta di Pere caramellate   231
Tortino di Patate al Rosmarino   111
Turdilli con Miele   216

U
Uova alla Diavola   41
Uova in Purgatorio   40

Z
Zeppole   222
Zucchine Agrodolci   28
Zuppa di Aglio e Patate della Mamma   29
Zuppa di Lenticchie Con Salsiccia   23
Zuppa di Pesce   21
Zuppa di Pollo con Polpettine   9
Zuppa di Pomodori con Crema   11